Charlayne Hunter-Gault

In My Place

Charlayne Hunter-Gault is known to millions of
Americans as the national correspondent for PBS's
MacNeil/Lehrer NewsHour. She lives with her family in
New York.

In My Place

Charlayne Hunter-Gault

Vintage Books

A Division of Random House, Inc.

New York

FIRST VINTAGE BOOKS EDITION, NOVEMBER 1993

Copyright ©1992 by Charlayne Hunter-Gault

All rights reserved under International and Pan-American Copyright Conventions. Published in the United States by Vintage Books, a division of Random House, Inc., New York, and simultaneously in Canada by Random House of Canada Limited, Toronto. Originally published in hardcover by Farrar, Straus & Giroux, Inc., New York, in 1992.

This edition is published by arrangement with Farrar, Straus & Giroux, Inc.

Library of Congress Cataloging-in-Publication Data
Hunter-Gault, Charlayne.
In my place / Charlayne Hunter-Gault.—1st Vintage Books ed.
p.   cm.
Originally published: New York: Farrar, Straus, Giroux, 1992.
Includes bibliographical references (p.).
ISBN 0-679-74818-0
1. Hunter-Gault, Charlayne.   2. Journalists—United States—
Biography.   3. Afro-American journalists—Biography.   4. Race
discrimination—United States.   5. United States—Race relations.
I. Title.
[PN4874.H83A3   1993]
070'.92—dc20
[B]   93-10511
CIP

Manufactured in the United States of America
3579B864

For my mother and father,.
who never told me I had to stay in my place . . .

And to the children of apartheid,
the last to take their place

Acknowledgments

Although this book bears my name as its author, many other hands, hearts, minds, and memories helped mold it. The names of many of them appear in these pages, therefore I will not repeat them here. Suffice to say that almost every name that appears made a contribution above and beyond the printed text. To them, I express my deepest appreciation and love.

There are others who are not a part of this immediate story, but without whom it could not have been told as is. Among them are Colonel John Cash, army historian, who, among other things, led me to Delores Lane of the Military Personnel Records Department in St. Louis, Missouri. Their immediate understanding of my needs helped me to almost effortlessly re-create my late father's twenty-year history with the army. Lt. Colonel Jesse J. Johnson, U.S. Army Retired, also falls into that category, along with the Chief of Chaplains, General Matthew A. Zimmerman, whose achievement as a Black man in the military affirms my father's pioneering struggle and faith.

"Due West of What?" owes much to Lowry Ware, emeritus

professor of history at Erskine College, whose love of his field and his and my hometown is infectious. Thanks to him for helping me walk through on my journey back.

To Laura Belcher McGee, my indebtedness for her thoughtfulness in offering and then generously donating the material collected by her late father, John C. Belcher, a sociology professor at the University of Georgia. His effort to document the role of the faculty in the desegregation crisis and the politics involved in the public reaction was immensely helpful.

I also want to thank Dovie T. Patrick and Charles Freeney of the Archives Division of the Woodruff Library of the Atlanta University Center for their timely response to my request for rare historical documents and Barbara Lowe, librarian at Frank L. Stanton Elementary School.

Also, whatever it is that is more than thanks to all my friends, like Dante Brown, who was always there no matter the hour when I called in desperation, saying, "The computer ate my homework"; to David Driskell, and the Reverend James Forbes of Riverside Church, whose understanding of the process of writing this book helped to sustain me, and to the late Barbara Pryor DeJongh, whose call from her hospital bed imploring me to "finish before I leave here" gave me one of my most compelling reasons to burn the midnight oil till dawn.

To Jonathan Galassi, whose gentle persistence and enthusiastic prodding caused me to write this book and complete it a lot sooner than I once thought possible, I extend my arms to wrap you in gratitude.

Even though William Shawn's name appears in the book, I make an exception about mentioning it here because his gifts as an editor and his instincts as a human being have been among the most important seasoning elements of my professional life, starting at the beginning, some twenty-eight years ago. It was *the* way to start a career and it is the best turn of fate that, as I added this dimension to it, he was here, gently and tenderly guiding me with his unique gifts.

My deepest appreciation to Dr. Kenneth Clark and his late wife, Mamie, whose pioneering studies showed the devastating psychic trauma suffered by young Black children under segregation who did not have the support system that I did. Their work was critical to the success of the *Brown v. Board of Education* case.

And then there are my helpmates, my soulmates, and my blood—my daughter, Susan, who researched, transcribed, and wrote delightful notes of encouragement that I would find in the most unlikely places; my son, Chuma, who gave me both the "splash-board" to tell my story even before I was ready, and the critical feedback when I was; and my husband, Ronald, who gives me my space because he understands my place.

And finally, to the Movement People, wherever they are, *A luta continua!*

Charlayne Hunter-Gault
New York, New York
April 30, 1992

Contents

Prologue

"She had been getting ready for her great journey to the horizons in search of people; it was important to all the world that she should find them and they find her."
—ZORA NEALE HURSTON, *Their Eyes Were Watching God*

On January 9, 1961, I walked onto the campus at the University of Georgia to begin registering for classes. Ordinarily, there would not have been anything unusual about such a routine exercise, except, in this instance, the officials at the university had been fighting for almost two years to keep me out. I was not socially, intellectually, or morally undesirable. I was Black. And no Black student had ever been admitted to the University of Georgia in its 175-year history. Until the landmark *Brown v. Board of Education* decision that in 1954 declared separate but equal schools unconstitutional, the university was protected by law in its exclusion of people like me. By deciding to apply to the university, Hamilton Holmes and I were the first to test the new law, and no one was sure just how hard it would be to challenge 175 years of exclusive white privilege. It would take us almost two years of fighting our way through the system and the courts, but finally, with the help of the NAACP Legal Defense and Educational Fund, Inc., and with the support of our family and friends, we won the right that should have been ours all along. With the ink barely dry on the court order of three days before, Hamilton Holmes and I walked onto the campus and into history. It would be the last time that whites could demand of me or any other Black person what they had demanded of Blacks since slavery—that we diffidently accept the secondary and inferior role they had consigned us to, under the paternalistic assurance that everything would be all right as long as we stayed "in our place." Until this moment, the fate of any Black who dared forget his or her place was often cruel if not fatal.

That we were now daring to define our place irrespective of white wishes or demands sparked, among other things, the raucous greetings by mobs of white students and other forces of white resistance who within forty-eight hours would hurl epithets, burn crosses and black effigies, and finally stage a riot outside my dormitory while, nearby, state patrolmen ignored the call from university officials to come and intervene. Tear gas would disperse the crowd, but not before I got word in my dorm room, now spattered with glass, that Hamilton and I were being suspended for our own safety. It might have been the end of the story but for the fact that the University of Georgia was now the lead case in a series of events that would come to be Georgia's entry into the Civil Rights Revolution. And we—like the legions of young Black students to follow in other arenas—were now imbued with an unshakable determination to take control of our destiny and force the South to abandon the wretched Jim Crow laws it had perpetuated for generations to keep us in our place.

The newfound sense of mission that now motivated us evolved for me out of a natural desire to fulfill a dream I had nurtured from an early age. With a passion bordering on obsession, I wanted to be a journalist, a dream that would have been if not unthinkable, at least undoable in the South of my early years. But no one ever told me not to dream, and when the time came to act on that dream, I would not let anything stand in the way of fulfilling it.

The desegregation of the University of Georgia is the point of departure for this book, but what made all of that possible is the larger story that I have tried to tell—the story of the kind of nurturing that made it possible for me to take the steps I did as a nineteen-year-old Black child of the South who didn't stay "in my place." It is a story of values—my family's values and those of the community that shared them. Values that are timeless, transcendent, and inclusive of all people who treasure and celebrate the limitless potential for elevating the human condition.

In understanding the source of those values, I believe it is possible to understand why I would stand before a riotous mob and not be afraid. (One clue is found in my grandmother's insistence that I learn and take to heart at an early age the words of the Twenty-Third Psalm —"Yea though I walk through the valley of the shadow of death, I shall fear no evil. Thy rod and thy staff they comfort me...") Or indeed why the experience of being yelled at and being told "Nigger, go home" did not leave me bitter. (One clue could be found at the separate and distinctly unequal Washington Street Elementary School in Covington, Georgia, where my parents and others labored to raise money to make up for the lack of resources allotted to the "colored" schools. One fundraising event culminated in the child raising the most money being crowned "queen." The year I won, the notion that I was a queen took up residence in my head and was nurtured by my family and community to such an extent that by the time I got to the University of Georgia, it was inconceivable that I might be the "nigger" they were talking about.)

In My Place, then, is above all the story of the people and their values that nurtured and sustained me and, in the process, provided me with the suit of armor and determination that I needed as I began my journey to the horizons.

—Charlayne Hunter-Gault
August 1993

chapter 1

Due West of What?

The first of many places that I would call "my place" was a tiny village tucked away in a remote little corner of South Carolina: Due West. There may have been bigger, better known, and happier places on February 27, 1942, but you couldn't have told my mother anything about them. Not even a difficult labor at home, which lasted four days, with the doctor popping in from time to time with encouraging words but little else, could diminish my mother's happiness.

When I was old enough to appreciate just what a remote little town Due West, South Carolina, was, and what a mostly country girl my mother was, I really became curious about how she came up with what then and for many years to come was a very unusual name. She explained that I was supposed to have been Charles. During the four years she had unsuccessfully tried to get pregnant, she had dreamed of having a boy. She would name him Charles, after my father, whom she adored. It would have been the third Charles in the Hunter family, and she had planned for me to have all the names of the two previous ones—Charles Shepherd Henry. If I had been a boy, I would have been called Henry, as was my first brother eight years later, because my grandfather was known to his friends and close associates as "Shep" and my father was called Charles, sometimes Chace, by his family.

For as long as I can remember, I loved my name. Mother chose Alberta as my middle name, in honor of my father's mother. My mother, her mother, my brothers, and my closest, oldest friends sometimes called me "Char," and I liked that, too, but it was a long time before I heard anything that sounded remotely like Charlayne. After a while, I heard the name Charlene—the way most people pronounced mine. And though I was always quick to correct them, most people still had trouble getting it right. I didn't like that part. But I did like the idea that people had to think about my name, and sometimes exert some effort to get it right. It was a long time before I ever asked my mother, who also had an unusual name—Althea— how she came up with Charlayne.

The conversation went something like this:

"Mother [I always called her Mother, because everyone else I knew called their mothers Mama or Ma and I wanted to be different], how did a little country girl like you, off in this isolated little town of Due West, come up with a name as different as Charlayne? Had you ever heard anything like it before?"

"Well," she said in her usual nonchalant and soft-spoken way, "I just made it up."

I persisted. "But how could you just come up with a name like that?"

"Well," she began again, nonplussed by my insistence, "I wanted it to be as close to Charles as possible and yet make it feminine."

And that, to me, always meant strong-and-feminine—which could cut two ways. In fact, whenever my mother would get annoyed with me in later years, like most mothers who have an unerring instinct for getting under their daughter's skin, she would say, "You're just like your father."

In those circumstances I didn't mind her saying that, because my father was quite a man. But when speaking in anger, my mother usually had that "nobody can tell you anything" tone of voice. And it hurt, because all I wanted was for her to think of me the way I thought of her—as smart, but also soft, beautiful, and feminine. At that point in my life I wanted more than anything else to be like my mother; I even worried whether I would be smart enough to come up with a wonderfully original name for my own daughter.

I didn't grow up in Due West. And yet ask any Southerner where he is from and he will tell you every place he has ever been from. I am no exception. I always say, "Well, I grew up in Georgia, but I'm from South Carolina. That always leads to the question of where in South Carolina, and I can always count on anyone I tell to ask me, "Due West of what?" And that is one of the things that have given me a strong sense of place. My place.

As far as I can tell, no one knows for sure just how Due West got its name. Since most people always ask, "Due West of what?" it is easy to assume that it was Due West of something. It is actually a town tucked away in a small spot in the northwestern part of the state, west of Abbeville and Greenwood. There is local history that traces it back to the days when it was the land of the Cherokees, who first used the term Due West in 1768. According to Donald Calhoun, in *The Golden Quill*, the town of Honea Path got its name from the corruption of a junction point in what is now Abbeville County, which the Cherokees had named Hee-na-heena, meaning "many paths."

According to Calhoun's history, sometime before the Revolutionary War, an Indian trader named Charles DeWitt set up a post near there that he called DeWitt's Corner. It was located on the Little River, the dividing line between the present Abbeville and Anderson Counties. Then came the Revolutionary War.

As Calhoun wrote:

The Cherokee Indians rushed with savage ferocity upon the exposed inhabitants of the frontier, and on the day rendered memorable by the Declaration of Independence, DeWitt's Corner was destroyed. [But, the story goes], a little army of militia was gathered together on a field near Hogskin Creek, and advancing into the Indian territory, they so decimated the Cherokees that they were forced to sue for peace, and concluded a treaty by which they acknowledged themselves vanquished. As if by a sort of poetic justice, this treaty was signed at DeWitt's Corner.

The trading post was never reestablished, but "some five or six miles southeast" the town of Due West sprang up. There is speculation that the name was a corruption of Dewitt's Corner, or possibly Duett's Corner, or Duesse's Corner.

Due West could easily have qualified as just another of South Carolina's one-horse towns, like Ninety-Six, Honea Path, Traveler's Rest, Prosperity, Society Hill, Promised Land, Moncks Corner. But Due West had a distinction that the others didn't: it was a college town. Erskine College was founded for white male students, in 1839, by members of the Associate Reformed Presbyterian Church.

As Calhoun recounted:

As for the inhabitants of this post, that story goes back to far earlier events in Scotland. In particular, a woman by the name of Jennie Gedes (there is a large clan of Gettys in the A.R.P. Church) made herself famous, or infamous, by throwing a footstool at the head of a bishop who attempted to say mass in the presence of the good Scotch Presbyterian brethren. It was here that the revolution began that culminated in the dissolution of the Presbyterian Church of Scotland, marked by the secession of a group led by Ebenezer Erskine, who quickly became known as the Seceders. The sons and the daughters of these early valiant seceders appear to have settled at this crossroad which came to bear the name of Due West Corner. And in the course of time Due West became the holy city of the A.R.P.'s, the Mecca toward which all the brethren of Psalm-singing faith turn in reverent awe.*

The church defined Due West, earning it its other, informal name, the Holy City. Its inhabitants were so religious that they referred to Sunday only as the Sabbath. According to legend, as recapitulated by Calhoun, they went so far as to decapitate a rooster who crowed on the Holy Day. "It is even rumored," according to Calhoun, "that

* Donald W. Calhoun, "Due West—An Objective Sketch," *The Golden Quill*, May 1938, pp. 4–6.

when Billy Sunday came to Due West to perform his gyrations before the people of the town, he was referred to not by his usual name but as William Sabbath."

My mother recalls: "You weren't supposed to do anything on Sunday but go to church—no reading the paper even. They had a train called *The Dinky* that ran each day to the next town, where it had to back up all the way back, as there was no place to turn it around. But it didn't run on Sunday."

Except for the college, there was little else to Due West. In fact, all there was of "town" resembled what a Hollywood set designer would have created to look like a small town—a mile and a half long and a mile wide. Main Street consisted of one drugstore, a few grocery stores, a lumber-and-paint store, a furniture store, a shoe-repair shop, an oil mill, an ice plant, a dry cleaner, a garage, four filling stations, a printing office, a barbershop, one restaurant, one hotel, three private boardinghouses, and a doctor's office, which at one time was a miniature hospital. Even if you drove slowly, it would have been easy to drive right through Due West without realizing a town was there.

Being born in a town called Due West would have been enough to give me a distinct sense of place. But I was born in 1942, and being Black in those days meant not only that Due West was the place where I was born but that people of color—Negroes or colored people in those days—had their place. The area where we lived was situated around the Mt. Lebanon A.M.E. Church. It was called Rabbit Stew. Here again, no one is quite sure why. But WPA researcher Ben Carlton, canvassing for the WPA in 1938, came up with two explanations, both equally plausible. He wrote that the name "derived from the fact that soon after 'freedom' several negro families moved to the outskirts of Due West in what was then pines. Rabbits were cheap. One of the elderly Negroes, from whom I got some of my information concerning [Mt. Lebanon] said his uncle's 'fondness for rabbits' caused the name." But that's where a lot of the Black folks lived, in an assortment of mostly ramshackle, unpainted houses of various sizes, on craggy, unpaved streets. In 1938, there were some 105 white families and 50 Negro families in Due West. Like my grandmother, most of the Black folks worked for the white people of Due West—either for the college as maids, janitors, and the like, or in the homes of people who worked for or were in some way associated with the college.

My mother's people were from Georgia. But sometime after my grandfather, Rochell Brown, died, my grandmother, Frances Wilson Layson Brown, was asked by the Todds, a white family for whom she had worked in Covington, Georgia, to come to Due West to take care of their mother, who had suffered a stroke and was confined to a wheelchair. Unlike some white folks she had worked for, the Todds were good employers, and I never heard any complaints about them. When Black folks stayed in their place, they got along just fine with the white folks of Due West.

Not long after my grandmother moved to Due West, old lady Todd died and my grandmother married a part-time bricklayer named Ollie Jones. Few people could understand why, although one long-time resident of Due West speculated it was because "opposites attract"; another ventured that it might have been their shared love of baseball. They had a garden, where they grew a lot of the food they ate, and also a modest cotton field, which was a source of additional income for them. It was her third marriage—her last and her worst. But before it got bad, my mother moved to Due West to live with her. My mother had been living with my father, who had just begun his career as an army officer at Camp Livingston, Louisiana. She was in the early stages of her long-awaited pregnancy and having a rough time of it. I'm not sure whether it was a need to be nurtured by her mother, whom she was extremely close to, or a desire not to be a burden on her newly commissioned young husband, but she made the decision to go to Due West and remain there until I was born. She remembered that on December 7, 1941, she sat pregnant and heavy-hearted, listening to the stunning and foreboding news, on the old radio, that the Japanese had attacked Pearl Harbor, declaring war on the United States.

There was no hospital in Due West—only an infirmary associated with the college. Ollie Jones's sister, Jenny Vauss, whom I called Aunt Jenny, worked as a nurse there, and also as nurse/midwife to Dr. W. L. "Buck" Pressly, one of the two physicians in town, highly respected by both Blacks and whites. (Interestingly enough for the times, the other was a woman.) It was a comfort to my mother that we lived next door to Aunt Jenny. Anybody seriously ill either suffered through it, died, or went twenty miles to the town of Anderson. My mother once had what the doctor diagnosed as appendicitis, and he sent her to Anderson to have her appendix removed. When the pain persisted long after the tiny intestinal organ had been cut out and placed in a jar of formaldehyde on the mantelpiece in the bedroom, my mother told the doctor that he must have taken out the wrong thing. She told me he said, "I took out what I went after." And that was that. Years later, my mother told me that she believed the reason the doctor ordered the operation was that he knew she had just gotten an army check of close to $700 from my father. I asked her how he would have known and she told me that everybody in Due West knew everybody else's business, especially if it came through Western Union. It was wartime and money was scarce.

My mother recalled: "We had ration books and I had purchased a little Ford car, so I'd collect the neighbors' books in case I ran into scarce items like fatback, butter, cheese, etc., when I shopped in Abbeville or Anderson . . . Sometimes we'd go to Honea Path and other small towns where Jenny and Wallace [her husband] had family or friends. Erskine College, founded by Dr. Pressly's family, was being used as an army base, and since my mother's sister-in-law was a nurse at the infirmary, I never had to worry about gas stamps. The soldiers would give them to her."

There was a CCC camp for Negroes on the outskirts of Rabbit Stew. My mother says she can remember some Black folks saying, "Thank God for Hitler," not because they were unpatriotic or liked Hitler, but because the war brought desperately needed work to the poor folks of Due West.

My mother supplemented her income—and, I suspect, filled some of her lonely hours—by teaching school. She did not have a college degree, but she had graduated from Hyde Park, one of the most prestigious high schools in Chicago back then. My mother remembers that Nat "King" Cole, who was just starting out, used to play for their high-school dances. I think she overcame some of her innate shyness and enjoyed going around with some of the most popular young people in Chicago at the time.

My grandmother had sent her to Chicago to live with my grandfather's sister. When I asked her why, she said that her parents were deeply committed to her getting a good education and didn't feel she could get it in the colored school in Covington. There was an additional factor: her parents were concerned that some of the white men in Covington had their eyes on my mother, who was quite beautiful, and although their shy young daughter stayed mostly at home, they had sent her away to protect her from advances that they could have done little about.

At Hyde Park, my mother learned typing and shorthand, and got a good grounding in all the basics. She loved writing reports, and once pulled out one of her favorites—on the Standard Oil Company—when I was preparing one of my first long papers in school.

I would suspect that the high-school education she received "up North" was far superior to anything in either Black or white high schools in the South, and maybe even the equivalent of some Southern colleges. It certainly helped nurture the love for learning—especially reading—she inherited from my grandmother and grandfather. For as long as I can remember, my mother devoured books, often reading one a day. And she spoke well—with a Southern drawl, to be sure —and always with perfect grammar. She loved to work crossword puzzles, too, and had a gift for understanding the meaning of words. We always had a highly visible dictionary in the house.

Calhoun describes the "colored school" in Due West four years before I was born. He wrote:

It exists, and that is about all. The facilities consist of a large frame building, probably used in the pre–Civil War days, which contains rooms which are bereft of blackboard facilities to speak of and blessed by only the roughest of seating arrangements. The windows are mostly conspicuous by their absence, and the roof undoubtedly leaks. As to the type of instruction afforded, I do not have any specific information, but if it is influenced by the environment, it is poor indeed.

In 1940–41, the WPA built a new school named after George Washington Carver, improving upon the physical features of the old "colored school," but not on the facilities. The school where my mother taught first through third grade was, as she put it, "in the country"—several miles outside town—and was comparable to, if not worse than, Calhoun's "colored" school in Due West. When I asked her about how she got the job without a college degree, she said, "The white folks didn't care what the Black folks got, so all they cared about was that I was willing to do it. It was the preacher at the church we went to that told me about the job."

Five years later, halfway across the state in the town of Summerton, the Reverend J. A. Delaine and a group of Black parents, including Harry Briggs, a Black mechanic, petitioned their local, all-white school board for help—not even in bringing the poor Black schools up to par with the white schools but just to get a bus so that the Black children, like the white children, would have a somewhat easier time going the often long distances they had to travel to their little country schools. The school board turned them down, and they went to court, asking then not just for a bus but for school buildings, services, and education equal to whites. It was to be the first in a long series of steps that would lead to the United States Supreme Court's decision that not only outlawed such segregated and unequal school systems but provided still another road leading me to my place in American society.

The preacher who told my mother about the teaching position was the Reverend B. J. Glover. Like the Reverend Delaine, he, too, was a social activist, "using his pulpit as a platform for social reform. He promoted a variety of causes never particularly popular among Southern whites."★

Black folks were not allowed to vote in those days, and the Reverend Glover, who had been sent away from his home in nearby Promised Land (pronounced locally as Promiseland) and had returned to Due West after training in theology up North, at Wilberforce

★ Elizabeth Rauh Bethel, *Promiseland* (Philadelphia: Temple University Press, 1961), pp 215–17.

University in Ohio, had that on his public agenda, too. In the late thirties the Reverend Glover attempted to register at the Abbeville County Courthouse (Abbeville was the county in which Due West was situated). As recounted in Elizabeth Rauh Bethel's *Promiseland*:

> The clerk routinely administered the literacy test required by the 1895 state constitution; and Glover, literate in three languages, easily read and interpreted the passages from the constitution as they were presented to him. The clerk had no guidelines for such a situation and quickly conferred with other officials, leaving Glover on a bench in the courthouse corridor. The clerk returned and dismissed Glover with a simple and final decision: "I just can't register you." There was no additional explanation. Glover left the courthouse quietly but filled with deep emotion. The following Sunday, he rose to his pulpit in Due West and "talked about black people registering to vote and the unfairness" of his Abbeville courthouse experience.

Such episodes drew the attention of whites, including the Ku Klux Klan. And one day, between Due West and Greenwood, they confronted the Reverend Glover. As he later told the story: "A group of white men stopped me at that time and asked me my name. I told them, but I didn't say 'yes, sir' and 'no, sir.' It was five to begin with." It was said that Glover's cool dignified responses further enraged the angry group of white men, for he failed to follow the proper Southern pattern of Negro deference.

Glover continues:

> They took me from there in a car, blindfolded, out in the country . . . They did every kind of thing you can imagine. I was stripped completely. I wore nylon shorts, and I can still hear them talking about my nylon shorts. They beat me and made me say "yes, sir," and made me do all kinds of personal things. They were sexually cruel, talking about my sex organs and things like that. They made me do things. They would do it and talk to me. "What you doing, nigger? Why don't

you leave things like they are?" The KKK said they had to make an example of me. I was an uppity, smart nigger from the North. I had come back with Northern ideas. They came up with the idea of beating me, and they did . . . for five or six hours. I fought until I couldn't fight anymore. Then they left me for dead in the woods.

But the Reverend Glover survived. His assailants, all known in nearby Promised Land, were never brought to justice.

It was the seeds of such experiences, as shared from the pulpit of my mother's church, that were sown in her consciousness as I lay developing in her womb. It would be a generation before they made a difference, a generation after the morning of February 27, 1942. In a bedroom of the small unpainted frame house that was within eyeshot of the church, my mother lay suffering perhaps the greatest pain she had ever known. Labor started on Wednesday, and by Friday there was still no sign that I was ready to enter the world. Dr. Pressly, who had been stopping by daily, and who probably didn't want to work on the weekend, told my mother she was going to have the baby that day, come hell or high water. She vaguely remembers that he gave her something, and for the next several hours he worked and worked, trying to maneuver my head out, alternately inserting a pair of metal clamps, then his hands. Despite her own pain, my mother remembers screaming for the doctor to "stop mashing the baby's head. You're going to mash it to death."

When I finally did emerge, she said the sides of my head were bruised from the imprint of the clamps, and the space on my forehead between my eyes was red from the apparent pressure of a thumb. My head also was so ill-formed that for days my mother and Aunt Jenny took turns massaging it, trying to get it back to its original round shape. But I cried spontaneously—all nine pounds of me. And, despite the fact that I was not the boy my mother had been anticipating, she felt herself the luckiest woman in the world. I asked her later if she was frightened. "No," she answered. "Momma was there."

There were no telephones. A telegram to the army base in California where my father was then stationed told him the news. For four and a half months, my young mother struggled with her new baby. She told me, "You didn't like to sleep at night, and I would often rock you half the night. Mr. Ollie said I used to start off singing church songs, and by the time I finished I'd be singing the blues."

After four and a half months, during a trip to my father's people in Florida, Mother got word that my father wanted us to join him. She wasted no time and left straight from Florida by train for the long trip across country. It took something like four or five days. She said it wasn't too bad, because we had a sleeper. A white woman with a baby was company for a while, but during one conversation the woman "confided" to my fair-skinned mother that she was really upset that the previous night a "nigger" had boarded the train and slept in the bunk above her. After my mother told her that she didn't see anything wrong with that, the conversations came to a halt. My mother spent the rest of the trip taking care of me and silently enjoying the scenery.

My father had been preparing for our arrival by gathering autographs of famous Hollywood people who had performed on the post after I was born. Two of the most well-known radio personalities of the day, Jack Benny and Eddie "Rochester" Anderson, were among them. Years later, I would look at those autographs in the little pink-satin autograph book my mother had carefully tucked them into and feel really great—not so much because I had the autographs of these stars, but because it was clear to me that my father had made sure that they all spelled my name right.

The next few months in Riverside, California, were to be the closest I would come to having my father and mother together and us living as a family. At first, we stayed with a nice Black lady who was a Christian Scientist. Then my parents found a small apartment, but before they could move in, my father got orders to report overseas, to North Africa, the scene of the most intense fighting between the Axis forces under Field Marshal Rommel and the Allies, led by General Montgomery. It would be months into 1943 before the Allied forces could claim victory. Meanwhile, rather than go all the way back to Due West, my mother decided to go partway and settle temporarily in Cleveland, where her half brother lived—Robert Layson, my grandmother's son by her first marriage. He and his wife lived in a house behind an apartment building and were happy to have my mother and me, but my mother recalls that for her it was wrong from the start.

Mother said: "I knew the moment I got there I couldn't live there. Cleveland was so dirty. So much concrete and no grass. Just grease all over the place. And I always kept you so clean. As soon as we got there, the pretty little white things I had on you got dirty and you got dirt all over you. It was the first time you had ever been dirty. I got in touch with Momma and she came up and we rerouted our belongings back to Due West."

Once there, the two women grew even closer. I think they had ceased to be mother and daughter and had become each other's best friend. And they both needed a best friend. My grandmother's husband was an alcoholic and was becoming increasingly abusive. So my mother rented a small house on the highway that ran through town and she and my grandmother moved.

My mother lived for the days when "Old Man Wharton," a friend who walked to town to collect the mail, would come back down the road and, spotting her from a distance, would begin shouting, "I got it! I got it! I got it!" all the way down the road, so that she and the whole neighborhood would know that a letter had arrived from my father. But, she said sadly, there weren't many. By now my father, in the North African theater of operations, was one of the few Black chaplains serving overseas at the time, fighting both the war and the racists who regarded the all-Black fighting forces with suspicion and often treated them with contempt and disdain.

He was always pretty closed-mouth about the bad experiences, not even telling my mother until after he had returned home that he had been wounded and was awarded the Purple Heart as a direct result of enemy action somewhere near Bari, Italy. But he did tell us the story of his experience walking through an Italian town. He said that the local people kept running up behind the Black soldiers and lifting up their jackets. My father spoke fluent Italian, among several other languages, and when he asked them why they were doing this, one of the Italians told him it was because the white American soldiers had told them to stay away from the Black soldiers because they had tails. When he told us that story, my father was more bemused than bitter, almost as if he pitied them for their ignorance and fear. The pictures he brought home, bearing such warm inscriptions as "To My Dear Chaplain Hunter," and often signed "Affettuosamente," illustrated what little effect the story had on the Italians—especially the Italian women at whom the warnings were certainly directed. Still, it was surely a demanding and trying time for men like my father, who were expected to act as liaisons between the men and the white leaders. Even though the chaplains themselves were leaders, they had to defer to the white commanding officers. There were no Black commanding officers.

Meanwhile, my mother began preparing for the time when my father would be coming home. She corresponded with Mrs. Mary Daniel Martin, a wealthy Black lady, and eventually decided to buy a house from her in Covington, Georgia. She told me, "I felt we would enjoy life more, as I had lived there so long, and I wanted to be away from Due West when Charles came home." And so we left my first place before I really came to know it, but not before it had become a part of me.

chapter 2

Covington, Georgia

The first place I really knew as home was Covington, Georgia. Compared to Due West, it was a teeming metropolis, but in actuality it was a small town in the northern part of the state. It was a place where my mother's family had roots, and finding my own place among the many branches of those roots was sometimes difficult, and occasionally mysterious. For most of my childhood, I would remain in the dark about a lot of it.

The street that we lived on—Brown Street—was actually named for my great-grandfather, but no one in my family really talked about it. That's because Ike Brown was white and never married my great-grandmother. It was my mother who told me the story, with neither pride nor embarrassment, but rather matter-of-factly.

Here is what she said: "My father, Rochell Brown, went by the name of his father, Ike Brown, who was a rich white landowner with farms and stables and a huge white colonial home, where he lived with his mother until his death. He never married. But my Grandma Josephine bore his child, and he took care of her. He gave her a nice large house, painted yellow. Not many Black folk lived in painted houses. It had six big rooms, with front and back porches. She never worked for anyone—kept barrels of flour and sugar, and had all the groceries she wanted, and she dressed, as folks said, 'like a queen.' She was a mixture of Cherokee Indian and white, the color of bronze, with long, straight black hair. And she was full of life. When I would go to visit her sometimes, she would be cleaning up and she would have the gramophone playing and she would be dancing all around while she dusted the tables and made up the bed."

It would appear that the churchgoers in the community didn't think too much of my Great-grandma Josephine's way of life, or so it would seem from an anecdote my mother relayed: "Ma Josephine told me about going to church on Sunday, dressed to kill, and she would have the whole pew to herself. Nobody would sit next to her."

"Did that bother her?" I asked.

"Naw," my mother replied. "Not in the least." But then my mother added, she wasn't sure. Maybe it did. But if it did, she bore it silently and kept on living as best she could, with what she had.

As for the father of my grandfather, she told me: "Ike Brown recognized my father as his son, and my father rode his horses and played at his house. My father had a brother, George, who was a barber for the white trade, and he taught my father the trade. George moved to Calhoun, Georgia, where he killed a white man in the center of town and got away. He then went to the Klondike to search for gold. He wrote for a while, then disappeared. My Aunt Fannie Mae—the one I lived with while going to school in Chicago—was also white, and had been adopted by my grandmother. She later found George out West, where he had passed for white and married a white woman and had a family.

"My grandmother did finally marry a Black man named Lindsay, and had a daughter, who was named Althea. My father was working as a barber. The shop was owned by a wealthy Black family named Daniels and was the only Black business on the town square. My daddy shaved and cut hair for all the prominent white people. The chief of police, the sheriff, the bank president, the postmaster were all friends of his. The sheriff had a large farm, and when he went for meat or produce, he'd come by our house and give Daddy whatever he wanted from the farm.

"Mr. Daniels had a well-equipped shop. He had two bathrooms with tubs. At that time, some white folks and a few Black folks had tubs in their bathrooms. Most, though, had outdoor toilets and bathed in tin washtubs. The two tubs in the shop stayed busy—25 cents for a hot bath. Shaves were 15 cents and haircuts 25 cents. Most times, Daddy had four other barbers, who were Black, working for him. He was a very handsome man, fair—he looked white—with soft brown hair and a sweet smile. He dressed in very fine suits, all of which came from the postmaster, Mr. John Calloway. They also raised fox terriers together and Boston bull pups. My daddy had a boy dog and a girl dog named U-Know and I-Know. He was happy most of the time, because everybody respected him. He felt as important as any of his white friends, and they treated him as one of them. Whenever the sheriff made a run on the bootlegger, he'd go by the barbershop and tell Daddy to come on over to the courthouse and get a couple of gallons of what he said was 'good moonshine.' "

Ike Brown had promised to buy my grandfather his own barbershop and, in fact, had discussed it. That was on a Sunday. On that Monday, he had a heart attack and died. The white members of the family sent for my grandfather, to tell him that Ike Brown was dead and to ask him to shave him and cut his hair, never allowing that my grandfather just might have wanted a little time for his own emotions or grief. Although my mother remembers his saying it was the hardest thing he ever had to do in life, she said he also charged them ten dollars. When I asked why, she told me: "He said he knew that that was the last he'd ever get from the Browns, now that his father was dead, and so he decided to get all he could."

On my grandmother's side, the roots were equally tangled. Her mother, Ellen Wilson, came from Macon, Georgia. When she was a teenager, in 1879, her mother allowed her to go with a white family, the Harrises, to be a companion for their children. As my mother told me the story: "Just a child herself, she became pregnant by the son of the family. When the Harris family found out she was pregnant, they sent her back to her mother. Her mother took her in, and life went on. Everybody in that family, including my mother, looked like pure Caucasians, although their grandmother was part Indian, so they had long, black, silky hair.

"Back in Macon, Ellen married a Black man named Dave Wilson—which is where my mother's last name came from. Dave Wilson was a cruel man, and Momma said she could hear her mother crying many nights because of his meanness. She became ill and stayed ill and in terrible pain for a long time. Momma said she passed part of her intestines before she died. She had cancer of the uterus. All that time, she was suffering at home, because Black people just didn't go to the hospital."

My grandmother was extremely close to her mother. All her life, she had a habit of writing her mother's name any time she had a pencil in her hand. Sometimes, my mother told me, she would sit for a long time, just writing "Ellen Wilson, Ellen Wilson, Ellen Wilson." It was a minor miracle that my grandmother could write at all, for, as my mother recalled, "Momma used to say that when she got to the third grade and could read and write, her momma thought that was enough."

That's when Ellen Wilson took her daughter, Frances, out of school and started her working for white folks. But she already had developed a curiosity about the world and a love of learning, so she never stopped educating herself. She was probably the first news junkie I ever knew. In Covington, we subscribed to three newspapers—the *Atlanta Constitution*; the *Atlanta Daily World*, which was the oldest Black daily in America; and the Covington *News*. Every day, she read each paper from front to back. And we always listened to the news on the radio. H. V. Kaltenborn was a name I remember from my childhood.

Like her mother, my grandmother had unhappy marriages. The first was to a man who, she used to tell me, was "one of the prettiest men who ever walked on this earth." His name was Robert Layson, and he was a tall, light-skinned Pullman porter, with black, curly hair. She thought he surely must have loved, because with his looks and his Pullman-porter job, with its spiffy-looking uniform, he could have had just about any woman he wanted. But he chose to marry her. And she was carried away with him.

Soon after the marriage, however, she found out that he was a womanizer and, in fact, had a white woman who bought him silk underwear and pajamas. My mother says he told my grandmother all this. She told me, "He bragged about her and told my mother that the reason this woman bought him all those things was that she did not want him to come to her with clothes he wore when he was home with my mother, who she knew was Black."

My grandmother bore him a son, Robert Layson, but after a while she could no longer tolerate his behavior and she divorced him. Robert Layson was a teenager when my grandmother married Rochell Brown.

It was a marriage made in heaven, my mother later recalled. Rochell Brown adored my grandmother, and by the time they married she was over her childlike infatuation with the handsome Pullman porter. For a while, they lived in Macon, Georgia. Sometime in the latter part of 1917, my grandfather and grandmother and her son boarded a northbound train, joining what became the "Great Migration," the dramatic series of mass moves that started in 1910 and saw somewhere between 300,000 and 1 million Blacks leave the South and enter the cities of the North. While some were hoping to escape the "debbil in de white man," according to Florette Henri in *Black Migration*,* more often than not, as it was with my grandparents, it was a combination of factors, not the least of them being the search for a better, more economically secure life. World War I had created new industrial plants up North, and the speed with which Blacks began fleeing the South was so swift that the Macon *Telegraph* was moved to sound an alarm about the potentially disastrous effect this migration would have on the Southern economy. "Everybody seems to be asleep about what is going on right under their noses," the paper editorialized. "That is, everybody but those farmers who have awakened up of mornings recently to find every male Negro over 21 . . . gone—to Cleveland, to Pittsburgh, to Chicago."†

While most Northern cities got their fair share of Black migrants, Detroit got the most, with a population that by 1920 became eight times as great as it had been in 1910. This period gave birth to the "Motor City," which years later, transformed by Black talent into Motown, would provide the music of the Movement of which I was

---

* Garden City, N.Y.: Anchor Press/Doubleday, 1976, p. 51.
† Henri, p. 72.

a part. But for now, it was seen as providing economic opportunity for Black people woefully in need of it. And it was to Detroit that my grandparents went.

My mother remembers what her mother told her of the move: "They lived in furnished rooms that were cramped and unattractive, and they didn't find any better times up North. In fact, my father just found Detroit too big and too impersonal for his liking. It was so different from the kind of Southern places he had always known and loved. My mother got a job at a hospital there, and soon after that began to feel sick. She got so sick that she made an appointment with the hospital for an examination. She told me that both Daddy and my stepbrother, Robert, didn't want to get home first that afternoon because they were so afraid to learn what was wrong with her. She said the doctor said, 'I'm sorry, Mrs. Brown, but you are pregnant.'

" 'But, Doctor,' she said, 'my baby is eighteen years old, and my husband is gray-haired.'

"That was a good joke for a while, but Daddy said, 'My baby will not be born in Detroit. We are going home to Macon.' And he said that when he got on the train in Michigan to go to Macon he was going to take a laxative, sit on the toilet on the train, and say, 'Shit on Michigan,' and he'd do it all the way back to Georgia."

Althea Ruth Brown was born on May 20, 1918, in Macon, Georgia. They had a Black doctor, but Althea was listed on the birth certificate as being white. And, of course, being the daughter of my grandparents, she was extremely fair, with gray eyes and brown, straight hair.

Shortly after my mother was born, my grandmother had an interesting experience. My mother described it: "A friend of hers worked for a Jewish family there—the Wachtel and Waxelbaum family—and they needed a maid. The lady, Mrs. Pearl Wachtel, came to see her, and of course Mother explained that she had a young baby. Mrs. Wachtel told her to just bring the baby with her. She fell in love with me as a baby and I looked white, so while my mother worked, Mrs. Wachtel kept me herself. I slept in her bed and she begged my mother to give me to her. She said no one would ever know, and explained all the advantages I could have as a rich white girl. Now my father was the proudest gray-haired father in the world, and he would hear nothing of this."

When my mother was three years old, they moved back to Covington. The Daniels boys had died and the family needed someone to run the barbershop, so my grandfather took over and his business flourished. And then a second big surprise—another child was born, my Uncle Rochell.

My grandmother continued to work for white people, most of whom treated her well—until she was hired by a Captain and Mrs. Cooper. He was a conductor on the railroad. My mother probably would have remembered the Cooper story in any event, but there was a twist to it that had all the makings of poetic justice.

Here's what she recalled:

"Mrs. Cooper had a granddaughter, Renee, who was a few years older than I was, but I played with her in her back yard playhouse while my mother cleaned house. Mrs. Cooper was the only white person I can say was mean. My mother ran home one evening so she could cook our supper, and while chopping wood, she fell out cold. Mrs. Cooper was having her bridge club, so after the doctor came and said it seemed that Momma had a brain tumor and would have to go to Atlanta to the hospital, Momma told me to tell Mrs. Cooper that she was sick and could not come back and serve the bridge club. Well, Mrs. Cooper came to the back door after I knocked and started saying, 'What is it? What is it?' and I said, 'Momma can't come back because . . .' But before I could tell her how sick she was, she slammed the door in my face. I was eleven, and I just didn't know what to do. When I got home, I found out that when the doctor went to Daddy's barbershop and told him about Momma's attack he had a stroke. They said she had a brain tumor and they would have to operate. My father refused. He told them, 'I'll never let you cut open her head.' She recovered, but Daddy was never quite the same after that.

"Now, the first time I ever heard of the University of Georgia was when I played with Renee. She talked of going there, and of course, I knew I'd never be able to. When Momma sent me to Chicago to high school, Renee went to the University of Georgia. A few days after getting there, she and a boy went horseback riding. Her horse kept acting up, so the young man jerked the bridle and pulled the horse's head down. Renee went over the horse's head, fell, and broke her neck, then died. I felt bad about Renee, but I could never get over how her grandmother treated Momma. I soon forgot about all that, and never thought about the University of Georgia. Not for a long time. And I certainly never, ever would have dreamed that a child of mine would go there as a student."

My mother didn't go to college. Instead, she came back home from Chicago and got a job working as a secretary for the Covington branch of the Black-owned Atlanta Life Insurance Company. She lived at home and also helped my grandmother, who took in washing and ironing for some white families—the president of the bank and the pharmacist among them. My mother remembers that there was a big round black pot out in the back of the house that my grandmother used to boil the clothes in. "I used to iron all those white shirts for the president of the bank," my mother recalls. "I could iron them just like the laundry. Momma didn't like to iron. She said it made her sick. I also ironed all the gowns from my daddy's barbershop and those little-bitty towels. He must have had a hundred of them. He had a more dignified job, but a haircut was only a quarter, a shave 15 cents, and a shoeshine a dime. So we had to work hard to make ends meet. My mother's job as a cook paid two dollars a week."

To supplement their income, my grandmother also sold toilet articles—face cream, lotions, and what one customer referred to as "body odor" (deodorant). "Black folks didn't have any cars in those days, so Momma and I walked everywhere we went. We'd walk to Oxford, and we sold to workers at the cotton mill in Porterdale, and that was about five miles. Sometimes we'd hitch a ride with Mr. Shoats, who had a bus that would take the workers out to the cotton mill early in the morning and back at night. But most of the time we walked."

With all that, however, the work that took up most of my grandmother's time yielded no monetary gain. She was devoted to her church—Bethlehem Baptist, believed to be the oldest Black church in the county. Although Martin Luther King, Jr.'s maternal grandfather was one of the church's pastors, from 1896 to 1902, the man around whom a legend grew was the Reverend George W. Woodson. As my mother tells it, "He would preach for two hours and nobody would move. The church would be packed with Black folks, but during the service whites would come and sit on the banks and listen." My mother continued: "Your grandmother was in the Missionary Society and everything the church had to offer, and was usually the president. Because I had a pretty good handwriting, and I had studied Gregg shorthand in high school in Chicago, I could take good notes, so I was always elected secretary."

My grandmother was quite an organizer. One of the things she helped organize, along with a doctor who had come to Covington from the West Indies, was a club called the King David's Council. My mother said it was like a burial society; people paid dues, and when they died the families would get something like fifty dollars for the funeral and burial. "They'd set up these little societies in small towns all around Covington and they'd have meetings and conventions. Just like the Masons and the Elks. You know, there just wasn't a lot for Black folks to do, so these societies would have programs and picnics—things like that. I think people joined for the fellowship. And while these weren't religious clubs, religion was at the center of everything, so there was a religious flavor. Momma was really good at this, and she always kept busy. She was so intelligent, although not educated. I always said that if she'd had a little education she would have been a powerful woman, because she was as smart as she could be."

Both my mother and grandmother made a lot of speeches, and often my mother, having had a more formal education, would help my grandmother with her preparation and delivery. Once, when my grandmother was running for the presidency of one of the many clubs she belonged to, she and my mother were working on her delivery. "We were in the living room and I was sitting in a chair and Momma was practicing in front of me," my mother recalled. "She got to the line where she had to say, 'And to you, my worthy opponents,' and she read it as op'onnents. I said, 'Opponents.' And she repeated 'Opponents.' But then she would start all over again and get to the word and say 'op'onnents.' We rehearsed and rehearsed. Finally the night came and she was delivering her speech and got to the line and said, 'And to you, my worthy op'onnents.' She knew immediately that she had said it wrong, but she kept on going, and in spite of her goof, she won anyway. We laughed about that for a long time. She had such a wonderful sense of humor.''

It was through church speaking that my mother met my father. Just out of Atlanta's Gammon Seminary, the dashing young minister had come to Covington in March 1937 to pastor the St. Paul A.M.E. Church. Although my mother was a Baptist at the time, the A.M.E. Church was next door to their house. As she recalls: ''There were quite a few unmarried young preachers, and they were all searching around. Charles was going around with a young Covington girl who would send him little notes and give him presents.''

At the time my mother and father met, she had been seeing another young minister, DeQuincy Newman, who was also a friend of my father's and went on to become one of the great voices of the Methodist Church. Like my grandmother, my mother was very active in their church. She remembers: ''I was in everything for young people that they had at the church—the Baptist Young People's Organization, and there was a social club that my mother was the matron of.''

On the night she first met my father, who was pastoring a small church in Covington at the time, she had just given a speech at the New Hope Baptist Church, in which she said that the Baptist Church was ''traveling at an oxcart gait in an airplane age.'' She explained it this way: ''We were always trying to interest young people and bring them into the church. I just didn't feel that the church was doing enough to show that they were really interested in them. It's the problem the church has always had. Not enough programs really geared to young people. We didn't have a lot of teenage pregnancy and things like that, but we had some wild ones, and the church just wasn't being aggressive about going after them. They preached from the Bible, but didn't apply it to modern-day problems.''

After the program, she remembers, ''Charles came over and introduced himself and complimented me on my speech. He was a lot taller than I was—he was about six feet and I'm about five foot four—so I had to look up at him when he talked. But he was very charming, and after we talked a little while he asked if he could see me again. Four months later, at the A.M.E. Annual Conference in Atlanta, we were married by Bishop W. A. Fountain, in the parlor of his house on Boulevard. I hadn't been expecting it to happen that day, but I was sort of expecting it to happen any day, so every time we went out on a special date I would wear this little light-blue dress I had bought. On a hunch, I put it on that day, too." After the wedding, they drove back to Covington.

"Old Roman!" my mother recalls my father bellowing as the newlyweds entered my grandparents' home in Covington. "Old Roman" was the affectionate nickname my father had given to my grandfather soon after they met, probably because of his Romanesque features. "I've made your daughter my wife," he boomed.

"Like hell!" my grandfather roared back. "Like hell you have."

And with a great sense of satisfaction that he had bested the "Old Roman," my father, gentler now, responded, "Oh yes, I have."

I asked my mother if she thought the fact that my father was dark-skinned had anything to do with my grandfather's objections to him, and she said no, quite emphatically. As light as they all were, they always identified themselves proudly as Black, even when they could have easily passed as white in some other location.

My mother thinks that my grandfather probably would not have approved of any man who wanted to marry her—"He just didn't think anybody was good enough"—but especially one who was fifteen years her senior (he was thirty-three, she was eighteen) and one who most probably would take her away from Covington. In fact, at the conference, the annual meeting at which the ministers received their church assignments, my father had just been named to St. Philip's, in Atlanta, so the Old Roman's unease was altogether justified.

At that point, my mother left the Baptist Church and joined the church of my father and his father, the African Methodist Episcopal, the denomination established in 1819, with Richard Allen as its first bishop. Allen, a former slave, broke with the Methodist Church over their insistence that Blacks sit in seats separated from the whites. In staging a walkout at the St. George's Church in Philadelphia in 1787, Allen is widely credited with starting "the first protest movement by Negroes in America . . . the first attempt on the part of Negroes to strike for dignity and respect for personality."★ The words "He who would be free must himself strike the first blow" infused his church down through the generations, including the Reverend J. A. Delaine's, the A.M.E. minister who started the case that ultimately led to the Supreme Court's outlawing segregated schools, and Linda Brown, the schoolgirl from Topeka, Kansas, whose name that landmark case bears and whose father, like mine, was an A.M.E. minister.

★ Howard D. Gregg, *The A.M.E. Church and the Current Negro Revolt* (Nashville, Tenn.: no date), p. 7.

chapter **3**

212 Brown Street

The house my mother bought for us in Covington was at 212 Brown Street. It was not the largest on the street, but I thought it was the nicest. It was a comfortable four-room house, to which my mother added a kitchen and a modern bathroom. She also screened in the front porch, where she and my grandmother would sit at dusk, talking to each other. I can remember many nights falling asleep in my twin bed, in the bedroom I shared with my mother, listening to the sound of their quiet conversation, which was as soothing and as comforting as a lullaby. We had a large back yard, where my grandmother had a garden. She grew collard greens, tomatoes, okra, corn, squash, and other vegetables, and she also had lots of flowers. She loved flowers, and it may be because of her that I do, too. I hate to throw out a cut flower until the absolute last sign of life has left it.

My mother and grandmother also raised rabbits. I loved having them in the yard as pets, although they were never let out of the cage next to the house; but I also loved eating them when my grandmother fixed them. They multiplied so fast, I never felt guilty eating the ones she cooked. She always did all the cooking for the family. She was a superb cook, and I don't remember ever seeing her stick to a recipe.

Even if she read one, the dish always ended up being her own original creation. It was a dash of this and a smidgen of that. She was patient and allowed me to help her in the kitchen—mostly letting me lick the thick buttery cream icing from the bowl, at first; then, when I got old enough, she allowed me to come in and experiment with my own creations. I used to watch her use food coloring to make the icing yellow, and once, when I got ready to bake a cake for my younger brother's birthday, I decided that since he was a boy he should have a blue cake, so I used blue food coloring in the batter, which we always made from scratch. It turned out sort of bluish-green, but my grandmother never made any reference to how it looked; she just praised me and said it tasted really good.

Between our house and the last house on the street—a large three-story place called the Daniel House, which by then was broken up into rental units—was an empty plot of land that made an excellent, albeit barren, playground for me and the many children in the neighborhood. The first time I ever tried out the new bicycle I had received for Christmas, I got on it and rode straight across that land, and smack into a mulberry tree. I was scratched up and bruised a bit from the encounter, but the tree remained a constant in my life. I ate from it as soon as the berries turned dark purple and juicy, and I climbed it often, feeling that its upper branches, high above ground I knew so well, held out the promise of revealing the old tree's secrets.

We also had a peach tree—a source of bittersweet memories for me, for it seemed as if my mother was always telling me, "Go get me some peach-tree tea." By that she meant that I should break off a slim switch that she could whip me with, usually on Sundays, because I had been too squirmy in church. During what I thought were interminable services, which sometimes went on for as long as three hours—and I had already been there earlier for Sunday school—she would start out by elbowing me; when that didn't work, she would pinch my arm. Inevitably, when that didn't work, she would lean down to me and whisper the dreaded words: "I'll see you when we get home." The dreaded "peach-tree tea." A bigger offense than squirming in church was bringing her a scrawny switch. If I had to be sent back for a bigger switch, it meant the beating would be twice as hard and maybe twice as long. By the time she finished with me most Sundays, my legs would be a mess of welts, for I had to stand there and take it. I dared not run. But I did scream!

Anyone in the neighborhood who wasn't deaf had to know what was going on at 212 Brown Street, because I was unrestrained in my response. I'm sure nobody thought two cents about it, because, while not every child in the neighborhood got a dose of peach-tree tea, similar punishment was a common prescription for most of them. In fact, if one of their parents "caught you wrong," it was perfectly acceptable, if not desirable, that they administer their own punishment on the spot. My first-grade teacher once slapped me because she mistakenly thought I was hiding a classmate's handkerchief with a nickel for lunch tied in the corner. And while I was emotionally hurt because I was innocent, and she did slap me hard, I never mentioned it at home, because I knew that the teacher had such license.

What I found hard to understand was that all the while my mother was beating me she would be crying herself, and sometimes, long after I had gotten over the stinging dose of peach-tree tea, I would hear her off in some other part of the house, sobbing. I know now that it must have been due to the stress of my father's long absences, but she never talked openly about just how sad and lonely she was. By the time we moved to 212 Brown Street, I was almost four years old and my father had been overseas almost all my life.

From time to time, he would send presents. Once, he sent me a beautiful matching coat and bonnet from Italy. My mother took a picture of me in it and mailed it to him. And he also sent her a beautiful gray tablecloth embroidered with colorful bunches of fruit. She never used any of the things he sent. She would open them, admire them, and pack them away. She didn't like to show off.

My father returned to the United States in October 1945, two months after the war ended. We drove to Atlanta to meet him, and I remember sitting on his lap, soaking in his smells—brass and Dentyne chewing gum and pipe tobacco. But he was not home in Covington for long. He was assigned to Camp Atterbury, in Indiana. He asked my mother to come along, so she hastily packed up and we joined him.

It was a good time for us, for the most part. We lived in a rented room upstairs in the home of a Black widow lady and often went to the base with my father for dinner. The soldiers loved and respected him, and my mother was a favorite of the cooks in the officers' dining room, where German prisoners-of-war had probably replaced Blacks as waiters. The mess sergeants would often make special dishes for my mother if they knew she was coming.

By this time, Black and white officers were eating together. My father seemed to be comfortable with the situation, although I can remember an embarrassed silence during one time when we were eating a meal that included gravy. I noticed that my father, who was seated across the table from me, had a lot of gravy left on his plate and no roll. While I didn't know my father well, I knew that he liked gravy, so I reached for the roll on my plate and, as I held it in the air in his direction, during a moment of absolute silence at the table, I called out, "Here, Daddy, sop up your gravy."

My mother thought it was funny. My father pretended that I had not spoken, as did everyone else. I didn't understand it at the time, although I still remember the sinking feeling that the gesture hadn't had the effect I had intended. I wanted so much to please my father and make him glad to be home with us. But this kind of social integration was still rare, and off the post the sight of a Black officer was rarer still. Once, when my father and mother and I were walking down the street in Indianapolis, the town nearest the camp, we encountered a group of white men who took one look at my father and his captain's bars, which he had been awarded only the year before, and as we passed, one said quite loudly, "Well, I'll be damned. I've seen everything now." If my father heard it, we never knew it.

Being on post with my father really made me feel special, because everyone treated my mother and me with the respect they showed my father. But these times were short-lived, as was the entire period at Camp Atterbury. It seems as if no sooner had we arrived than my father received orders to leave again. In fact, it was five months after he got to Atterbury that he was assigned to Korea, where tensions were rising over its recent war's-end division into the Soviet North and the U.S. South zones of occupation.

My grandmother was staying in our house in Covington, and once again my mother decided to go home to her. My father drove us to the train station, and the last thing I remember is seeing him standing there waving to us as our train pulled out. My mother was crying.

Back in Covington, we picked up right where we had left off. Since we had the first, and for a long time the only, television set on the street, our living room was always full of neighborhood kids watching *Kukla, Fran and Ollie, Howdy Doody*, and Arthur Godfrey. I even wrote Arthur Godfrey a fan letter once, and was awestruck by the postcard he sent back, signed.

Since most people didn't have television, the movies remained popular with us all. That's what Saturday was for, all afternoon. We would get our 15 cents and walk the few blocks to the edge of town, where the colored theater was situated. The show, as we called it, would be packed with noisy, boisterous young people, excitedly waiting for the screen to light up. There would be previews of coming attractions, newsreels, and cartoons, and then a serial, like *Pogo Man* or *Tarzan*, and a cowboy movie, which we would see all the way through. The big favorites were Roy Rogers and Dale Evans ("Happy Trails to you, until we meet again") and, of course, Trigger, Hopalong Cassidy, Zorro, etc.

Every now and then, as a special Friday-night treat, my mother would take me to see some other kind of picture. One that always stuck in my mind was *Pinky*, with Jeanne Crain in the title role. It was very different from what we used to see, and a very different kind of movie for that time. It was the story of a young, fair-skinned, Southern Black woman who had been studying to be a nurse up North. She got engaged to a white doctor, but after deciding that she would never give up her Black heritage and concluding that the relationship would never work, she returned to her Southern roots. Oddly enough, she discovers these roots after the white woman her grandmother works for falls ill and she is called in to nurse her back to health. The woman dies, leaving Pinky her estate. The dowager's family contests the will, because its members can't bear the thought of a Black woman getting her hands on all this property. They sue, charging Pinky with unduly influencing their sick relative. But Pinky fights back and wins, and turns the estate into a nursing home and school for Blacks. Everybody was talking about this movie when we went to see it. Ethel Waters played the grandmother and Ethel Barrymore the dowager.

Sometime during the movie, when Pinky was on screen, in the semidarkness of the movie theater I could see my mother's face. I remember turning to her at one point and whispering that she was "my Pinky." She just smiled and kept on watching the movie. And in that moment she did look just like Jeanne Crain.

Despite the fact that I was darker than my mother—I had sandy hair that was fine but kinky—I was often taunted about my color during my years at Washington Street School. It usually happened after school, as I walked on this one particular route, a shortcut, with my friends from Brown Street—my best friend, Betty, and her younger sister, Shirley. Whenever we collided with the girls from Short Street, a rough part of town where people were always fighting, stabbing, or shooting somebody—especially on Saturday nights—I would break out in a sweat, because I knew I was in for trouble. The kids there were bigger than most of us, liked to fight, and were always picking on somebody. If I happened to be there when one of them started something with some other girl, they would push me to get into it, literally and figuratively. "Go'n, white girl," they'd shout at me, pushing me from behind. "Git her." A circle would form, and everybody would get into it. "Yeah, white girl," they'd yell, "git her! Git her! Git her!"

I hated to fight and hated these scenes, because there was no way out. If I didn't hit the other girl, I would get hit, and since I didn't have any beef with anybody, I usually ended up getting hit. But I didn't dare tell my mother, because she would have gone to the school and reported it to the principal. I tried to summon the words my grandmother had taught me: "Sticks and stones may break my bones, but words will never hurt me." But it was small consolation. They only left me alone when I took the long way home.

My mother and grandmother never had such problems among the people who knew them in Covington—at least not that I was aware of or ever heard them talk about—and just about everybody knew them, including the rough, grown-up crowd on Short Street, with whom they got along just fine. They all called my grandmother "Mis' Frank," and my mother "Altha' Ruth." They didn't socialize a lot, minding their own and not other people's business, unless somebody got sick or needed help. In that case, they were always there with something practical, like food, or with an offer to run an important errand in our car. My father, on the other hand, stayed in the street most of the time he was home on leave. In fact, whenever he did come home, he spent more time on Short Street playing checkers with the old men than he did at home. If my mother wanted to find him, all she had to do was get in the car and drive to Short Street, and there he'd be, sitting under a chinaberry tree, deep in a checkers game. That was one thing about my father: he was sometimes described as arrogant, but I've always felt that that was because of the supreme self-confidence he exuded, never acting as if anyone could "put him in his place." His mother used to say it was because she let my grandfather's somewhat haughty sister be the one to "walk him around the house" when he was a baby. Those were the days when recovery after childbirth was long and confining, and you stayed in bed for weeks, sometimes wearing a hat to prevent catching a cold. The only way a baby got any fresh air was when a relative or somebody close to the family would "walk him around the house." And it was believed that the baby would be "marked" by the first person to do so. Despite his "mark" of arrogance, my father never put a distance between himself and others, regardless of what they did for a living or how much education they had. More than once, he used to quote me Rudyard Kipling's lines:

> *If you can talk with crowds and keep your virtue,*
> *Or walk with Kings—nor lose the common touch.*
> *Yours is the Earth and everything that's in it,*
> *And—which is more—you'll be a Man, my son!*

My father was full of heavy messages like that, from as early as I can remember. Sometimes they made sense and sometimes they didn't. One of the times they didn't was when I had to deal with the girls from Short Street. Betty Wright and I never had fights. But we did argue, and when we did, especially on weekends, there would be tension on Sunday morning, because we always walked the half-odd mile from Brown Street to Short Street, where the Sunday school was located. The church was next door to my Great-grand-mother Ma Josephine's house, although she was long dead when I started going to St. Paul. If Betty and I had fallen out, I would go up to her house with a note that said something like, "Let's don't be mad anymore. Let's be friends." I would leave the note, and a few minutes later Betty would emerge, and we would walk to Short Street, usually with Shirley in tow.

Betty and I were not just best friends; she was my first soulmate. Shirley and I got into trouble together—like the time we decided to smoke a wild weed called rabbit tobacco in the bathroom off our back porch. We rolled it up in newspaper and lit it and, after a couple of puffs and coughs, got caught by my grandmother, who could smell the smoke. Betraying me, she called my mother, whereupon I got a whipping and was sent to bed in the middle of the day. Shirley got a whipping, too. The next time, we tried snuff. It always looked so interesting, protruding from inside the bottom lips of women on Brown Street, who from time to time would spit, propelling halfway out into the yard a long, thick string of brown saliva that had been mixing with the snuff inside their mouth. That part wasn't enticing, but the snuff inside the little round boxes always contained a whiff of strawberry or peach. Or maybe that was just the power of sug-gestion from the label—Sweet Dental Peach Snuff. At any rate, the suggestion was not powerful enough to penetrate my tastebuds. We didn't get caught "dippin'," but we didn't have to. I was so sick after that first dip that I didn't have any wish to do it again.

But it was Betty with whom I daydreamed. We were going to leave home. I would become a doctor, and Betty a nurse. When the word got out around the neighborhood, some of the local boys wanted to know if we wanted to *play* doctor first. Being good Sunday-school girls, we declined.

I loved to go to Betty's house. Upward of seven or eight people lived in four small rooms, with low ceilings. But to me they seemed more cozy than cramped. Our house was airier, with higher ceilings and more spacious rooms, but being alone, except for Horace and

Tommy and a gaggle of other dolls and imaginary friends, made me wistful. Especially when I had to come in before dark. My house was quiet, and being an only child, I spent a lot of time entertaining myself. That's when I would read stories or make them up, sharing them with Horace, Tommy, and the other dolls, whose names changed regularly, along with the little dramas I made up.

I got part of my sense of drama from the radio. On special nights, we all listened to what we used to call "the stories," from the Mutual Radio series *I Love a Mystery*. The scariest was *The Shadow* ("Who knows what evil lurks in the hearts of men?" the low, mysterious voice would ponder as the door screeched open. "The Shadow knows"). I wouldn't miss that one, or "Jack, Doc and Reggie," three guys who were that era's Indiana Jones, only scarier—(especially *The Temple of Vampires*, where they were always in some monastery where the doors creaked, strange creatures in long habits floated about threateningly, and someone or something was lurking, ready to strike and suck your blood. By the time I got to bed at night, I would be trembling with fear, knowing that one of those creatures was going to come after me in the night and suck my blood and nobody would know until it was too late.

My mother let me spend the night up the street at the Wrights' house every now and then, and that was heaven to me, piled up in bed with Betty and Shirley—Sarah Ann was older and didn't have much to do with us, and so was Jimmy. It was at the Wrights' that I learned all about onion sandwiches—onions between two slices of white bread, smeared with mustard, salt, and pepper. Or, in the absence of onions, mustard sandwiches, and sometimes, in the absence of mustard, salt-and-pepper sandwiches. What may have been born of necessity for the Wrights, I saw as a rare treat.

The few close friends my mother and grandmother had lived a long way from Brown Street. When they did visit, it would usually be on Sundays, after church (and after my peach-tree tea). We'd get in the car and drive across town to visit Mr. Joe Baker and his wife, Hattie; or, in the opposite direction, Mrs. Emma Zanders and her husband, Elec, whose name was probably Alexander or something like that—all I ever heard was Elec. I don't think they had electricity, because their house was always dark and musty. But once a year, at

Christmas time, Mrs. Zanders baked us one of her special cakes, a musty-tasting walnut-filled layer cake, with a sugary glazed icing. The older Mrs. Zanders got, the harder it was for her to see, and the more walnut shell got into the icing. Even so, the cake was one of the treats I looked forward to all year. The Zanderses seemed very old, from my earliest memories of them. But most of my mother's friends were those she shared with my grandmother, and most of them were closer to my grandmother's age. I guess that may be why I have always enjoyed the company of older people, and how I learned from an early age to "be seen and not heard" in their presence.

chapter 4

So'Circle

We took occasional trips to visit our cousins—multitudes of them—in Social Circle (widely known as "So'Circle"), a Georgia town even smaller than Covington. Sometimes Betty and Shirley would come along, and we'd all pile into my mother's station wagon with the greatest anticipation. We never stopped in the town but went straight to our cousins' farm. Well, not quite straight if it was in the summertime. That was when the bushes along the narrow little dirt road leading to the farm were loaded down with plums—yellow and purple ones—and blackberries and scuppernongs, a grapelike fruit that we'd suck the insides out of and save the hull. My grandmother would soak them several times, then make the most delicious pie. For the other fruits and berries, we always had little sacks or containers in the car, and all that I didn't eat right off the bushes—dusty and delicious—we packed to bring home.

Our cousins were an odd assortment of shapes and colors; local folks called them "Black whites." My grandmother's first cousin headed the family. We called him Cuddin Johnny. Everybody around there apparently knew that Cuddin Johnny's mother, Mandy, a pure-bred Indian whose hair was so long she could sit on it and then some, had been taken into the home of a white couple in the area, and according to one of his sons, Cuddin Willie, "They used her as a slave girl to his wife and his woman to him. That's the way they was workin' it." Cuddin Willie told me that the arrangement was common for the time, and that there was no question that the husband was going to take care of the family. As for Grandma Mandy, he said, "She was just glad to have someone to take care of her." Grandma Mandy was the sister of my grandmother's mother, Ellen Wilson. Cuddin Willie said that the white sons of this family "can't face the Blacks." But, he said, he had a good time teasing them anyway. "When I see one of them in town, I call 'em 'brother,' and he'll say, 'I ain't none of your brother,' and I'll say, 'Oh yes, you are, and Black was there first.' "

Cuddin Johnny was a tall, gaunt-looking man who didn't have a lot to say. His wife, Cuddin Millie, was part Indian and part Black, and was what Southerners would describe as "a little piece of leather but well put together"—a tiny, wiry, dark figure who had given birth to fifteen children. As the children grew up, many of them repeated the pattern; I think it was Cuddin Ruth who, with ten, had the most. That was one of the reasons I enjoyed going to the country; there were so many kids that there was always someone my age to play with. Our visits didn't have much of a pattern; we made them whenever my mother or grandmother had a notion to go for a ride. I think it took less than an hour, but it was still a big adventure to go.

The summertime was the most fun, until our cousins had to start picking cotton. In those days, the school calendar revolved around cotton-picking time, and so long after I had started back to school, my young cousins were still going out into the cotton fields every day. I went with them once, and started off enthusiastically enough, walking the long, dusty rows, plucking the soft white bolls off the stalk and depositing them in a cloth sack slung over one shoulder. But a little of that went a long way. Not that I got tired—I was just bored with the endless repetition. Whatever curiosity I had about picking cotton was satisfied for me early on. My cousins were amused and joined me later—much later—back at the house, after they had finished a much longer day's work.

Cuddin Johnny had been a sharecropper on a farm owned by two white brothers. Several of his and Cuddin Millie's children were born on the farm, although they took the name Ivy from an earlier white farm they had lived on; that's how most Black folks got their names in those days after slavery. One of the brothers died, and the survivor made a deal with Cuddin Johnny. He sold him seventy-seven acres and allowed him to pay it off as he sold his cotton. Cuddin Johnny sold cotton in the fall of the year, and eventually paid off the debt. Cuddin Willie told me, "We made a good living. We's on the farm, so we didn't go hungry. We was raggedy, but we never got hungry."

In addition to tending the cotton fields, they grew vegetables and raised hogs and cows. Fall was hog-killing time, so we'd go down on a Saturday. By this time, there'd be a little nip in the air and we'd have to wear sweaters. But there would always be a place to warm up, near one of the big black pots with the wood fire going underneath and some wonderful concoction of stew brewing inside. My favorite was Brunswick stew, which seemed to contain some of everything that had been grown on the farm that year—corn, tomatoes, assorted parts of the pig, and only heaven and Cuddin Willie know what else.

As the stew in the pot was cooking, my cousins would prepare the meat for winter storage, dressing the parts of the pig to be laid out in the smokehouse and salted and then hung until about February. There would be meat from the smokehouse all winter—hams, shoulders. Breakfast with fried ham slices and red-eye gravy slopped all over grits and biscuits—the best food I ever ate! (Hence, "Here, Daddy, sop up your gravy.")

They got their milk from the two cows—buttermilk and sweet milk—and made their own butter from it. They also had sugarcane, which they would take to the mill and squeeze the juice out of. Then they would boil that and make a kind of sweetener for tea cakes, gingerbread, and other goodies. As Cuddin Willie said, "That and a glass of buttermilk, and you could go all day." We'd be there for hours, but sometime before dark, laden down with good, fresh food, we'd get in the car and head back to Atlanta.

What was as wonderful as the food at these gatherings was the feeling. Our cousins were always so glad to have us visit. The first one to spot us would call to the others, and they'd stop what they were doing to run to the car and throw their arms around us, hugging and kissing us all the way up the house; inside, the smells of tobacco and snuff and field and earth and hickory wood and smoke enveloped me, connecting me to them and a way of life that was so different from my own.

The only thing I didn't like about being there was when I had to use the toilet. It was in a little wooden shed in the back yard, an outhouse that had no running water or electricity. Inside was a bench-like wooden structure that had a round hole for you to sit over. Below was a bucket that collected the waste and was removed from time to time, emptied somewhere out in the woods, and sprinkled with lime. I would hold myself until I almost burst to keep from having to go to the outhouse. Although they kept it as clean as they could, I hated the smell, and I always imagined that as soon as I sat down and exposed my bare bottom, a snake or some other creature was going to spring up and bite me. But sometimes I just had to go, and when I did, I almost always got lightheaded from the combination of fear and holding my breath the whole time I was in there. But I knew better than to say anything about the outhouse. If I had, my mother would surely have smacked me right in the mouth (or threatened to wash out my mouth with soap).

chapter 5

115th-Between-
Lenox-and-Fifth

Not all my summers were spent in Georgia. In fact, I hardly ever spent the whole summer at home. My grandmother was a real adventurer, and I was her favorite traveling companion.

I first knew exactly where I was going to spend the fifth summer of my life when my Great-uncle Henry, who had met my grandmother and me at Penn Station, New York, as we arrived from Georgia, said to the cabdriver, "A Hundred-Fifteen-between-Lenox-and-Fifth."

Central Park, a mass of tiny green patterns, reminded me of the country. But once the green park gave way to the city, I saw nothing that reminded me of anything I'd ever seen before. All around me were tall, cold-stone buildings with expressionless faces. As far as I could see, there were no hills or sand or clay or grass; nor were there blossoming dogwood trees—or any trees at all—to identify the season. It was June, and in Georgia the crops were flourishing in summer sun and rain. But when the wind blew cold in my face, I realized that summer came late to this place. It was definitely not a Georgia June day, on which I would begin the summer without shoes.

Later on, my impressions of 115th Street changed with the scene.

My spirits lifted on the days when children my age played hopscotch, jumping in the chalk-drawn boxes on the sidewalk, or when they shot marbles that weren't really marbles but bottle tops weighted with candle wax. These children spoke a fast, musical language that I did not understand, and even when they spoke English, I often had to beg their pardon and ask them to repeat. Their names, instead of being Betty Jo and Mary Ruth and Sarah Ann—my friends back home—were Ana and Maria and Alaina. The boys were Tonio and Mario and Filipe, instead of Jimmy and Eddie and Pete. In the summer when it was hot, the neighborhood young cooled off in the water from fire hydrants opened by boys who appeared from around the corner and disappeared like wisps. The children also cooled off with the grape-ice, orange-ice, and lemon-ice cones that cost a nickel and had little effect.

At home, we had no havens from the heat. Instead, my friends and I crawled under houses, some of which were raised high off the ground by brick pillars, and looked for dust-covered bugs making their way in and out of the soft brown earth. We suffered from the heat only when there was nothing else to do, and when there was no one in the calaboose behind my house to talk to. We'd wander around the boxlike prison—altogether different from the red-brick jail where the more dangerous criminals were held—trying to find some crack that would allow us to see inside. But the cracks were always too small, so we had to be content with the sound of the voices inside and a slither of light.

The icehouse two blocks away, past the corner veterinarian's and up a dusty alley, was always a source of interest in hot weather. We were never allowed inside, so all we saw were huge blocks of ice being hauled out onto the ramp to be cut up and sold to individual purchasers, or to be carried away on trucks that had ICE in dull-orange letters on their sides.

There were not many places to wander to on 115th Street. The hallways leading into apartment buildings were darker and more forbidding than the calaboose back home. Absently, one day, I walked into a strange building and climbed the first flight of stairs, but since I was alone, I left hastily. Above the street there were always people in the windows, looking down on me and everything else that moved.

Out of the corner of my eye, I once saw a man sleeping in a basement alcove. He was a stranger (nearly everyone was), and the children's screaming voices failed to wake him, but they gave me comfort.

The nights on 115th Street were more vivid than the days. In my great-uncle's house, part of the hallway casually became the closet, and the part next to that became a bedroom. The house was laid out like the train that had brought my grandmother and me there. Years later, I learned it was called a railroad flat. As I lay in bed, the smell of leather luggage and mothballs made the night seem to close in around me. I missed the intimacy of the nights back home, where the soft and barely audible voices of my mother and grandmother on the porch made something warm and lovely of the night, where a few dogs barked and howled, sounding far off and dreamlike.

The sirens on Lenox Avenue frightened me at first, and would not let me sleep. One night, I tumbled out of bed and walked to the front of the house, where there was one window. For as far as I could see, people were walking along the street or standing languidly around their stoops, careless of the night or the sounds it brought them. Near the corner, people, colored by red and green and orange and yellow neon lights, stood gesturing and laughing about some secret thing that I could never know. Somewhere along the street, a bell rang with predictable regularity. It was the ragman, who got little for his time. Perhaps the nights would have come easier for me and would have seemed more like home had there been more windows. At home, every room had several windows, and the houses next door were not too close. But the windows on 115th Street were blinded by the buildings next door—they were almost close enough to touch—so I could not see the stars.

Mornings came quietly to 115th Street, unlike those in my home, where at daybreak, hungry, clucking chickens and silent rabbits had to be fed. Most of my mornings there—in fact, most of my days anywhere—I spent running. I cannot remember walking anywhere in summer. I remember occasionally sitting long enough to dress a paper doll, but my mother always made me come in at early dark, so I had to run and run and run to stay ahead of the day.

During our visit in New York, my great-uncle's wife, Lucille, got in touch with my father's brother, Ted, and Uncle Ted used to come to take me on wonderful adventures. Ted was a lot different from my father. He was more like my mother's brother Rochell— fun-loving, with lots of women friends, including Lucille's sister, Alleen—all of whom competed to do nice things for me, hoping, I guess, to please Uncle Ted. He didn't discourage them. In fact, just the opposite. "Mary, the baby needs a pretty little outfit to go this place or that," he would say to one. And the next thing you'd know, I'd have it. If I showed up dressed in a new outfit and one of the other girlfriends got wind of where it had come from, I'd have another one.

My uncle was "running on the railroad" as a Pullman porter, and in between runs he'd take me around his haunts in Harlem, up and down Seventh Avenue, to 125th Street, which then was internation- ally known as the "crossroads of Black America." Street-corner preachers declaimed on ladders, affirming and promoting Black Na- tionalism, and Wednesday night at the Apollo Theater was Amateur Night. Uncle Ted would tell me about Sarah Vaughan, who, he said, used to live in the same hotel as he did. He said that every time she went up to the Apollo on Amateur Night, "she just couldn't win for anything." He said she finally got a boyfriend who played the saxophone—or perhaps some other instrument—and it was this man who brought her out. She married him, went back and won the contest, and went on from there. At least, that was Uncle Ted's version of events, which he passed along to me. Right or wrong, I bought it—and all the other excitement he generated about Harlem in those days.

One day, he and one of his girlfriends took me to Coney Island. I had never seen anything like this giant playground, but I was not intimidated by the big rides. In fact, I dragged my uncle onto the Ferris wheel, the rubber cars, the merry-go-round. I tried and tried to get him to take me on the roller coaster, but, for once, he refused to grant my request. "Oh no," he said, chuckling and shaking his head. "You'll never get me on that thing. Your old uncle's heart's not strong enough for that." I settled for cotton candy, which I thought was the most wonderful thing I had ever had to eat. Well, along with candy apples.

I loved my Uncle Ted. Although he had features like my

father's—especially what my family calls the "Hunter mouth"—prominent, with a full top lip, that opens into a wide smile—he and my father were as different as night and day. He loved a good time, and he was so relaxed. He got along with the street people, but on a different level from my father. Ted was more of an "of the people" man. My great-uncle's wife, Lucille, was also a lot of fun. She had numerous bottles of real red nail polish and would let me use them. I used to polish my nails several times a day—something I would never have done at home, because my mother never used nail polish.

Lucille worked as a maid for some white people a long train ride away from 115th Street. In fact, one time she took me with her. Everything was very different from where we had come from. There was space, with lawns and wide streets, and the house was bright and airy, with lots of white and green, like the houses white people had back home, only nicer, I thought. They smelled different—not bad or anything—just different. I didn't see any of the people, but my aunt later sent me some clothes they had given her that she thought I could use. Although my mother always bought me the best clothes, she held her tongue about the secondhand white people's clothes because she felt Lucille thought she was doing a good thing. Lucille had never been South to visit, so I'm sure she had no idea how we lived. As for me, I was just thrilled to get a package from Lucille. My favorite was a green pleated wool skirt. There was something about getting a present from "up North" that was special. If anybody thought anything about the hand-me-downs, nothing was said. I wore that green skirt everywhere. It was so grown-up and sophisticated-looking.

My grandmother always loved baseball, and once we got on the subway and went to Ebbets Field to see the Brooklyn Dodgers play. I don't remember much about the game except the names of the pioneering Jackie Robinson and Roy Campanella; they were heroes to Blacks everywhere and maybe especially in little segregated Southern towns. Their breaking of barriers in baseball said, "And maybe one day we can do it too." On that day in New York, they were all my grandmother talked about for the rest of the day.

Somebody usually went places with us, but my grandmother was not at all intimidated by New York City. There were times when she and I would go out alone and get on the subway. We never got lost. She was so adventurous and full of curiosity about everything. On the train ride North, we made many friends. We usually exchanged the food we had packed for the trip with other Blacks in the segregated section of the train, because we couldn't eat in the dining car. But nobody seemed to mind. On that train, I had some of the best fried chicken I ever tasted, and I also was introduced to brownies by a girl my age who was traveling with her grandmother. As our grandmothers talked about only God knows what, the girl taught me how to wiggle my ears. It took a good part of the overnight trip, but I had it down pat when I said goodbye to her at Penn Station in New York.

When it came time to leave 115th Street, I had nearly forgotten what I'd left at home. Everything I hadn't brought with me—bicycle, bottle dolls, tree swing—I had learned to do without. I now knew how to make marbles out of bottle caps weighted with wax. It had not been a lonely summer. Maria and her friends and I promised to send cards at Christmas. Our parting wasn't sad. I left, promising to come back the following summer. But it would be many summers before I returned, and when I did, it was with totally different eyes.

chapter 6

Washington Street School and St. Paul A.M.E.

Back in Covington, all my playmates were getting ready to go to school. I was as big as they were—I was usually the tallest and almost always the youngest in most of the groups I belonged to when I was growing up—but at age five I was not old enough to go to school. I decided to accompany Betty, anyway, just to see what it was like. Nobody seemed to mind, so I kept going, day after day after day, and at the end of the first term I heard my name being called to come up to get my report card. At the end of the year I was promoted to second grade.

Every morning I eagerly got up and dressed and ran up the block to the Wrights' house. There were four Wright children of various ages. Their father, Mr. Buddy, worked for the dry cleaner, whose steam used to spew out into their back yard. Their mother, Mis' Zenobia, almost always had a headache. There were a lot of school-age kids on Brown Street, so there was something resembling a procession as the street emptied out each morning. Usually Betty and I walked together, unless we had had one of our falling-outs. The school seemed like a long way to us, I guess because we were little, and because we dawdled and sometimes stopped at Mr. Feets' store to look around, perhaps buy a penny's worth of gum or candy, or maybe just look at Mr. Feets. He was in a wheelchair and was so crippled by arthritis that his body had shriveled up and all you could see of him was his head and feet. But he was independent, close to self-sufficient, and he hated being called handicapped.

Anyway, the school was actually less than a mile away. A near-mile of adventure and fun, most of the time. Especially that first year, when everything was so new and not quite real, since I wasn't supposed to be there.

It was called the Washington Street School, Washington Street being a dusty red-clay road, unless it rained, at which time it turned into a muddy red-clay road. In wintertime, it would get so cold that we put our books against our chests and our hands inside our sleeves and walked backward up the hill to school. It was the only school for Black children in Covington, and it was fairly representative of how Black schools were treated by the all-white school boards that were in charge of them at the time. Because few Blacks were able to afford college, classes were large and the teachers had to carry a heavy load. "We just didn't have much of anything," recalled my third-grade teacher, Miss Sara Francis (Thompson Hardeman) later. There was no science or laboratory equipment, no playground equipment; in fact, barely a playground, other than the gravelly expanse of red clay in front of the school.

There also was no lunchroom, although in the basement there was a concession where you could buy a snack of milk and peanut-butter crackers for a dime, and for fifteen cents lunch, usually a boiled pig ear or a fried-fish sandwich or a hot dog. We'd put lots of mustard and hot sauce on the sandwiches—and eat them along with bags of pigskins.

Sometimes, when the white schools had surplus orange juice, the school officials would tell us to bring quart jars to school, and they would fill our jars with the juice to take home. At times there were apples to take home.

The school didn't have money for other things like crayons, art materials, or even books for the library. But there was an active Parent-Teachers Association, and my mother got very involved in that when it came to raising money for the school. Every year there was a contest: the student who raised the most money was crowned queen of the school. There would be a big program that night, and no one knew right up to the last minute who was going to be queen, because everybody was still counting the money right up to the last minute.

I can remember my mother and grandmother sitting off to the side, dipping into their laps, counting out what seemed like thousands of pennies, nickels, and dimes that they had brought to school wrapped in white linen handkerchiefs. They would finish counting, turn in their money, and wait. I thought I would explode waiting for the final tabulations. When the winner was announced, I could hardly believe what I was hearing: "Our new queen this year is Charlayne Hunter." My mother had raised something like $113 and a few cents, and we were far ahead of the next person. I got a "diamond" tiara and a Bulova watch.

Black adults, like our teachers, were aware that there was a difference in the distribution of teaching equipment and library materials between the Black and white schools, but, as Miss Sara Francis told me years later, "we just had to do as best we could." Even the lady that fixed my hair, Perry Lee, who was also one of Uncle Rochell's girlfriends at the time, had a hair fashion show to raise money to help put things in the library. Some of the older girls and teachers wore her "upsweeps" and "waves." I was the model for the "baby-doll curls." I also helped sell doughnuts, although Perry Lee imposed a condition on me. "It's okay to help," she told me, "but after you get your lesson."

The teachers really worked hard, too, both at teaching us and at preparing themselves. Many of them had little else to do, so they kept going to school. Miss Sara Francis, for example, would teach all week and then drive to Atlanta to take special classes at Morris Brown, a Black college founded by the A.M.E. Church, on the weekend. She got her master's degree in education that way. As a result of their going to school all the time, Miss Sara Francis said, they found out, after schools were desegregated and they had more access to information, that many of them were better qualified than the white teachers. But the system was such that it was separate and secret, so we never knew just how much they and we were missing. Our teachers labored to keep us from feeling we were missing out. "They wanted to teach," was how Miss Sara Francis put it. "It was like a mission. They felt they had to see that their children learned."

And learn I did, devouring the *Weekly Reader* with a passion. "See Dick. See Jane. See Spot. See Dick run. See Jane run. See Spot run." Over and over and over. Repetition and memorization were the hallmarks of education at Washington Street School. And if you got it wrong there would be hell to pay.

"Hold out your hand, miss," I can still remember Miss Mary Wright saying sternly. I would hold out my hand and that stinging old brown leather strap would come crashing down onto it. But I refused to cry. She could break it in my hand before I would cry. And she sometimes seemed to try. Betty remembers to this day the four licks she got for missing "piano" in the spelling bee.

Learning didn't stop at school, though. At Sunday school, we had to memorize Bible verses, Bible stories, and parts for plays—especially at Easter. Miss Mary Wright's counterpart at St. Paul A.M.E. Church was Miss Sally Benton. I think both those ladies were born old. Miss Mary always wore a black suit and a white blouse that buttoned high up on her neck. She had a stern countenance and gray hair, which she wore in a bun. What Miss Mary Wright and others did for us at school, Miss Sally did for us, almost single-handed, at church. Betty and I always talked a lot, and Miss Sally would get after us about talking and laughing in Sunday school. She could be intimidating, reminding us that this was no time to play.

We didn't have any Sunday-school books, but Miss Sally would give us three-by-five cards with a picture of Jesus or some other holy figure on them, along with a piece of Scripture we might have to memorize. I once had to memorize the story of Jonah and the Whale and tell it to the entire Sunday-school class. Miss Sally didn't have a strap—she didn't need one. A look from her was enough.

Her big thing was the Easter program. We'd work for weeks memorizing our speeches and getting ready for the Easter Day program, which was held in the afternoon, following church. Getting your Easter Day outfit was one of the highlights, if not *the* highlight, of the year. We'd shop for days for a dress and shoes, a little hat and a pocketbook. My mother would sometimes make my dress. It was really a special day that we all looked forward to. No one more, however, than Miss Sally. It was the day when all her hard work paid off and she could put us on display so the entire congregation could witness the fruits of her labors. The program never changed from one year to the next. One by one, according to age, we'd get up and say our pieces, as we called them, filling in between with the same songs every year. "He lives, He lives, Jesus lives within my soul . . ." and "He Arose." I had such a vivid imagination that I would be transported to the tomb as I sang at the top of my voice, "He arose one Easter from the dark domain and he lives forever with the saints to reign. He arose. He aro-ho-hose . . . Hallelujah, Christ arose."

Although Easter was a kind of climactic moment for Miss Sally, she didn't stop there. She had us all in the Junior Missionary Society. We would have meetings all over Covington in the homes of various church members, and one of us would always have to say, "Thank you for opening your doors for us and welcoming us in." We'd then have a kind of off-site, weekday Sunday-school meeting, studying Bible verses and religious stories. Then we'd get milk and cookies.

We hated to go to Miss Sally's home for the meeting, because she had a houseful of cats and they spoiled our appetite. They were all over everything and we just assumed that they were all over the food, too. We would just pick at the food, but none of us dared to say anything, lest we hurt her feelings. Just as we never spoke about the ice cream she used to make for us to sell to raise money for the Junior Missionary Society activities. She always boiled the milk until it burned and you could taste it in the ice cream. We knew how really good homemade ice cream tasted, because Mis' Zenobia used to make it.

We didn't have anything like day camp or sleep-away camp, but in the summer we had Daily Vacation Bible School, and also, Miss Sally used to take us to the Sunday-school convention, which was kind of like a sleep-away. The conventions would be held in nearby towns like Conyers, Lithonia, Social Circle, Monticello, Shady Dale, and we'd go on Wednesday and stay through Friday night. We would stay in the homes of different church members. We had Bible lessons and programs, and usually, on Friday nights, there would be a big musical featuring different choirs. The convention was a lot of fun because it made us feel grown-up, and we also got a chance to flirt with boys. At night, after the services, we could go for a walk, usually to a small roadside store-café where they sold sodas and candy, and we'd get a chance to talk away from the ever-watchful eye of Miss Sally. We didn't stay out too long; otherwise, the people we were staying with would come and get us, and also tell Miss Sally. We didn't want to cross Miss Sally, or let her down, because she really believed in us, and like Miss Sara Francis and Miss Mary Wright and the other teachers that I had as I was growing up, they taught us to believe in ourselves.

chapter 7

Florida

The summer of 1948, when my father returned from Korea, we went to Fort Lauderdale to visit his parents. My grandfather was pastoring at Grant Memorial, one of Fort Lauderdale's biggest churches. Everybody knew my grandfather "Shep" Hunter. He was an old-time evangelist-type preacher renowned throughout the state for his preaching and singing. Once, in Africa, I ran into an A.M.E. bishop, Richard Chappelle, Sr., whose late father had been a contemporary of my grandfather, and he described him as "a legendary figure . . . one of the great preachers of his day." Bishop Chappelle went on: "He was a preacher's preacher, and the phrase we use in the church is that he could tell a story. They would come from miles around to hear Shep Hunter preach."

The difference between my father and my grandfather as preachers was that my father was a minister—more cerebral, less theatrical. In the pulpit, my grandfather was as dramatic-looking as he was dramatic, six feet tall, medium frame, with smooth blue-black skin accentuated by his completely bald head and Ipana-white teeth. He would get wound up during a sermon and, crouching low, would run from one side of the pulpit to the other, back and forth, in a frenzy of preaching and singing that would rock the building from its foundations to the rafters.

"I got two wings to fly across Jor-dan!" he would half sing and half shout as he shot across the pulpit. "And the world can't do me no harm."

He would sing, "Got two wings to veil your face," and some sister somewhere in the congregation would call out, "Jesus! Two wings!"

"I've got two wings to fly across Jordan, haah!"

"Two wings!"

"I've got two, two, two wings."

"Two wings."

Once Poppa was on a roll, he could go for hours, and no one would think about leaving.

Another sermon he was famous for was "Dry Bones." That one was taken from the Old Testament, in Ezekiel. When the Children of Israel were wandering in the wilderness: "The hand of the Lord was upon me, and carried me out in the spirit of the Lord, and set me down in the midst of the valley, which was full of bones. And caused me to pass by them round about: and, behold, there were very many in the open valley; and, lo, they were very dry." The passage provided a major theme for sermons, and the message could go in a lot of directions. The message my grandfather chose was that no matter how low or far down a person got, he could always rise up. Like the dry bones. And Poppa would talk about the "bones in the valley, disconnected and lying in the dust." He would work in the gestures. The bones would begin to click, and he would begin to sing the old Black spiritual that was adapted from the Scripture: "Ankle bone connected to de leg bone . . . leg bone connected to de knee bone," and on and on till the whole body was back together, and Poppa would shout, "Now hear the word of the Lord," and he would start singing, "Dem bones, dem bones, dem dry bones," over and over.

My grandfather also used to preach from Revelations, which my

Uncle Ted said was rare for most preachers. When I asked him why, he said simply, "Too deep."

After every sermon, my grandfather would sing. My Uncle Ted's favorite was "Jimmy Knight's Repentance." As Uncle Ted told it: "That was a song about a guy, maybe he was a gambler, but he repented and came to the church, and that's when he got the inspiration to write the song." It was also the story of my grandfather.

The congregation seemed never to tire when Poppa got going. But I tired, and sometimes other members of the family did. My Grandmother Hunter, whom we called Momma, was a saint in her own right. She started every day by reading from the Bible. The Psalms were her favorite, and she taught me the Twenty-third Psalm. So devoted was she to the word of the Lord that as I recited the Psalm I could actually envision myself walking though the valley of the shadow of death, a slightly damp, cool, solitary place, smelling of nasturtiums and reminding me a lot of the passageway between the church and the parsonage in St. Augustine, Florida, another place my grandfather pastored. But when Momma Hunter said, "I shall fear no evil," I took heart, learned the lines, and got on out of that valley . . . "Thy rod and Thy staff they comfort me . . . all the days of my life."

At noon, every day, no matter what she was doing, Momma Hunter stopped and walked the short distance from the parsonage, which was usually next door to the church, and entered the church, most times alone. There she would pray and meditate for an hour. I would sometimes creep to the side door and see her in there, transfixed, transformed, a little too mysterious for me.

Friday she fasted and prayed all day.

I think in some ways she was more religious than Poppa, who once, in anger, cursed in front of us.

"Oh, Poppa," she said in her usual half-doting, half-chiding way, "you know you shouldn't speak like that about the Lord."

But my grandfather, sorely agitated, would not repent, and shot back, "Oh, be quiet, Momma. Sometimes I think you got too damn much religion."

On one particular steamy-hot Florida Sunday, as we sat in the back of the church, sweating and fanning with the paper fans supplied by somebody or other's funeral home, my grandfather was on one of his rolls. He had reached a crescendo and seemed to be winding down several times, only to rev back up again, as if the spirit had grabbed him and told him to keep on connecting "dem bones," or whatever. At one point, my grandmother said quietly, "I wish Poppa would look at his watch." Whereupon I stood up on the church bench and yelled, "Poppa, look at your watch!" Poppa heard me, grinned his big, wide, beautiful grin, and paused for a moment. "I guess it is about time, baby," he said. But instead, he used the pause to pull out his white pocket handkerchief and mop his shiny wet brow, and then proceeded to preach for at least another thirty minutes. My grandmother sat there with a beatific smile on her face, but I could hear an occasional sigh.

Shep and Alberta Hunter were a real team. They had met in the small town of Monticello, Georgia, and had married when she was twelve and he was sixteen. While the rich, dark face of my grandfather revealed a trail from Africa, his family could take me back only as far as Barbados. Like many Blacks in the area around Monticello, my grandfather at one time worked in the phosphate mines. My grandmother's brother, "Unca" Dave Johnson, who lived to be over one hundred, used to show people the holes where he shot dynamite into the phosphate. The Hunters may have come from Barbados, but in Florida they, too, were mixed up with the Indians; in fact, there was one sister who was called "Poca Hunter."

My Uncle Ted told me a story of my grandparents' marriage this way: "He had to get permission from her brother, Unca Dave. And Unca Dave told him, 'Now, if you hit her, when you see me coming, you better cross over to the other side of the street, 'cause I'll kill you.' My father always believed that. He never did fight my mother. Never did."

My father was born when my grandmother was fourteen. Poppa was strong and could be domineering. Momma was a small woman who widened out as she got older, a rich reddish-brown, with a lyrical voice that had the smooth, round quality of a pearl. I never heard her raise her voice or complain about her life, even when Poppa was on a rampage.

"All I've ever known was Poppa," I once heard her say.

At the same time, Poppa always said that if Momma told him not to do something, he wouldn't do it.

That started before Poppa got "the call" to preach. From the beginning, my grandfather placed a high value on education. Uncle Ted: "Education was important, because my daddy made it important. He said, 'Get an education, boy. That's gonna be your salvation.' And it extended to all of us, including Momma. We went to the same school, my mother, my daddy, my brother, and me. All at the same time. My daddy was going to Edward Waters to take up theology. It went all the way from kindergarten up. And we started going there, too. Momma was a second-grade student. I was in fourth grade. Momma learned to read and write right there. Daddy would go home and ask questions, and we'd try to answer as best we could. Momma would be there, too, asking questions. Just like a little kid. Boy, I thought that was the greatest thing in the world—for the four of us to be going to school at the same time. Everybody loved it."

My father once gave me an example of how my grandfather influenced him at an early age. He said he was thirteen and Poppa told him he was spending too much time in the streets; he was to come inside and devote more time to his studies. "Study words," he remembered Poppa telling him. "If you master words, you will walk with kings and queens." Years later, during the Second World War, when a tour of duty took my father to Jerusalem, King George VI and Queen Elizabeth II came to review the troops. Because they were concerned with morale, they sought out the chaplains, including my father. That night he wrote from the King David Hotel to his own father, thanking him for his advice years before. "For today," he wrote, "I walked with both the King and the Queen."

Momma Hunter was also a teacher in her own right, and had special ideas about how the children of the preacher should conduct themselves. "Never mistreat anybody," she would say, "no matter how nasty they might be to you. They might be the very ones who are feeding you. We have to live from the people, and you have to show them your gratitude."

Under segregation, the Black preacher held a special status in the Black community. He was looked upon as a leader by both Blacks and whites; and because he was paid strictly out of the coffers of his congregation he had a degree of independence that allowed him to deal with whites, if not on a legally equal footing, certainly in a way that was more dignified than if he had had to rely on them for his living. Everywhere my grandfather went, whites and Blacks alike respected him. Whites, as well as Blacks, called him Reverend Hunter. Like my father, he also loved to spend time with the "buddy boys," as my uncle called them. And he was very much at ease with them, perhaps because he was once a "buddy boy" himself.

To the younger ministers, he was like a master teacher. My Aunt Louise, my father's younger sister, put it this way: "He taught the younger ministers how to succeed in their churches, how to get their sermons together. And then he would tell them how to keep their wives from interfering in church work. He would tell the wives, too. They would sometimes come and talk to Momma. And they would say, 'Well, Mother Hunter, how can you stand that?' And she would say, 'Well, do you realize who is taking care of you?' "

There was a very formal side to my grandparents. They never left their bedroom without being completely dressed. My grandmother would have fixed her face and her hair, and put on high-heel shoes. You never saw her in house shoes or without a pair of stockings. And you never saw Poppa in house slippers, either. When he finished shaving his face, he would shave his head. Every morning. Used Noxzema. Every day he wore a dark suit, a white shirt, and a black tie. Shoes shined.

Momma Hunter always set a formal table and insisted that everyone sit down to the meal. If you complimented her about the food, she'd laugh and say, "Aw, it ain't nothing. Let's throw it outdoors to the dog." In the evening, the table would be set long before dinner. Parishioners just dropping by would see the table that way and apologize, assuming they had intruded on my grandmother's preparations for company. "Oh no, it's all right," my grandmother would say reassuringly. "I'm having company. My family. They are my company."

Grace was said at every meal, and everybody had to repeat a Bible verse. I liked "Jesus wept, Peter crept, out the back door and down the step," but at my grandparents' table I knew to stop after He "wept."

It was hard to imagine this very well-dressed, formal-looking man on the muddy banks of some river, casting a rod into the dark running water and struggling as the pole arched forward to rein in a bream or a catfish. But it was easier to imagine my grandfather than my father. In fact, my father would also be immaculately dressed, but would never fish. When he took my brothers fishing, he would stand on the banks of the river reading the Bible while they cast their lines. But fishing was my grandfather's passion, and long before any of us were up on Sunday morning, he would rise, put on his dress pants and a long-sleeved shirt, gather up his poles—he used only wooden reeds—and his worms, and he was off in his dark maroon Buick, with its own set of fins, poles poking out the window, slicing through the Florida morning's blanket-heavy heat. He never caught fish just for sport—only enough for the family's breakfast. By the time he got back, Momma Hunter would be up and piddling around the kitchen. He would hand over the fish, which she would clean and have ready by the time we woke. Our alarm clock was the penetrating smell of frying fish and baking biscuits. There would also be a pot of grits bubbling on the stove. Poppa always ate a big breakfast, because it would have to last him for all the various services throughout the day. Plus, he needed fuel for that mighty evangelical engine inside his body.

My grandmother was probably the first person I knew to be into health food. She always used olive oil on her grits and she drank nothing but goat's milk. Except for me, nobody else in the family followed her lead. But I was always eager to try new things, and convinced myself that I really liked them. While my mother protested that I shouldn't drink all of Momma Hunter's milk, because it was expensive, my grandmother let it be known that anything she had was mine, and we winked at each other and downed another glass of goat's milk.

chapter **8**

"From Little Acorns"

After a good long visit in Florida, we drove back to Covington, and not long after that, my father left again. This time to Fort Benning, Georgia.

One day, my mother called me into the bedroom and handed me a book. I loved books, and we had a lot of them. I was excited to be getting another one. But I was totally unprepared for what happened next.

"I want you to read this," my mother began. "It's called *From Little Acorns*, and when you finish it, I want you to let me know, so we can discuss something."

I eagerly took the book from my mother, who at that moment was wearing the softest, most beautiful smile I had ever seen.

"All right, Mother," I said. "I'll read it right away, and I'll come and get you when I've finished."

Oh boy, I thought. This is going to be great fun. I had long ago decided that there was no one smarter than my mother, and to have her want to discuss a book with me made me feel really grown-up.

The book had a blue cover, with a drawing of an acorn on it. It started out by telling the story of the seed of the fruit of the oak, the acorn, and how this little seed gets fertilized and one day grows into a mighty oak tree. From there, the book continues its discussion of seeds and fertilizer, and pretty soon it's talking about eggs and ovaries and menstruation and sperm and eggs and fertilization and babies. Ooooohweeee, I thought as I devoured the words, ravaged the paragraphs, and swallowed whole pages at a fevered clip. Wonder why my mother gave me this book to read.

By this time, I was seven years old and I had heard things from my friends about the birds and the bees, but it was all pretty vague, and mostly nasty. I could never quite imagine just how the things they were describing could actually take place. A weenie in a bun was graphic enough, but even my vivid imagination couldn't make the leap to Peter and Mary, the names we called our private parts. Whenever the subject came up among my friends, we were mostly wide-eyed and giggling as one of the older girls in the group— like my cousin Shirley, who used to come and visit from nearby Oxford—would try to describe menstruation, which everybody called "menustration." I asked questions like, "Well, do you swell up when it happens?" And my cousin would say, "Naw, fool. You just bleed." And then she would tell me about how men and women "did it." She said she "did it" with a boy in their outhouse, and it sounded pretty unappetizing to me. These conversations were always far away from the house, or under the house, or someplace where we could be sure no adult could overhear. After all, we were talking about something grown-up, mysterious, and bad. We could get a whipping for talking about stuff like this. And yet here was a book with everything in it—and with pictures, too! And of all people, *my mother* gave it to me. I couldn't believe it.

The first time my mother casually inquired about whether I had finished the book, I panicked. "Not yet," I said, and darted out of the room. But I knew we had to have this conversation eventually, so not long after that I went up to her in a quiet moment and said, "Mother, I finished."

"What did you learn?" she asked softly.

"Well," I said, not being completely sure of exactly what words I should use to describe all that I had read, "I learned about the little acorns that make trees and the ones that make babies."

"What did you think of that?" she asked.

"Oh, it was interesting," I answered.

"What would you think of it if I told you I had a seed that was now growing inside me?"

"I don't know," I answered, starting to feel red and flushed.

"You are going to have a little brother or a little sister," she said.

"You mean a *baby* brother or a *baby* sister?" I asked, emphasizing the word "baby" as if it were the first word in a new foreign vocabulary I was learning.

"Yes, that's what I mean. You are going to have a little brother or a little sister."

I had enough sense to know that this was a momentous occasion, that the situation called for me to say something important, worthy, but I was so overwhelmed with all this new information and this impending reality that I was having difficulty coming up with something I felt would suggest that I was mature enough and smart enough to have merited my mother's confidence.

"Well, you really had a lot of acorns in you, didn't you?" I finally managed to say.

At that, my mother reached for me and gently placed my hand on the rounded, protruding belly that I must have been too busy to notice before, and I stepped into the zone of another one of the mysteries that would enchant my childhood.

In the dead of winter, as I snuggled in my bed under mounds of quilts and blankets, I was awakened by my mother's screams. I bolted upright in bed, trying to determine if I was dreaming. A silence followed. I decided that I *was* dreaming. I lay back down, and as I drifted back into sleep I heard it again. My mother's painful cry. "Oh! Oh! Oh!" I was not dreaming. Something terrible was happening to my mother. I needed to find out what it was.

As I threw my gangly legs out of the small cot I was sleeping on—now in my grandmother's room—they collided with my uncle Rochell's body, which was lumbering over to my bedside. He was reeking of alcohol and crying, having been ejected from the "delivery room" by the doctor, moments earlier, and told to "go out in the back yard." Before I could say anything, he took me in his arms, patted my head, and began to assure both me and himself, "Everything going to be all right." And then, between his own barely containable sobs, he told me, "You're going to have a little baby brother or sister in the morning."

My heart began to pound inside my uncle's warm and slightly smelly embrace. I stayed with him until his sobs subsided, then crept to the door of the room where my mother was and pressed my ear against it. There were no more screams. I was relieved but anxious. My uncle was now asleep on my bed, snoring. I walked over to my grandmother's bed. She was not there, but the white doctor was there, sound asleep. I was confused, so I crept back to my uncle's side and fell asleep, not knowing that the doctor had left my mother with Mis' Myrtis Evans, the midwife, with instructions to wake him when the baby's head became visible.

When I woke up, I was led into the room where my mother was, all clean and quiet, and I was introduced to Charles Shepherd Henry Hunter III. He was wrapped in swaddling clothes, like the image I knew from Sunday school of the Baby Jesus. And he was lying next to my mother, who looked radiant, if a bit tired. I decided right then and there that I would be the one she could depend on to help her through whatever she faced with this swaddled creature that had caused her so much pain.

It was February 19, 1950, six days after my father's birthday and eight days before mine. What a birthday present! We decided to call him Henry. That's because all the other names were in current use. Regardless of the task—whether it was changing a smelly diaper or rocking Henry to sleep on the porch—I was available. As the neighborhood once used to hear me reacting to a dose of peach-tree tea, they could now hear me singing, as my mother once did for me, every church song or ditty I ever knew, sitting on our screened-in front porch with the baby in my lap. Once, after a fairly sustained period of singing at the top of my lungs, in which I think I temporarily forgot what my primary mission was, I returned from being lost in my rhapsodic reverie to look down and find the baby sound asleep, probably in self-defense. As I looked at him, I started to get up. Somehow I slipped out of the rocking chair and lost my hold on the baby. Although he hit the floor with a thud that I thought was loud enough to wake even the somnolent drunks in the calaboose, no one, not even my baby brother, realized what had happened. For my part, I was terrified. He slept so soundly on the floor that I thought surely I had killed him. I grabbed him up, rocked him back and forth, held my head down to his nose to confirm that he was not breathing, only to feel a faint but wonderful wisp of air from his nose onto my cheek. I squeezed him with an intensity that woke him up, and I happily started my singing all over again, from the beginning and with a passion that neither my baby brother nor the neighborhood had ever known.

On June 25, 1950, North Korean troops invaded South Korea. Five days later, the United States entered the war. In the early weeks of the conflict, the only defenders standing before an aggressive wave of North Korean troops were four army combat units, poorly prepared for fighting and woefully undermanned. By August, the first American war dead began returning home.

Over my mother's protests, my father returned to Korea two months later—fifteen months after he had left the first time. She begged him to stay home, pleading that she needed him, we needed him, and questioned why he had to go again. She argued that he had done his duty. It was not a good conversation. My father accused her of being unpatriotic. That ended the discussion. And so we said goodbye once again, and the man in our lives went back to the battlefield, where, he said, he was most needed.

In Korea, Black soldiers were performing heroically at this stage of the war. On July 25, the all-Black 24th Infantry Division attacked and seized Yechon, achieving at least a symbolic victory.

Another all-Black unit—the 999th Field Artillery Battalion—was soon under way from the States as part of the 3rd Infantry Division out of Fort Benning, Georgia. Among its men were my father and Second Lieutenant Grover Dubose. By the time they reached southern Japan, Allied victories at Inchon had all but ended the war, so they were held in reserve until the Chinese entered the conflict in support of the North Koreans in late October. Lieutenant Dubose recalled what it was like for the various Allied positions:

"They brought us in when they detected that the Chinese were getting involved. They started swarming across the Yalu River. We started falling back as our forces began withdrawing along the main supply route. There was no way in hell we could have stopped them. They were coming at us like ants. We were killing them like flies. They were walking over each other, picking up the weapons of those who were slain. That's where the term was invented, I think—hordes. The hordes of Chinese. I have no idea the number of people they committed to that—whatever they thought it took. They overwhelmed us with numbers. We couldn't kill them fast enough. There were more of them than we had bullets. So we retreated and came to the South.

"Our job initially was to keep the roads open for the first Marine divisions and the 7th Army Division, which were retreating from the Choson reservoir in the northernmost part of Korea. That's how far up we were, and boy, was it cold! It was bitter, bitter cold, and we were very, very ill-equipped as far as clothing was concerned. We had regular clothes that you could use, say, in the United States, but we had no outer protective gear. I'm talking about North Korea, where temperatures were sub-zero for days on end. We were not only fighting the enemy, we were fighting the weather. It was very, very tough, actually, and I don't think we even got winter gear until sometime in February, when we started to get the right shoes, parkas, and sleeping bags. We were in combat. We were fighting day and night against the Koreans and the Chinese. Anything in sight that moved. Now, it was pretty easy to identify the Chinese from the Koreans because of their clothing. The Chinese had quilted, down-filled, beautiful coats and caps with flaps.

"Your father, the chaplain, was all over the place because he was visiting the different batteries. We were the last people out, since we had to blow up the ammunition dumps. I know we were the last artillery unit, because we were sitting right on the beach. When the tide got high, water would come right into the tent.

"I've commanded subsequent to that artillery batteries from

Alaska, battalions in Germany and Vietnam, but the pride in that unit—nobody compared to it. I never served with a unit that had more *esprit de corps*, that was more professional than that group. Never served in a unit that could shoot like that unit. We could move into position faster than anybody I've ever seen. And our morale was very high, thanks, in part, to people like your father. He was always very upbeat. Everything was going to be okay; things were going to get better. He loved the soldiers, and they loved him. They had problems, they went to see Chaplain Hunter. Far away from home. Wives screwing off. They were getting letters saying, 'I want a divorce,' and all this. No matter what was going on, the first thing a soldier wants to see is the chaplain."

My father was also called in when army officers established a recreation club for the white enlisted men downtown in Pusan. Black soldiers were not allowed to attend. After my father was called in to negotiate, a separate club was established in the Black work area. There were one or two Black officers in Pusan. Lieutenant Jesse J. Johnson and Percy Roberts. According to Johnson, who retired as a lieutenant colonel, they had to pay club fees but were not allowed to attend.

"A Chaplain Hunter came to visit our unit today," wrote Lieutenant Percy Roberts in his diary. "He preached a two-fisted sermon that made us all feel good."

Chaplain Grey Johnson was there, too. He later told me about the soldiers: "They were just babies, many of them. And they'd be in a line, firing shoulder to shoulder. I would see five or six laid out there dead that I knew. Like the lieutenant that went by and I said, 'I'll see you tomorrow.' And tomorrow never came for him. When you're going through it, your mind is as tight as a drum; you don't make wrong moves. Too many people depending on you. But I got to the point where I couldn't go to a briefing. I couldn't stand it. Black men dying in the service of a country that didn't give a damn about them back home. I'm not a pacifist, but I just got to the point where I couldn't stand it. I think it was a conflict unique to chaplains. Like me. Like your father."

Sometimes, back home, I would get a glimpse of the pain my father silently suffered. He would be preaching a guest sermon on

Sunday morning, and would bring the battlefield into the pulpit. He talked of the time he was running through the rice paddies, fleeing the "enemy," running past a mortally wounded young soldier who asked to be turned over before he died and stopping to turn him over . . . and taking out the Bible and reading to him—"I am the way, the truth, and the life . . . He that believeth in me, the works that I do shall he do also. I go and prepare a place for you . . . that where I am, there ye may be also. In my Father's house are many mansions: if it were not so, I would have told you"—in the rice paddy in a far-off land, a soldier dying for freedom, democracy, fighting for a country that back home still kept him "in his place," but fighting and dying for the ideal of American freedom and equality, if not for himself, then maybe for his children. Or the chaplain's . . .

chapter 9

Atlanta

Some time before my father again returned, my mother announced that we would be moving to Atlanta. I received this news with mixed emotions. I did not want to leave Betty, but I had been hearing about Atlanta from the two Wyatt sisters who had come from there with one of our relatives to visit us. The one who was my age, Eloise, had gotten me really excited about going to Atlanta and to her elementary school and being in Miss Quarterman's class. She said Miss Quarterman was the best teacher and had the best class in the whole school. So when the time came, I tearfully said goodbye to Betty, Shirley, and the whole neighborhood, and promised to keep in touch.

Atlanta was totally different from Covington—by comparison, a sophisticated, cosmopolitan city with a sense of itself that was as strong in the Black as in the white community. It was a pride rooted in the history of what the Reverend E. R. Carter called the "Black Side," the Atlanta of the "sons of Ham," whose property ownership dates back to the turn of the nineteenth century, when Mary Combs sold her house and land to buy her husband out of slavery; and who, according to the Reverend Carter,

. . . notwithstanding the effort to close every avenue which leads to trade-learning against the Negro, the Black Side of this city has surmounted obstacles, leaped over impediments, gone ahead, purchased the soil, erected houses of business and reared dwellings, which show architectural skill and taste, and, as Mr. Crumbly said, if given a white man's chance and let alone, will accomplish what any other race has accomplished or can accomplish.★

Much of Black Atlanta's sense of itself emanated from its world-renowned institutions of higher education, also established in the 1800s: Spelman College for women, Morehouse men's college, Clark and Morris Brown Colleges, the Interdenominational Theological Center (formerly Gammon Theological Seminary), and Atlanta University, which produced some of Black America's most outstanding scholars, educators, writers, poets, theologians, lawyers, and other professionals—names that constitute a *Who's Who of Black America*: Horace Mann Bond, father of Julian Bond, John W. Davis, Mattiwilda Dobbs, E. Franklin Frazier, John Hope, Maynard Jackson, James Weldon Johnson, Mordecai Johnson, Martin Luther King, Jr., Lucy Laney, Rayford Logan, Benjamin E. Mays, James and Samuel Nabrit, Eugene Dibble, Ira De A. Reid, Walter White, and Whitney Young, Jr., to name a few.

It was from his base at Atlanta University at the turn of the twentieth century that W.E.B. Du Bois took on Booker T. Washington, opposing the doctrine he laid out at the Atlanta Exposition of 1895, in which Washington said to whites: "In all things that are purely social we can be as separate as the five fingers, yet one as the hand in all things essential to progress." He went on:

To those of my race who depend on bettering their condition in a foreign land or who underestimate the importance of cultivating friendly relations with the Southern white man . . . I would say, "Cast down your bucket where you are—

★ E. R. Carter, *The Black Side* (Atlanta: The Black Heritage Library Collection, 1894; reprinted, 1971), pp. vi, 13.

cast it down in making friends in every manly way of the people of all races by whom we are surrounded. Cast it down in agriculture, mechanics, in commerce, in domestic service, and in the professions."

Du Bois attacked Washington, accusing him of preaching a "gospel of Work and Money to such an extent as apparently almost completely to overshadow the higher aims of life." Thus provoked, Du Bois wrote his historic essay "The Talented Tenth"—a reference to his belief that one-tenth of educated Blacks would lead the masses out of ignorance and despair. He argued:

If we make money the object of man-training, we shall develop money makers but not necessarily men; if we make technical skill the object of education, we may possess artisans but not, in nature, men. Men we shall have only as we make manhood the object of the work of the schools—intelligence, broad sympathy, knowledge of the world that was and is, and of the relation of men to it—this is the curriculum of that Higher Education which must underlie true life.*

It was a debate that was still resonating in Atlanta when we arrived in 1951, and would in time touch my own life in a significant way.

We moved into an Atlanta neighborhood that was new to Blacks, a neighborhood of tree-lined streets and big houses which was in transition from white to Black. Typically, one Black family moved in and all the whites began to run. The house my mother bought was on Mozley Place. It was twice as big as our house in Covington, with beautiful grassy lawns in the front and back. The streets were paved just like the white folks' streets in Covington.

Another big difference was that the school Eloise attended and where I enrolled had a name that was more than a street destination. It was the E. R. Carter Elementary School, named for Reverend

* John Hope Franklin, *From Slavery to Freedom: A History of Negro Americans* (New York: Alfred A. Knopf, 1947; revised 1967), pp. 393–5.

E. R. Carter, the author of *The Black Side* and other works, and a prominent A.M.E. minister whom Bishop Henry McNeal Turner called "a preacher of the gospel [who] has few equals." The Reverend Carter was what came to be called a Race Man, as those Blacks were called who were engaged in contributing to and promoting the general advancement of Black people.

Attending a school named for a Black person was part of the way in which Black history was celebrated and passed on every day, as opposed to just one month out of the year. We learned Black history routinely, taught by people who understood that while it was not within their power to confer first-class citizenship legally, they could prepare us through the power they knew no one could deny them: the transmission of a heritage that we could be proud of and inspired by. The public-school system did not provide our schools with books or other materials that contained that history, as they did the white schools with books that contained mocking depictions of it. Eldridge MacMillan, who once taught in the Atlanta public schools, told me of a discovery he made after he was assigned to a former white school that had just been turned over to Blacks. The school still bore the name of the Confederate general Nathan Bedford Forrest, who has two historic distinctions: the line he spoke during the final battle of Atlanta ("Get there first with the most men"); more significantly, he was the founder of the Ku Klux Klan. "I had gone to look in the room that had been the library and I saw some books lying over in a corner," MacMillan told me. "I'm not sure whether they did it deliberately, but among the books was one that had a poem, 'Nigger, Nagger, Ragger, Tagger/Going to the Mill/Up the Hill,' and it had illustrations of Blacks looking like minstrels in raggedy clothes, croaker sacks, looking shiftless and lazy. That's what they taught their white children about Blacks." I don't know what their sources were, but Black teachers, most of whom were churchgoers, probably got a lot of that history in the church and somehow managed to pass it on.

I was so excited to be going to this school that I had heard so much about and to be a part of Miss Quarterman's special class; only when I got my class assignment, Miss Quarterman's name was nowhere on it. I was assigned to Miss Murphy's class. I was devastated. I went to the principal's office. Surely there has been some mistake, I said. I was supposed to be in Miss Quarterman's class, with my friend Eloise. And all the good students. No, there had been no mistake. Miss Quarterman's class was full, and Miss Murphy was taking the spillovers.

It was clear to me from the start that Miss Murphy's class was the one for idiots. The students were throwing things, running around, and leaving the room at will, while poor Miss Murphy, all four dumpy and waddling feet of her, was totally incapable of gaining control. I often asked to be excused to go to the bathroom, so I could look in on Miss Quarterman's class. They would all be seated, quietly listening as she explained something or other. Nothing like the relentless chaos going on a few doors away down the hall. Once, I went in and sat, thinking maybe I could just will myself into the class, but when Miss Quarterman noticed me she inquired about whether or not I was lost, and since I was unable to lie I was politely asked to go back to Miss Murphy's room.

"But don't you have any room for just one more?" I asked in my most plaintive voice. The answer, of course, was no.

I was upset by not being in Miss Quarterman's class, and I was also getting physically sick. Every day I had pains in my stomach so bad that when I went to the bathroom, I would double over. I would go back and tell Miss Murphy. She would send me to the principal's office, and from there I would be allowed to leave school. I walked the distance of about a mile from Ashby Street to Mozley Place, showing up at home in tears and in pain some thirty minutes later. I think my mother initially suspected that it was a case of heartbreak over not being in Miss Quarterman's class, but when the problem persisted she became so worried that she took me to the army hospital at Fort McPherson, where all army dependents in the area went for medical treatment. It was a place I knew well, because for the last several years, while we were living in Covington, my mother had been a frequent patient there, undergoing several operations for rectal problems.

Initially the doctors examined me for appendicitis, but when there were no white blood cells or any other signs of infection, they ruled that out. They gave me something for indigestion and sent us home. The next day, it was the same thing all over again. I developed stomach pains and was again allowed to leave school. My mother took me back to Fort Mac. Although I was only ten, I was very tall and the doctors wondered if I might be having pre-menstrual symptoms. I was always the youngest and the tallest in my group of friends and always had the biggest feet. I used to complain about it, until one day my mother said, "Just think of it this way: you're planted on a firm foundation." That was some consolation, but not enough to keep me from asking for a half size smaller when I went to buy shoes. In fact, it wasn't until the much admired first lady Jacqueline Kennedy let it be known that she wore a ten, more than a decade and much damage later, that I started being honest with myself about my shoe size. As it turned out, I was not pre-menstrual, but the doctor decided that something was really going on with me and he made a valiant effort to find out what it was. At one point, he asked me to open my mouth. I was perplexed, but I obliged without protest. When I did, and he looked in, he frowned.

"Where are her teeth?" he asked my mother, barely masking his astonishment.

She explained that she had taken me to the dentist in Covington once when I had a minor toothache. He was the only dentist in town, and he was white. He saw Black patients only on a certain day, when there were no white patients, and treated them in the cramped little lab where he made dentures and cleaned his equipment. It was caked with plaster and cluttered with dirty instruments. It also smelled like bad breath and outdoor toilets. It seems he never considered simply filling the minor decay in my teeth, which were permanent molars. Instead, he pulled them—two on one side and two on the other—all in one sitting. I remember going home from the ordeal and sleeping the entire afternoon and night, waking only to wipe the malodorous bloody drool from my mouth and shift to a position on my pillow which was not wet. The dentist not only neglected to prepare me and my mother for the pain I would suffer following the extractions, and to tell us what we could do to alleviate it, he also never told my mother that these were permanent teeth, and he failed to advise her that they would need to be replaced with some kind of denture. As time wore on, I learned to "gum" my food just like the old folks did.

"No wonder she's having stomachaches," the young army doctor said to my mother. "She has no way of masticating." Which I correctly surmised meant chewing. (That was the first time I had heard *that* word, which I immediately filed away for future use.) I was then sent to the post dentist, and there began a lengthy process of getting partial bridges to replace the empty holes in my mouth.

Somehow during this process I really did begin to feel better, and managed to console myself somewhat about not being in Miss Quarterman's special class. I don't think I learned very much that year, but when E. R. Carter held its annual fund drive, I came in once again with the most money and was named queen, "Miss E. R. Carter."

By this time, I had made a lot of friends and we would walk home together in large groups, similar to the ones in Covington, although without the acrimonious taunts about my color. In fact, Eloise was even fairer than I was, with wavy "good hair," and no one ever referred to her color in any way but positively.

Inevitably, though, arguments would break out; this time, however, there were few real physical fights. In fact, not only was I relieved of being taunted and pushed into slapping-and-hitting fights, I had now developed something of a reputation as a wordsmith and was treated with great respect and usually held in abeyance until near the end, when I would be called upon to administer the knockout punch, the *coup de grâce*. It wouldn't happen until after everybody else had exhausted his or her cursing vocabulary and all the "dozens" they knew—the insults game in which loved ones, especially 'yo' momma,' got put down in rhythm and often in rhyme ("She got jaybird hips/she got sparrow thighs/she got alligator feet/and terrapin eyes. Yo' momma"). It could get a lot worse—especially the sexual innuendo. But invariably the verbal combatants would run out of dozens and curse words. When that happened, my group would turn to me and say, "All right, Charlayne, thrown some big words on 'em."

I lived in the dictionary, always looking for unusual words. Besides the jokes in *The Reader's Digest* my mother used to read aloud to my grandmother and me on the front porch, which often made us laugh until tears ran down our cheeks, we also used to study the new-word section and take the test to see how many words we knew the meaning of before turning the next page to find the answers. So when called upon in this way, I would just start stringing every polysyllabic word I could remember, scoring big "Oooooowees!" for my side. For example, by calling someone "an antidisestablishmentarian antediluvian antebellum anus spot," I got their attention and, better yet, shut their mouths, especially since no one had the slightest idea what I had really said.

The first boyfriend I had at E. R. Carter was in Miss Quarterman's class. His name was William Guest, and he was also Eloise's boyfriend and the boyfriend of another girl who became a good friend of mine, Ruth Ellis. He told friends he liked Eloise for her "good" hair (earlier, he had dated Charlotte Cherry for her "red hair"), Ruth Ellis for her shape, which was extraordinarily well developed in the sixth grade, and me for my face and legs. Not being especially studious, Ba' Bruh, as he was called because he had an older sister, wasn't impressed with extensive vocabularies or other attributes of the mind. That was fine with all of us at the time; at least, most of the time. Anyway, I was convinced he liked me best, because one day after school he bought me a bottle of Jergen's lotion—the kind that was milky white and smelled like almonds. He said I should use it on my fine legs.

Sometimes, on Sundays, we would go to Mt. Moriah Baptist Church, where William and his cousin Gladys sang in the "Sunbeam" choir. Although they also sang on Saturday nights at the Royal Peacock nightclub on Auburn Avenue from the time they were about nine years old, never in our wildest dreams—well, perhaps in theirs but not in ours—did we think they would become one of the most popular and enduring rhythm-and-blues groups of our generation. But they did, as Gladys Knight and the Pips, with Ba' Bruh, because of his complexion, now widely known as Cousin Red. We would also go to Mt. Moriah's Sunday-school picnics, where, on long walks in the woods, Ba' Bruh would sneak a kiss.

Although Atlanta was the big city, the constant and sustaining elements of my life were the same as they had been in Covington. Everybody I knew went to Sunday school and church. At first, my mother started attending a small A.M.E. church not far from our house. But I had heard about Big Bethel, which was one of the largest churches, in Atlanta, and I went there a few times with some friends. I persuaded my mother to join Bethel. I liked its powerful bigness, and I liked the challenge of carving out a place for myself in it. I flourished there, as I had at St. Paul, playing the piano for the Sunday school and getting involved in all the activities, including Easter and Christmas programs. Despite all my practicing and playing, I was not a very good piano player. But nobody ever seemed to mind that I missed a few notes from time to time, and I wasn't embarrassed enough to quit. Big Bethel was a beautiful gray-stone church with a tower bearing the message "Jesus Saves." It was situated in the heart of the legendary thoroughfare known as "Sweet Auburn." Since the late 1800s, Auburn Avenue had been one of the identifying symbols of Black progress and pride, one of the most dynamic Black communities anywhere in the world, a place where Blacks owned property and flourishing businesses, practiced medicine, pharmacology, and law, wrote insurance and published newspapers, entertained and engaged in vigorous political activity. John Wesley Dobbs, grandfather of Atlanta mayor Maynard Jackson, is said to have been the originator of the title "Sweet Auburn," because this one was so distinct from Black sections in so many other towns he had visited that were "on the wrong side of the tracks."

Big Bethel, along with Wheatstreet and Ebenezer, were a major part of Sweet Auburn's history, and all had renowned ministers. William Holmes Borders, of Wheatstreet, and Martin Luther King, Sr., of Ebenezer, among them. In Big Bethel's basement, in 1881, Morris Brown College held its first classes.

Regardless of whatever else was happening in the lives of its members in the larger society during the week, the people who entered Bethel Church on Sunday walked with the confident assurance of belonging. There was, as they loved to say, "no slow walking and sad talking." One of the most exciting programs of the year, and one of the church's big revenue producers, was a play which nearly the entire congregation either participated in or attended. It was called *Heaven Bound* and it was a Black version of the Passion Play. My favorite character was the Devil, who dressed in a red costume with a long tail and carried a pitchfork, because of how out of character the man who played him was—Mr. H. J. Furlough, the stern, no-nonsense principal of David T. Howard, one of Atlanta's three Black high schools.

As much as I loved Sunday school, I was less fond of church. I much preferred the break in between Sunday school and church, when my friends and I would go across the street for milkshakes or malteds at the drugstore named for and owned by two prominent Black businessmen, Clayton Yates and L. D. Milton. Sooner or later, however, I would have to go back inside, find my mother, and stay there until the service was over. I still had a hard time sitting through long sermons and services where the collection plate was passed for various reasons several times throughout the morning, while the preacher exhorted the congregation to "dig just a little deeper now." But by this time, I had grown beyond pinching and peach trees.

It was a good thing, too, because soon my mother would have another one to train in the ways of good children in church. My father had returned from Korea in September 1951, and Franklyn Rochell Hunter was born July 26, 1952. My mother had informed me somewhat less ceremoniously than before of the pending arrival, and I remember not being as thrilled as I had been the first time around. I thought one brother was enough. Also, I think some of the intimacy I felt being in the next room and at least hearing the birth of my first brother was lost this time, because my mother delivered at Fort Mac. When we used to drive up from Covington to visit her, after her surgery, my Uncle Rochell would sneak me in to see her, as he had to do again this time. But it was several days before I saw my new baby brother. He was named Franklyn Rochell after my Grandmother Frances and my Grandfather Rochell.

As for my other brother, it was classic sibling rivalry from the start—one that lasted well into their adult life. While they were preoccupied with each other, I was able for the most part to be preoccupied with myself. Because I was so much older than they were, in some ways it was as if I were still an only child.

By the end of the first school year, enough Black families had moved into our new neighborhood and enough white families had moved out that it was announced that the elementary school in the district would be turned over to Blacks in the fall. That meant I would not be returning to E. R. Carter. I was really disappointed, because by now I was comfortable with Carter and had hopes that I would be in the class with my friends in seventh grade. But that was not to be. Most of the ones I had grown close to remained at E. R. Carter. I and a few others from my neighborhood started thinking about entering the "white" school that fall.

The white school was a beautiful school, at the top of a hill, overlooking an expansive park: Mozley Park. I couldn't imagine why the white people would want to leave such a wonderful place. But we were happy to have it. Nowhere I had ever lived did Black people have access to such a park. There was a huge swimming pool, with a big shallow part and a separate deep part. Next to it was a large clubhouse, with showers and changing rooms downstairs and a beautiful hardwood dance floor upstairs. Because there was no other facility like it anywhere in Atlanta, it drew crowds of young Black people. I divided my time between the swimming pool and the dance hall. Because I was tall for my age, I got a lot of attention from older boys. I think that's why I never learned how to swim. I always had too many eager teachers. Sometime that summer, I met an older guy whom I immediately developed a crush on. His name was Robert Dabney, known to all as Bobby, a junior in high school. He was tall, had big muscles, and was very cool. I found out he played football at his high school. He paid me absolutely no attention, but every time he came on the scene, all I wanted to do was watch his every move.

By the end of summer, as usual, I was more than ready to go back to school. My unhappiness over leaving Carter had now turned into guarded anticipation about entering the "white" school on the hill.

Of course, once I had climbed the hill and walked through the doors for the first time, there was nothing white in sight—only the ghost-whites that I conjured up as I climbed the stairs to my class-room and as I sat down in one of "their" seats for the first time. It was a strange experience, being in one of "their" schools. It even smelled different. Not better or worse, just different. At first, we all thought the tall, willowy principal, a Miss Post, was white. But it turned out she was not. About the only thing the whites left was the school name, Frank L. Stanton. He had been the poet laureate of Georgia. The school song, "Sweetes' Li'l Feller," was adapted from his poem of the same name, and we had to learn to sing it at assembly programs. At first, none of us wanted to learn this white song—especially with all the dialect, which seemed to mock us. But the teachers said we had to learn it, and in time, lacking any alternative, we came to sing it as our own.

> *Sweetes' li'l feller—*
> > *Everybody knows;*
> *Dunno what ter call 'im,*
> > *But he mighty lak' a rose!*
>
> *Lookin' at his mammy*
> > *Wid eyes so shiny-blue,*
> *Mek' you think dat heaven*
> > *Is comin' clost ter you!*
>
> *W'en he's dar a-sleepin'*
> > *In his li'l place,*
> *Think I see de angels*
> > *Lookin' thoo' de lace.*
>
> *W'en de dark is fallin'—*
> > *W'en de shadders creep,*
> *Den dey comes on tip-toe*
> > *Ter kiss 'im in his sleep.*

> *Sweetes' li'l feller—*
> *Everybody knows;*
> *Dunno what ter call 'im,*
> *But he mighty lak' a rose!*

I think there was some debate about whether or not to keep the school name. But in the end, the powers that be—who weren't Black—decided to keep it. It wasn't long before I was completely comfortable at Stanton, name and all. At home, I talked about the new school a lot, as my brother Henry, now three, sat in rapt attention.

Shortly after school opened, I happened to look out the window one day and I saw a little boy walking up the hill alone. Wearing only a diaper, he presented such a curious sight that it held my attention. Pretty soon I realized it was Henry. I quickly asked to be excused, and by the time I got to the door, there was Miss Post, holding my brother's hand. She turned to me and calmly said, "He says he's your brother and he wanted to come to school with you." I was, of course, embarrassed.

"What are you doing here?" I asked him as he grinned victoriously at me.

"I wanted to go to school with you," he said happily, beaming with pride both in himself and me.

Neither my mother nor my grandmother nor I could figure out how he had managed not only to get out of the house unnoticed but to find his way down Mozley Place, over two blocks to the larger Mozley Drive crossing, then choose the right turn to head up the hill to Stanton. I didn't know whether to smack him or hug him, but there was so much love in his little eyes that I just took him by the hand and led him back home.

I had a good year at Stanton. Having started on an equal footing with all the students there, I adjusted quickly, getting involved in school activities and making myself useful to the teachers.

As we were nearing the homestretch of my final year in elementary school, on May 17, 1954, the Supreme Court handed down its landmark *Brown* decision, unanimously ruling that racial segregation in the nation's public schools was unconstitutional. The "separate but equal" formula and farce that started with the 1896 Supreme Court *Plessy v. Ferguson* ruling that mandated racially "separate but equal" railroad carriages, and that as the venerable Atlanta *Constitution* columnist Ralph McGill put it, by the thirties had become "a heavy weight on the nation's conscience," was now to be consigned to ignominious history.

Ruminating on the stunning decision in a London hotel room, McGill put it this way (in *The South and the Southerner*): "For two years the more violent voices, including those of political leaders, had been proclaiming that the court would not dare reverse the ruling of 1896. Few heard those who were declaring that in the last half of the twentieth century the justices couldn't do anything else."

The case had its roots in several states, including my native South Carolina, but it bore the name of Linda Brown, of Topeka, Kansas, whose A.M.E. minister father had filed the case on her behalf. Like many thousands of young Blacks all over the South, five-year-old Linda Brown had to pass a white school and ride a bus in order to get to the Black school all the way on the other side of town. But there came a time when the Reverend Brown decided that little Linda had traveled long and far enough, so he decided to offer his young daughter as a test case, hiring the NAACP Legal Defense Fund, which was assembling cases all over the South, to help them out. Clearly, none of us was in a school that was anywhere near equal to the white schools. Even as late as 1960, in one of the most comprehensive studies ever done on Black Atlanta—"A Second Look"—the Atlanta Committee for Cooperative Action revealed that Black students, who on average lagged two years or more behind their white counterparts, "have been known to attend classes for weeks without being able to secure textbooks required for their courses; meanwhile, the practice continues of supplying Negro students with used or outdated texts discarded by Atlanta's white students." The study also pointed out that "many black students had to travel ten miles a day to reach a school that will admit them; [and that] double sessions continue in about half of the Negro public schools."

Even so, in Atlanta I was probably better off than I would have been if I had still been in the small town of Covington. It was also true that, for some time, having seen the rising court challenges to

Jim Crow education in other places in the South, the white establishment had been upgrading or building new Black schools all over
the state. As Ralph McGill wrote in *The South and the Southerner**:

> About two years before the 1954 decree, the Deep South,
> with almost frantic urgency, began to do something about
> the much relied-on, much-ignored *Plessy* decision. To the
> sound of hammer and saw, and to the Wagnerian bellow of
> oratory in their legislative halls in behalf of emergency bond
> issues, the South began to build modern schools for Negroes.
> Bond issues and building authorities mushroomed. It was an
> almost compulsive confession that the schools [had] not
> been equal and that there had been no previous will or
> intent to make them so. Privately, too, there was considerable
> self-accusation. "We should have done this years ago," they
> said. "Then maybe we could have prevented all these court
> cases."

If the *Brown* decision created a stir in Black or white Atlanta, it
didn't reverberate down to seventh grade. I'm told that Black teachers
discussed the decision among themselves, with some not knowing
exactly what it was going to mean, others fearful that it would
threaten their jobs if they had to compete with white teachers, who,
they felt, had the power, if not the superior training. Others, like
Miss T. I. Jones, who later was one of my high-school English teachers, told me when I was making a documentary in 1979 that at the
time of the decision she was "quite elated, because I felt that this was
a time that meant that we would have better opportunities for our
students, and certainly it would offer them an opportunity to advance.
I realized that at the time, that it would take some time for us to feel
the full effects of the court ruling. But I must say that I didn't realize
it would take this long!"

Indeed, for some time to come, the closest any Black student in

* Boston: Atlantic Monthly Press, 1959; reprinted 1963, pp. 22–23.

Atlanta would come to going to school with white students would be with the ghost-whites I imagined at Frank L. Stanton.

Henry McNeal Turner High School was probably one of those schools built by the white establishment to help them defend against integration. As such, it handpicked its faculty and administration and was far and away superior to either of the other two Black high schools in the city—Booker T. Washington, which for generations was the only Black high school in Atlanta, and David T. Howard, which was built later.

When I got to Turner in the fall of 1954, it had the reputation of being *the* school for the Black *crème de la crème*. The surrounding neighborhoods ran the gamut, from lower to upper middle class, and featured some of the nicest Black homes in the city. Turner was about another mile beyond Stanton. Most days, a gang of kids from Mozley Place walked together, picking up other friends along the way. The school was named for Henry McNeal Turner, another A.M.E. bishop, also originally from South Carolina, who had served as a chaplain in the Union Army and then in the Reconstruction legislature of Georgia, with a distinction that earned him great enmity among whites, who, he once said, had accused him "of every crime in the catalogue of villainy."

At Turner—the school—the legacy of the man resonated throughout its classrooms, where the idea of Du Bois's "talented tenth" was alive and well in the minds of many of the teachers. As for me, in those early days of school, when the waning summer heat was reaching a comfort level and an occasional breeze through a classroom window felt like a loving embrace, I was wide-eyed with the joy I felt about moving to a whole new level of being. With sponges in the tops of my bobby socks and starch in my crinolines, I was ready to be a serious teenager, perhaps serious enough to get a little more serious attention from Bobby Dabney, who that year was entering his senior year and was one of the Big Men on Campus.

I loved high school from the first day. Especially the part where you changed classes after homeroom. It was so different from elementary school. There was even a school bank, started by Mr. V. C. Nash, to help students learn how to handle money responsibly. At Turner, I felt so grown-up. So free. So *high school!* Some of my friends from Carter and from Stanton, like Charlotte Cherry, whom I kept in touch with, lived in zones that required them to go to Washington High, now Turner's archrival at every level, especially in sports. But I was now a real green-and-white Turnerite, and I couldn't imagine being anywhere but there.

Not long after I had really gotten settled in at Turner, my mother called me to her one day and said she had some news. "We're going to be moving to Alaska," she said in her usual nonchalant way. My father had been stationed in Alaska since April 1954, but it had never occurred to me that we would deviate from our routine of living in two different locations.

I was incredulous. I think I wanted to faint, if not die. I couldn't believe I had heard what had just come from my mother's lips. But for the moment all I could bring myself to ask was "When?"

"As soon as we can get packed and get our furniture on the way."

"But why?" I was able to ask, my voice starting to crack as I now had a slightly fuller understanding of the implications of her words.

"Well, I just think it's time we lived with your father, together, as a family."

I had become so used to our family as it was, my mother and grandmother taking care of each other and us kids and every other conceivable thing, that it would not have entered my mind that perhaps my mother felt that two young boys needed a man's hand and his daily example. And I was not predisposed to consider it now, even though my grandmother, whom we were leaving behind, tried to get me to understand. For all the years that she had lived with us, she had never tried to interfere with my mother and father, and would have been the first, I think, to encourage my mother to join him. She had many friends in Atlanta and Covington, too, and it was not that far away. She was still in good shape, and at that time she could take the bus for the hour-long trip without any problem.

Within short order, I was pretty well beside myself with grief, even though my mind refused to see the end of my wonderful new world of Turner High School. I would not be consoled, even though my mother promised that I could take all the furnishings in my room, which I had just redecorated like a room I saw in a magazine. I had a blond-oak bedroom set, with a bed that had a bookcase headboard, and a blond oak hi-fi and record player. My curtains were the latest in magazine-bedroom fashion—three different-colored floor-length panels of white, blue, and pink, a solid-pink bedspread and three different-colored throw pillows to match the colors in the curtains. It was my private sanctuary at the front of the house, separated from the living room by sliding doors and from my brothers in the back part of the house. When I wasn't playing the piano in the living room, I would shut out one world as I closed the sliding doors and open up another: my world of reading, listening to pop music on the radio, playing my records, talking on the telephone. Most of the time, my family would be in the back of the house watching one or the other of their favorite television programs—my grandmother's was wrestling; my brothers' were cartoons (my mother preferred reading in the middle of all that). But there was always a lot of confusion during these times, because my brothers were always fighting and my mother was always shouting at them to quit and occasionally spanking them. So I preferred to be as far away as possible. My mother tried every now and then to get me to join the family, but I usually declined. Depending on her mood, she might call me antisocial, but she never insisted. I was more than comfortable being alone; I thrived on it—a fact that would be my salvation a few years down the line, when I had absolutely no choice. As for my room, I loved it, all right, but I did not want it or me to go to Alaska.

But even as I would not reconcile myself to moving, in time I started to face the dismal reality—especially when one day the movers deposited huge round crates and cardboard cartons throughout the house. So before they packed up my red, leather-bound *World Book Encyclopedia*, which I had received one Christmas from Santa Claus, I pulled out the first volume one day and shut myself up in my room and read all there was about this frigid place that was so far away and barren that for many years after the United States purchased it from Russia in 1867 for $7,200,000 it was called "Seward's Folly" or "Seward's Icebox," after the Secretary of State who pushed for and brokered the deal. Thereafter, "folly" became my favorite word for this venture my mother was cheerily determined to undertake, but I kept it to myself (I had better), nurturing it as a small, secret payback for what she was putting me through. What none of us thought about at the time was the irony that in the year of the *Brown* decision I would be going to a white school, after all.

chapter **10**

Alaska

Not surprisingly, Alaska opened up a whole new world of experiences and adventures, starting with the plane ride from Atlanta—our first. What a way to get introduced to flying, crossing the entire United States in one fell swoop! The plane stopped at various points along the route for refueling, including Chicago, where my mother's aunt's husband came and kept us company at the airport. He was so excited that he kept turning to strangers, saying over and over again, "This is my niece and her family, and they're on their way to Alaska." Every time I heard it, it was as if I had been slapped, and tears welled up in my eyes again and again. The stops along the way underscored the distance we were traveling, and by the time we arrived at the Anchorage airport, I was convinced that we had traveled to the end of the world. As we stepped off the plane, I couldn't help wondering what really was going on. We couldn't be in Alaska, I thought, because there was no snow in sight. Just brown, muddy ground. But disappointment was now for me a threadbare emotion, so I just shrugged it off and never even asked why there was no snow.

Somehow my brothers had managed not to kill or maim each other on the long flight, and my mother bore up well. When she stepped off the plane, she looked fresh and lovely. My father was more excited than I ever remember seeing him. He hugged and kissed my mother, then me, then swooped up each of the boys and gave them big hugs. They seemed slightly overwhelmed by it all, probably due to the fact that they were by now exhausted, and maybe also because, in fact, this man who was now effusing over them was the occasional visitor who would come home and summon them to the door shouting, "Boys!" as if he were ordering troops: "Fall out!" Their father was someone they hardly knew. But from that moment on we were in Alaska, in the military, and in our father's world, and we would learn more about him and his life than we had ever before known. And that, along with my other experiences in and out of school, would go a long way toward preparing me for what lay ahead, just a few years down the road, back home in Georgia.

Our housing was situated in an endless complex of two-story, boxlike, adjoining structures that from the outside all had that same dull, monotonous, military-barracks look. Inside, depending on the size of the family, the individual apartment configurations had only slightly more variety. Ours was a duplex, with a living room and a small dining room adjacent to a small kitchen on the first floor and, at the top of the stairs, three bedrooms, in descending order of size. I got the medium-sized room in the middle, which was barely big enough to hold my beloved bedroom suite and only one set of my curtains from the magazine picture.

Shortly after our arrival, the wife of one of the other chaplains stopped by and brought us sweets, and started acquainting us with some of the protocols of on-post living. Like most army families, they had lots of children, and in short order we knew all the details of where I would be attending school. I didn't look forward to it at all. I just wanted to shut myself up in my room and, like the legendary grizzlies I had read about in my pre-trip research, hibernate all winter.

What a winter it was! A week after we arrived, so did the first snow, the transforming element whose pervasive whiteness would challenge us mentally, physically, and symbolically. Of course, it was more snow than I had ever before seen, since I could remember only frost back home in Georgia. But this was the vision that had always danced in my head as long as I could remember, along with sugar-plums and Dasher, Prancer, Donder, and Blitzen. What I had seen on the Christmas cards with old St. Nick, and never dreamed either that it was real or that I would wake up one morning and have to walk to school in it. But walk I did. Only a few blocks from my apartment, but in temperatures that dropped to 30 and 40 below. Actually, it wasn't that cold to my body, wrapped as I was in fur-lined boots and a swaddling parka, and it was also a dry cold that you didn't feel, sometimes, until it was too late. There were a lot of cases of frostbite among the soldiers at the infirmary; I saw some of them when my older brother had to be taken there, blood pouring all over the clean white snow, after being hit by my younger brother between the eyes with a toy pistol.

The school I enrolled in was called Ursa Major, after one of the two great northern constellations, also known as the Great Bear. Determined as I was to be unhappy, I soon met my first big disappointment. Eighth grade was still *elementary school*! I had lost not only my place but my freedom, too. It seemed as if I had been demoted, which made me feel even more betrayed by my mother. But she was so busy setting up housekeeping and being introduced around the post by my father, who seemed so proud of her beauty and good taste, that I don't think she noticed.

There was another difference, and it was a big one. I was not just the only Black student in the class, I was the only Black student in the school. I didn't know quite what to expect. My father had given me a little talk going in, saying that I shouldn't be too concerned that there were no other Black students, because I was as smart as any of them; that I had a first-rate mind—he loved the phrase "first-rate mind"—and that they would all respect me when I demonstrated it.

I didn't have any particular attitude about the fact that the other students were white, but I was anxious about how prepared I was to compete. Not only was this a white school, in effect, but I was coming in late and therefore was already at a disadvantage. Somehow, although we never really talked about it per se back home, somewhere in my psyche was something that said white education was superior, and it wasn't too much of a leap to conclude that so were white people. But I think I was able to mentally draw the line at the people, because of all the positive reinforcement I had gotten from my father and the rest of my family. White people were not superior; they were just *different*.

All these students were real military brats, as regular army kids were called and, as such, changed schools approximately every two years, when their fathers' assignments changed and they rotated to another post. I assumed that this meant that as world travelers they had broad exposure to all races, classes, and creeds. Little did I know that most of them lived in sheltered American enclaves, attending post or on-base schools, with limited contact with non-military and/ or foreign students. So travel was only a bit broadening. The military had been on orders to desegregate "as rapidly as possible" since 1948, after a historic executive order by President Harry Truman. In Alaska, my father was the only Black chaplain, and one of only a handful of Black officers. And as I was to learn in the coming months, the white students were affected by the same sometimes subtle, sometimes overt dynamics that existed in an army not yet fully desegregated or comfortable with the idea.

For example, one Sunday morning, a white soldier and his wife—both from Mississippi—were attending church for the first time since arriving in Alaska. When my father walked into the chapel, the woman said, "I sizzled." Years later, as reported in the *Atlanta Constitution*, she said, "It was hard to sit, and to listen, to a minister who was black. But I did not want to embarrass my husband, my family, or myself, so I sat still. It was against everything that was in me to do it."

The woman added, "I was hearing the words I had been hearing all my life. He was preaching the same Bible. His voice was terrific, I gave him that. He was educated and his sermon was prepared well. The first service over, since this was to become our chapel, I made the minister's color as minor as possible. As weeks went on, the sermons of this Negro became, to me, a source of great strength. His was a real talking acquaintance with the Lord."

After a time, the woman's husband had to have surgery. "The minister did his duty," she recalled. "And much more. He would slip in, but only for short stays, and seemed able to voice things which I held unsaid in my heart. I decided then that everyone should have the right to an education, be they white or Black, but they must 'earn position' after that. The chaplain 'earned position' with me. I attended chapel, and together we sent up prayers for my husband's recovery. That Negro minister helped, and my strength continued to come from his sermons."

But such conversions were hard to come by. For example, early on, my father took my mother out to a dance. During the course of the evening, one of the Black officers asked the wife of his friend, a white captain, to dance. The Black officer was Grover Dubose, now a captain, who had served with my father in Korea in 1950. He told me the story, which was confirmed by my mother: "We were at a battalion party and I was dancing with [my friend's] wife. The post commander sent word to the table by one of his aides and told this captain that 'we don't allow whites dancing with Blacks.' While I was on the dance floor! We finished the dance, but it put an absolute damper on the party for the rest of the evening."

Coincidentally, one of the most uncomfortable times I had at school also involved a dance. By the time the dance rolled around, I had become pretty comfortable in my school surroundings. Occasionally some of the students would visit my home, and once in a while I would be invited to one of their homes. I even remember once, not long after reading *Alice in Wonderland*, I was inspired to throw myself an Un-Birthday Party, and invited some of my classmates, along with my teacher, Fred Martin, and another teacher, his friend Rodney Delin. I decorated the living room and made all the other arrangements, let all the guests in, instructed them on how to act during this un-surprise party for my un-birthday, then left the apartment and closed the door. When I opened it a few seconds later, everyone in the room shouted "Surprise!" and I pretended to be surprised.

There were also other kinds of social activities that I participated in, including ice-skating for the first time in my life—there had been no ice like this in Georgia, and if there were rinks, we Black kids weren't allowed to use them. But I had been a good roller-skater back home, so I figured, How much different can it be? Down at the deeply frozen pond near our house, I put on the ice skates, got up on the ice, and in short order had my answer. A lot! I fell on my behind a few times, and I watched the white kids glide across the ice with grace and abandon. I felt like a klutz, but I was determined to be as good as I was at roller-skating. The only thing missing was the kind of friends I had when I was roller-skating. Good friends like Betty. I didn't have any of those on the ice—or anywhere else, for that matter. And besides, I hated the cold.

The Physical Education Department used to teach square dancing, polkas, and schottisches, none of which I had ever done before coming to Alaska. Those were white folks' dances. At least I had seen Dale Evans and Roy Rogers square dancing. And I had seen white people on television dancing the polka as Lawrence Welk played in the background. But I had never heard of a schottische. Having no other options, I learned them all, if not with total relish.

By this time, my mother was settled and was focusing on helping us children to adjust. The square dances were usually held on Friday nights, so at the beginning of each week she would start making me a new dress. It picked up my spirits some to have a new dress every Friday night, and she seemed to really enjoy making them for me. But there came a time when the school organized a more formal dance—and the army band was to play. It was a big deal, and of course, my mother made me a new dress. Nobody had a date as such, but all week long everybody had been talking about whom they were going to be with and whom they wanted to dance with. There was one guy I thought was cute. He had curly brown hair and played on the basketball team. In fact, he was really smart, and was a star on the team—just about the most popular and handsome guy in the class. And he didn't seem to be with anybody special. Until this particular dance, most of the dancing events didn't involve partners. But on this night there was slow dancing, and other dances that required a partner. All night long I sat around and no one asked me to dance. Then, close to the end of the evening, someone finally asked me: my teacher, Fred Martin. It wasn't exactly what I had in mind, but at least it got me out of the chair I had been sitting in all evening. I think everyone in the room took note of what had happened, although it didn't inspire anyone else to ask me to dance, as I recall.

On another occasion, I went with a group of my classmates to a teenage club near the school. The man in charge didn't want to let me in, because, he said, it was "members only." I asked him how

I could become a member and he gave me a big runaround. Later that afternoon, I told my mother, who told my father. You would have thought the Russians had invaded the post the way my father went into action. He insisted that I accompany him to the teenage club, where he confronted the manager, who backed down in a hurry. I was told that of course the chaplain's daughter could join, and why hadn't I said I was the chaplain's daughter, and on and on. He had thought I was an enlisted man's daughter, and this was a club for the children of officers.

I was really upset by the whole thing, and on the verge of tears. But my father told me that I shouldn't let it bother me. I said that it didn't and that I didn't really want to go there, anyway. And he said it was up to me, but then he said firmly, "You have to let these people know who you are." He continued, saying, "No, no," almost as if he wasn't talking to me. "You can't let them deny you, and I won't let them deny you or me. Not as long as I have breath in my body. Oh no. I've given too much to this man's army to have someone like that deny me and mine. Oh no. Go if you want. Don't go if you don't want to. But the choice is yours, not theirs." And then, true to his military side, he turned to me and barked an order: "And you will not be embarrassed!"

Despite the awkwardness on the social side, I managed not only to catch up academically—for I was indeed behind, not just because I had started late, but because the South was behind and Blacks in the South were even further behind—but I also got all As. Still, it was not an effortless exercise. I had had trouble with math since I had the mumps back in Covington in Miss Mary Wright's fourth-grade class and missed fractions and long division. And while I was a good reader, neither I nor anyone I knew back home had the kind of study habits I witnessed among these students. There was a lot of homework, and that came before anything else, because you would get called on in class the next day and it was a point of pride to know the answer, a humiliating embarrassment not to. I was petrified of being called on and not knowing the answer, so I applied myself with a diligence I didn't know I possessed, committing almost every word of every lesson to memory—especially the math.

About the only distraction from our classroom work was the

occasional moose that would wander down from the Chugach Mountains and take up residence on the snow-covered playground. The game warden would be called, but generally he was pretty ineffective, especially since it was an open secret that he had been chased by a moose and pinned under his car for hours, until the moose finally lost interest and wandered off, probably retreating to join the one that used to invade the garbage cans outside our apartment many mornings before dawn.

One of our most frequent visitors was the chief Army chaplain for Alaska, Colonel Paul Mauer, who was my father's cut buddy. He would often return from one of his swings around the territory with a side of moose or deer meat. Without my grandmother, my mother was now cooking more than she ever had before, and now she was really branching out. Although she had never cooked anything wilder than a rabbit or a possum, she outdid herself on the moose, marinating it in vinegar and onions and then cooking the stew out of it, as we used to say Down South, although not quite literally in this case, because it didn't mush up the way a good beef stew does when it has been cooking for hours. But my mother managed to cook the gaminess out of it, and it was not difficult to chew when she served it for dinner with my father's favorite dish, boiled white rice.

Colonel Mauer also introduced us to "squaw candy," which was a big disappointment the first time I bit into a piece, because, rather than something sweet that tasted like candy, it had a fishy taste. That's because it was not candy at all but cured whale blubber, given to him by an Eskimo chief way up North. The chief, he said, had also offered him his wife to keep him warm the night he spent in the igloo. When he declined, the chief thought it was because the wife was too old, so he offered him his daughter instead. An ellipsis followed that part of the story, as the gray-haired old colonel winked merrily at my father.

When the colonel told such stories, everybody roared, including my father, who didn't laugh a lot. In fact, my father was very conservative—even to the point of not wanting any alcohol in the house. My mother had made a few friends who would occasionally stop by with a six-pack, but my father never approved of her being too friendly or of her having even a beer, let alone a cocktail. That's why she found it so amusing when she and my father attended a Jewish seder and my father, unaccustomed to drinking anything, became quite tipsy on the Manischewitz served at several points during the ceremony.

I was too busy feeling sorry for myself, however, to notice that there was very little intimacy or joy between my parents. Something was wrong, but I didn't see it; nor, I suspect, did anyone else, for the chaplain and his wife kept up appearances, occasionally entertaining, and attending church and other activities on the post. What a handsome couple they were. My father continued to be a meticulous dresser, never leaving the house without his shoes spit-shined to mirror-like perfection. Somehow he also managed never to have mud on his shoes, despite its pervasiveness. And he had a closetful of shoes, all army brown—at least a dozen pairs lined up neatly in a row, one pair indistinguishable from another. And uniforms, too. Whenever the army changed uniforms, my father was always among the first with the most. My mother used to tease him because he was such a particular dresser that he refused to wear long johns, even on the most extreme sub-zero days. "You're going to freeze to death one day wearing those nylon undershorts," my mother said to him one day. But that made absolutely no impression on my father, who clearly had a style that made him happy and that he was determined to keep up, regardless.

Meanwhile, my real outlet was the piano, which my mother had put in the basement of the apartment building. I would finish my homework, rush down there, and play for hours on end. I had pages and pages of sheet music, which I bought with money I earned babysitting for other officer families on the post. I was in big demand because I was the chaplain's daughter, a trustworthy bet, and because at the age of twelve I was as tall as a sixteen-year-old and probably as confident, owing to my experience with my two younger brothers. I could change the diapers of infants and wrestle two-year-olds to the ground. As for the others, I could read them to sleep or sing them songs. I had a vast and varied repertoire that served me well.

I made a lot of money, especially after late-night parties, when the officers came in tipsy. I always got a big tip then. My special treat at the end of the week was the trip into Anchorage, the closest town, a little over a mile away, to purchase sheet music. My favorite that year was "Unchained Melody," which Roy Hamilton made popular on a record, followed by the blind singer, Al Hibbler. In fact, it became my anthem, with its mournful words of unrequited love. I especially loved the chorus about lonely rivers flowing to the open arms of the sea and sighing, "I'll be coming home, wait for me."

The search for the music helped obliterate the tawdriness of Anchorage: a rough-and-ready frontier town straight off the silver screen of that old Covington movie house; a place where Hopalong Cassidy and the Durango Kid would have felt at home riding down the middle of the town's one thoroughfare, Main Street, looking for trouble. Many of the people who populated Anchorage at the time were adventurers who had come to Alaska answering the "call of the wild," either looking for gold or to work on the railroad or the highway, or to service all the above. As for this time, while there was nothing left of those adventures, adventurers were still listening for the call, in spite of its diminishing clarity.

There was a small Black population, most of them living in ramshackle shacks and shanties. My father seemed to know every inch of their ground. Once, when I wanted to get my hair straightened, he drove me through a claustrophobic maze of these shanties, round one dark, rutted alley and up another, until we stopped in front of a structure that resembled a slightly larger version of one of the outhouses I had used in Social Circle. "Come on in, baby," he said to me without any sign of the hesitation I felt, so I got out of the car and followed him. In hindsight, I think there was a lot more going on inside than hair straightening, but the woman who fixed my hair was very respectful to my father and very kind to me, and she could fry some hair.

My father seemed at home everywhere he went, from the pristine, predominantly white officers' club on the post to Black and despondent Anchorage, known as "The Flats." As Byron Lewis, one of the young Black soldiers, put it years later, "He was the unofficial commanding officer of the Black soldiers and the unofficial mayor of Black Anchorage."

Byron Lewis was a New Yorker who had become a communications specialist during his time in the army. A private, he went from Fort Benning, Georgia, to Alaska on consignment. But, he said, most of the Black troops in his regiment were not there by choice. "The white troops I graduated with from Fort Benning got to go all over the world to fill out their communication assignments," he recalled. "I think the military didn't want to send us to Europe, because they thought we would enjoy that too much."

Byron had a beautiful tenor voice and sang in my father's choir. (My father's passion was singing, and he organized choirs wherever he served.) As one of his favorite young soldiers, Byron was often invited to our home. "Oh yeah," Byron recalled. "We liked to come to the house. It was like a home. In my barracks there were a half dozen guys who came to the house several times. We liked it. We also liked to come because you were there. I'd be going to the house and they'd ask me if I was going to see the Reverend (we called him "Rev"). I'd say, 'Yes,' and they'd all sit back and laugh. I'd grab my civilian clothes, and they'd say, 'Well, how's Charlayne?' And I would say, 'Oh, she's fine.' And then once I said, 'You know, she doesn't say much.' And one of them said, 'Well, man, do you know how old she is?' And I said, 'No.' And one said, 'Man, she's twelve years old.' But you were really tall. They said, 'Man, why you think she didn't say a word?' And they laughed at me all night long."

There was one young soldier who used to call the house and tell me I reminded him of his sister. I was afraid to tell my father—a fear that I found was justified when one day my father picked up the extension phone and heard the young man's voice. Since none of the twelve- and thirteen-year-old boys in my class ever called me, and since this voice was obviously deeper than that of any thirteen-year-old who might have been calling, my father immediately concluded that it was a soldier.

"Soldier!" he shouted into the extension phone, "what right have you got calling my daughter? State your name, rank, and serial number, and if you ever call her again, I'll have you court-martialed."

I never saw the owner of the voice on the other end of the phone, and after that day he never called again. I told my mother about it —well, actually she heard the whole thing—and surprisingly, she reacted sympathetically to the young soldier, who had told me he was nineteen. "I feel sorry for these young men up here without any girls to talk to," she said. "It's too bad."

It wasn't that my father didn't have empathy. Just not where his daughter was concerned. As Byron recalled, during his visits to the house my father would spend hours talking about the problems of the Black people in the military and in the town. "He really wanted to help Black people in Alaska, and he was fully conversant with their problems," Byron recalled.

"What were their problems?" I asked him, and he replied, "The problems were that the Black people who came up there to make money were pigeonholed into certain kinds of occupations. So they were the labor force. Just as we were in the military. There was a lot of loneliness, because it was a very small Black community. And it was definitely racist, because many of the white people who came up there were Southern. The military was there, and it was still a racist organization. So there were a lot of social problems in the Black community. Many of them got involved in illicit activities. There was a big Black prostitution community that serviced the whole base, and they had all kinds of problems, and they would call your father. For problems with the police. Domestic problems. All kinds of problems. Same as on base. The entire environment was in transition. You have to understand, the army was only just becoming integrated. It was the first time Black officers commanded white troops. And they operated in a very narrow environment. I think your father was one of the highest-ranking Black officers there, if not *the* highest-ranking officer. A captain. At the center of what I would call the emerging officer class. And he had the ear of the people who counted. So if you couldn't get a leave when you wanted one, and you knew someone was being unfair about it, that's who you went to. That's how I got to go home one time. I went to your father and I said, 'Can I get on a military aircraft?' And he said, 'What do you want to do that for?' And I said, 'Because I can't get out of here.' Your father was the type of person that would go right to the top.

"We had some really heavy problems, though. We had a big problem with alcoholism. Homosexuality. It was very hard for Black soldiers, because most Blacks up there didn't have families. You had all these men and very few women. Loneliness was a major factor.

And remember, the other problem was the weather. Those really long, severely cold winters. It was dark most of the time—dark when we went to work in the morning, and dark when we finished work. Fourteen to sixteen hours of darkness. We were really in a confined circumstance and an isolated environment. Your father became the person people would go to. He would try to do things that gave us more outlets. Which is ultimately how I got in the choir and why I spent so much time in church. He didn't ask you to do anything irrational. Nor to follow any particular belief systems. He dealt with what was real. His ministry was one of being where the deal was."

I remember, as did Byron Lewis, that my father was never far from his roots. Byron recalled: "People went to your father's services because they were different. Everything had a Black focus to it, although it was a military environment. The Blacks went to his services because it was like being home. You got a minister who gave you what you needed spiritually, but you also got the soul of a Black service."

My father also loved dramatics, as Byron remembered. "He'd have a particular sermon, and he'd pick the right hymns for it. He would come to the choir and he'd say, 'Okay, I'm going to start off and I'll get so far, and you start.' And he'd build dramatics into it. Now, you know, there's nothing the brothers like more than dramatics."

At the same time, my father was able to transcend race, because he related on a human level to everybody. My father's services were easily the most popular on the post, attended by all races and religions. And he made no distinctions in his counsel or his ministry. I heard him chide a young soldier for not calling his mother or father—"What kind of Catholic are you?" he asked—and then go on to deliver the gentlest of lectures.

Of course, as with his dress, my father was not without his vanity about his performance, and was always asking Byron or one of the chaplain's assistants for the count from the various services. At home it was a point of pride when my father could boast of having a bigger attendance than any of the white chaplains. I think it meant something to him that in this time of slow, begrudging racial transition, being able to appeal to such a broad cross section of the post population was one of the few tangible signs of progress and achievement for a Black officer.

I could appreciate my father's excitement. But what caused the big rush in *my* life was not the chaplain, even if he was my father, but the post mailman. That's who would bring letters from home. Every now and then I would get a letter from Bobby Dabney. He actually liked me—better, it seemed, when I was out of sight. In answer to a question I had posed in a previous letter, he wrote that "Unchained Melody" was a big hit in Atlanta and that, yes, he liked it a lot, too. Oh my God! When was I ever going to get back home?

When spring came, I was beginning to get hints that maybe I would know the answer sooner than the two more years we had to go. My mother started talking a lot about my grandmother and how much she missed her and how maybe my grandmother's health might be failing, and on and on like that. My father kept up his hectic pace, always on the go, from sunup to sundown. He was usually home for dinner, but often went out afterward to the servicemen's club, where the enlisted men congregated. Sometimes he would take me, but mostly he went alone. Somehow, even though he was an officer, I think he preferred the servicemen's club, because that's where most of the young Black soldiers congregated. Whenever I went with him, however, there were an equal number of white enlisted men coming up to greet him with enormous respect. I was proud of the way they treated him, and he was never aloof or arrogant, no matter how much they praised him. He always had time for each individual who approached him, which made it clear why it often took him so long to get home. It also helps explain why his services were the most well attended on the post.

Whatever was going on between my mother and father did not get in the way of our taking advantage of the spring thaw, which brought with it another wholly new experience for us. Spring brought nearly unending hours of daylight—the flip side of the long nine months of night that had just ended. Now we learned to put tinfoil over our windows in order to sleep during nights without darkness. Without definitive night, baseball games and some military maneuvers, including parachute drops, were carried out at unusually late hours, often as if midnight were actually occurring at midday.

It was during this season that we traveled a bit beyond the immediate perimeter of the post and Anchorage, up into the now lush Mt. McKinley range, out to where blanket-thick rivers of salmon fought valiantly against the current as they made their months-long, perilous journey back to their spawning grounds. I was especially fascinated watching the salmon swim upstream, preparing both to begin life and, in exhaustion, to end it. In fact, I was awed by this vision of nature as I had never been by anything before.

On one of these outings, we drove up to the entrance to a national park only to find it barricaded. My father's first instinct, as if he was personally challenged by a DO NOT ENTER sign, was always to ask, "Why not?" This time, when he did, a very polite ranger explained that there was an angry grizzly bear on the loose and that they were just waiting him out. It was an answer that more than satisfied my father, who got back in the car and drove us to another location.

We then visited an Eskimo village and gravesite that was the most joyful-looking burial grounds I had ever seen, with colorful little houses built over the graves. They provided a completely different insight into the stolid-looking, stocky Eskimos, with their leathery skin that looked as if it had been aged like squaw candy and bore no creases because they rarely smiled. In fact, to me, they seemed to be living in a place in their mind that was even more remote than the one they inhabited. The Eskimos made me sad. Except for their graveyards.

Very few Eskimos in and around Anchorage lived in igloos. In fact, very few anywhere in Alaska lived in igloos, except as temporary shelter while traveling, and most of those were farther north. But for the amusement of outsiders, from time to time they would construct an igloo in Anchorage and everybody would get a charge out of going inside and crawling around. I convinced myself that it was actually warm there.

When school closed in late spring, I had a feeling I had taken my last class in Alaska. And it wasn't long before my mother told us we were going home. It was a little vague at first, as if we might just be going for a visit, but then, when the round crates and square boxes arrived once again, I knew we were going for good. What I didn't know was what my father was going to do. In time, however, his demeanor revealed that we would be leaving him behind. In retrospect, I think that the distance from the earlier long separations just couldn't be bridged. But at the time I was too happy to be going home to care. I was returning home, and would be back at Turner High School in the fall. Besides, I figured, my father would probably be along sooner or later.

We left Alaska on MATS, Military Air Transport Service, flying first to Washington, where we changed to civilian aircraft, and then home to Atlanta. We had been gone only nine months, but they were nine months that would affect my life profoundly. Oddly, it was after I got home that I sang, for the first time with gusto, the Ursa Major school song:

> *We will remember our school days in Alaska*
> *And our school at Fort Richardson.*
> *Where the Chugach Mountains reach to the sky.*
> *Where the Northern Lights shine brightly on high.*
> *We will remember our school days in Alaska*
> *And our classmates, every one.*

chapter **11**

Turner

I was so glad to be back at Turner High School that I hit the ground running, determined to make up for what I still regarded as lost time. I joined clubs and went out for the basketball team, tried out for the majorette squad (although my real goal was to be the drum major), and started singing in the chorus. Meanwhile, it didn't take long for me to realize that I had advanced academically and intellectually beyond ninth grade. My homeroom teacher, Victoria Sutton, was also my English teacher, and soon after I turned in my first writing assignments and got As on my first few tests, she seemed to understand that I needed more of a challenge than what the classroom offered, so she took me into her special confidence, allowing me to come to her home and help her correct papers and assist in her preparations for other classes.

Mrs. Sutton was a tough, no-nonsense teacher from the old school, who believed in hard work, homework, and discipline. Many of the other students found her stern, and most of them were intimidated by her. But I really got on well with her, and I think I exceeded even her toughness when it came to giving red marks for errors in my fellow classmates' papers. (Thank God, none of them suspected

I was the pencil-wielding culprit!) Mrs. Sutton was married to a minister, and they had no children. I sensed that I helped fill that void, although in some circles, I was called "Teacher's pet."

Mrs. Sutton was extremely protective toward me, even to the point of jealousy over my relationship with another English teacher, Elsie Foster Evans, whose classroom was right next door. Mrs. Evans was also childless and had a student, Gloria Moore, who had a relationship with her similar to the one between Mrs. Sutton and me. Mrs. Evans taught piano, too, and Gloria was her most gifted pupil. She could play anything; I really admired her skill. She accompanied the school chorus, and occasionally, when she was absent, I filled in, albeit still missing quite a few notes in the process. But Mrs. Evans and I had a relationship on a completely different level.

Mrs. Evans was not tall, a bit stout, and diabetic. But she was so chic, sophisticated, and quick-witted that her heaviness was not a liability. What I loved about her was that she was never mundane. For example, she was given to quoting Shakespeare or some other literary figure in casual conversation, and was always making puns. Also, I enjoyed her relationship with her husband, Gilbert, which I got to observe often, because Mrs. Evans frequently invited me or Gloria or both of us to her home, a beautiful split-level house in a new part of town, where most of the Black people were teachers or postal workers and the like, and where most had two cars in their garage and the kind of home that led to Atlanta's being known in the Black world as "L.A."—Lovely Atlanta.

To an outsider, the Evanses' marriage might have seemed contentious. But it was really a loving, dynamic, emotional and intellectual union, full of energetic repartee. Like so many Black men in the South, Gilbert, a Hampton graduate, had a first-rate education. But regardless of their qualifications, Black men were shut out of the white world and its professions by rigid segregation, and unless they were self-employed, most of them ended up either teaching or working at the Welfare Department or in the post office. Gilbert, as we all called him, worked in the post office. He was a lot quieter than Mrs. Evans but every bit her intellectual equal. I remember once she called him a blackamoor (which sent me scurrying to the dictionary), and the honey-brown-skinned Gilbert shot back, "The blacker the berry, the sweeter the juice." Sometimes I found myself wishing wistfully that my parents could be like that.

If Victoria Sutton inspired my confidence, it was Elsie Foster Evans who helped me discover and nurture my passion. She was the advisor for the student newspaper, *The Green Light*. Like most of the other teachers at Turner, Mrs. Evans had to leave the South for advanced study that was available in Georgia only to white educators. She got her master's degree at the University of Michigan and had at one time worked as a reporter on a local Black newspaper, the *Atlanta Daily World*. While most of the staff on the school paper were upperclassmen, I got involved by volunteering to proofread articles for Mrs. Evans; I couldn't resist rewriting during the course of doing that. After a while, I found rewriting someone else's stories totally unsatisfactory and started working on my own articles.

Meanwhile, I studied the comic-strip character Brenda Starr as I might have studied a journalism textbook, had there been one. I had been reading the funny papers, as we called them, all my life, and along with Dick Tracy and Dagwood, Brenda Starr was one of my favorite characters. I loved her sense of adventure, and the adventures she was always having as the star reporter on the New York *Daily Flash*. I especially loved the mystery and romance in her life, a lot of which was supplied by Basil St. John, a one-eyed connoisseur of black orchids. The fact that Brenda Starr was a redheaded, blue-eyed white woman who worked in an all-white newsroom did not even register with me until, one day during my senior year, I had a conversation with my counselor about what I wanted to do after I graduated. "I'm going to go to college to study journalism," I said confidently. "I want to be a reporter." By that time, I had been editor of the paper for two years—the first junior ever to be appointed to the position, thanks to Mrs. Evans.

"You better hang up those pipe dreams and go on over there to Spelman [the Black women's college] and become a teacher," she told me in all seriousness. And while she didn't say it in so many words, it was clear to me what she meant: Journalism is a white man's profession; even your precious Brenda Starr is an exception! I later told Mrs. Evans about the conversation; she looked at me the way she usually did when she was about to cut with a verbal knife so sharp it left no visible marks, and said ever so sweetly, "Now, we know what to do with advice like that, don't we?"

Wilma and Carolyn Long were sisters, the daughters of Turner's first football coach, who had been promoted to principal of an elementary school just before I got to Turner. Carolyn was the older, a year ahead of Wilma and me. The three of us were almost always together—at school, on football trips, or at home on the weekends. Their mother taught at the city's one Black vocational high school, and loved to engage us all in discussions about current events, or anything else that happened to come to her mind at the time. She was a small, wiry woman who, like Elsie Evans, was bright and quick-witted and had a sharp tongue.

Mr. Long's brother, Francis, whom they called "Daddy Francis"—eventually so did I—was one of the counselors at Turner. Coming from a family of dedicated educators gave the Long children their first leg up. That, coupled with the fact that they had gone to the Black Catholic elementary school, ensured that they were better prepared academically than many of the students at Turner. A few of the Blacks who could afford it sent their kids to the Catholic school because it had an excellent reputation and a record of providing good instruction and training. The nuns were known for not sparing the rod. Many a Catholic-school student has told me about punishments suffered at their hands, including having the students' mouths taped shut for talking and their knuckles rapped with rulers for other infractions.

In the classes I had with Wilma, she stood out, as did the other students who had also come from Catholic school. They read more, were better readers, and were more articulate, and their math skills were also superior. Wilma was always helping me in math—although I did a lot better with geometry, algebra, and trigonometry than with basic math, getting mostly As and Bs. Because there was never any question that we would go to college, Wilma, Carolyn, and I always took college track courses. Under protest, I took one required home-economics class, cooking, which I argued I didn't need because of all I had learned from my grandmother. I did learn how to make white sauce. The other option was sewing—Carolyn's passion—but that was entirely too domestic for me. At that point in my life, although we were all interested in boys and each at one time or another had a boyfriend or two, nothing in my game plan involved domestic activity. I had even decided that I didn't want to have any children. Two younger brothers had been enough. In any event, I thought all such courses—for me, at least—were a real waste of time. I wanted to be taking Latin and chemistry and physics. (Well, I didn't really want to take physics, but it was expected of me.) And, indeed, we took them all: me, Wilma, and, among others, the quarterback of the football team and my fellow honor-society member Hamilton Holmes. "Hamp" and I were friends, and although we were not *that* close, we were close enough to kid each other, as I often did him about the way he wrote his name. He used large, cursive letters, always writing all three parts—Hamilton Earl Holmes. But I called him Hamilton "Ear" Holmes, because the *l* always seemed to get lost in the swirls.

We also were less than kind when Hamp had to speak before an assembly program. Despite the fact that he was a straight-A student, there were times when he was almost painfully shy, and he had a stutter which, when he was excited, would become more pronounced. That made us even more merciless. I don't think Hamp liked our poking fun at him, and I believe he thought we were all pretty silly, which we were. But we managed to bridge our different approaches to work and fun long enough to work together in the honor society and on other school projects. And in the final analysis, we respected each other's mind. That was important to me, especially where boys were concerned, because of an experience I once had had with my father. He had come home on leave, and my mother had told him that I had a crush on an older boy (I almost always liked older boys). One day, he and I were riding along together in the car and he asked me about it.

"Why do you like this boy?" he said.

"Well, I don't know," I answered, slightly embarrassed to be having such a conversation with my father, and also having no idea why he had brought the subject up.

"I hear he's a lot older than you," he said.

"Well, yes," I said, growing increasingly uncomfortable.

Then my father did something he had never done in his life. He slammed his hand down hard on my leg and, almost shouting, said, "Well, what do you think a young girl like you could possibly have to offer an older man? What do you know about anything?"

The blow to my ego hurt a lot more than my smarting thigh. My father had always told me that I had a first-rate mind. Even when I brought home a report card with four As and a B, rather than congratulate me on the four As, he would demand to know why I had not gotten five As. And now I thought he was telling me that I was not smart.

"A man who respects you is going to be interested in more than your body," he said, bringing up a subject that had never arisen between me and any boy, or between me and my parents. "And you are going to have to have something else to offer. What do you think you have to offer some boy now?" I was too humiliated to answer. But his words found their way inside me and took up permanent residence.

I was never interested in Hamp as a potential boyfriend. Besides, he always liked quiet, soft-spoken girls, like the high-school love of his life, Tony Mapp, who as a junior was still sucking her thumb in class and simultaneously twisting a lock of her hair. In any event, fooling with Hamp was in the same category of fun we had at Turner doing the unexpected. For instance, there was an annual talent show called "The Green and White Follies." Students would sing, dance, play the piano, recite. We had been content just to attend the Follies or work backstage or somewhere on the periphery until one year, Wilma, Carolyn, and another former Catholic school friend, Carmen Alexander, decided that we were going to perform. Nobody expected us to be in the Follies. Our talents were more on the academic side (which I should have learned when I went out for basketball). I also used to help with the script, losing it one time and rewriting the whole thing from memory moments before rehearsals were to start. So everybody was eager to see what we were going to do as performers.

We practiced a lot and in secret, and thought we sounded pretty good. We were planning to sing a song that was very popular at the time, although it's hard to figure out why from the lyrics—"Lollipop, lollipop/Oo-lolli-lollipop," was how the chorus went. The first verse went: "Call my baby lollipop/Tell you why/He's sweeter than an apple pie." And so on.

Well, during the big rehearsal, when it was our turn, we tuned up. "Oooooo," we sang . . . "La la la la la," we sang, still tuning up. And then, when the time came, we began the song, snapping our fingers to the moderate-pace beat. "Lollipop, lollipop," we sang, but just as we started into the "Oo-lolli-lollipop" part, one of us got the giggles. Then we all did, and for a minute the audience wasn't sure whether this was part of the act or not. But soon, when we couldn't stop laughing or start singing again, the audience realized that we were out of control and the whole place started cracking up. We were too tickled to be embarrassed, and left the stage falling into each other's arms, laughing all the way.

From then on, we stuck to things we had a talent for, like the Student Council, the Journalism Club, the Future Teachers of America (don't ask me why, other than it was a good club and maybe we were hedging our bets). We were also elected to the Junior Honor Society, and later the Senior Honor Society, the only two clubs determined by grade-point average. I was later elected president of the Senior Honor Society.

By my sophomore year, I was a full-fledged member of the *Green Light* staff, which I loved, because in many classes I was, if not ahead, so well prepared from the good study habits I had developed in Alaska that I often had lots of time on my hands. And generally, because I was well prepared for class, I often found myself daydreaming or becoming fidgety and talkative, asking for trouble. So, to avoid any problems with my teachers, I usually asked to be excused, citing a "pressing assignment" I was working on for *The Green Light*. Often, when I was walking the halls, I got ideas for articles from what I saw.

Sometimes I would wander down to the band room and talk with the band teacher. By this time, I had concluded that I wasn't going to make it as a majorette. I dropped the baton too often, among other things. And I couldn't get to be drum major without first having been a majorette. Wilma, who was now my best friend, played clarinet in the band, but she had been taking lessons a long time. It was too far along for me to make the band from where I would have to start, which was at ground zero, so that was out. But I loved the football games and the half-time shows, and really wanted to be a part of all that, so gradually, I began to try my hand at writing the half-time shows, and eventually I took over the whole thing, including announcing the shows and narrating them over the public-address system at the stadium.

I shall never forget one night after I had written what I thought was a really good script. As I was announcing the band's entrance onto the field, instead of saying, "And now ladies and gentlemen, the crack green wave of Turner High School," I said, ". . . the cwack gween wave," and I, along with the entire stadium, laughed so hard I almost couldn't go on. But I did, although for the next week it seemed as if every student in the school greeted me with "How's the cwack gween wave?"

If Turner High seemed an idyllic island in a sea of segregation, that's because it was. We were protected and isolated from most of the worst manifestations of segregation, hardly ever encountering overt hostility from whites. When we shopped at the downtown stores, we always ate before we left, knowing but not focusing on the fact that we couldn't get served in the restaurants in the stores or outside. And while our families had charge cards at the major stores—Rich's and Davison's among them—we usually went to shop only when we needed to buy shoes or dresses for a special occasion, like Easter or the first day of school (when we always dressed to the nines). The salespeople were not impolite, but there clearly was a difference between the way most of them treated Blacks and the way they related to whites. Once, for example, my mother and I were shopping together. Although we were standing side by side at the counter looking at some scarves, we were not talking to each other when the saleswoman came up. Ignoring me into invisibility, she smiled at my mother and asked quite nicely what she could do for her. When my mother said, "You have to ask my daughter, she's the one we're shopping for," the woman looked from my fair-skinned mother to me, and her entire demeanor toward my mother changed. She became abrupt and less polite. "Oh," she said, with near-derision, "I didn't see *her*."

In those days, things would have had to get a lot worse for any of us to simply walk away. Everybody shopped at Rich's, a huge multistory store in the heart of the city. Black Atlantans took great pride in how they looked. And I had heard more than one adult describe how good Rich's was on their return policy. "Child, I bought that dress, wore it that night, took it right back the next day, and they gave me my money back." Somehow, by handing out such crumbs, Rich's was able to keep Blacks from looking at the whole cake.

From time to time, things happened that intruded on our protected reality. The murder of Emmett Till was one such instance. It happened in August 1955, and maybe because he was more or less our age, it gripped us in a way that perhaps even the lynching of an older Black man might not have. "It was the first time we'd known a young person to die," recalled Wilma, who, like me, was then entering eighth grade. For both of us, pictures of his limp, water-soaked body in the newspapers and in *Jet*, Black America's weekly news bible, were worse than any image we had ever seen outside of a horror movie. Till was shot to death and mutilated, his body dumped into Mississippi's Tallahatchie River. His crime: he was accused of whistling at a white woman in a grocery store.

Most of us had heard our parents, grandparents, or some Black adult talk with fear and/or bitterness about the Ku Klux Klan—they were still meeting near Atlanta at Stone Mountain, one of the eight wonders of the world—and about lynching. But in our conscious lifetime such activity had greatly declined. And certainly there had been nothing as dramatic as the Till murder.

Carolyn, who was already in the ninth grade, remembers that her social-studies teacher, Miss Eleanor Bradley, spent the first week in class discussing the incident, bringing in articles and pictures. Still, that was all happening in Mississippi, and Mississippi, for us, was a world and a day away. None of us could ever forget the haunting gray image of the dead and waterlogged young boy; we just put it on hold.

One of the major events of our high-school years was when Carolyn, Wilma, and I decided to convert to Catholicism. It started, almost casually, when we occasionally attended Mass. Although no one in their family was Catholic, Carolyn and Wilma's interest was a hold-over from Catholic school. But by now, interest in the Catholic Church itself was growing among Blacks, owing to a much more visible and aggressive Church presence in the Black community. On our side of town, the Catholic Church had built a new church and a hospital, which was offering a better level of care to Blacks. In fact, a beautiful new hospital was a godsend, because Blacks were excluded from all of Atlanta's fourteen general hospitals. Of the 4,000 available hospital beds, there were fewer than 400 for Blacks, and those were at the aging Grady Memorial, the city hospital, to which Blacks gave the nickname "Bucket of Blood." There were also about 250 beds in three small private hospitals owned by Blacks.

I was attracted to the ritual and mystery of Catholicism, all of which seem to connect me more directly and more personally to the Deity. There was nothing during the Mass that disconnected me from that communion, compared with what I regarded as growing dis-tractions in my own church. The services in my church seemed to be getting longer and longer, and the preacher seemed to be more and more concerned with raising money than saving souls.

Ironically, I think that a lot of my dissatisfaction started after I returned from Alaska and the months of exposure to my father's services—brief, deep, and reverent—which I'd loved. Whatever the reason, Bethel and the A.M.E. Church had lost its aura, and after a period of instruction, I converted during my junior year. This came as a shock to my father, who was now stationed at Fort Jackson, South Carolina, but who was as much of a stranger as ever. Con-verting to Catholicism was my first serious act of defiance, which my father, though hurt, chose not to challenge. He once said, later on, that he was sorry I hadn't stayed to help the church overcome its problems.

Poppa ("Shep") and Momma (Alberta) Hunter, always dressed up for their family, whether they were having a party or not. Here they are celebrating their fiftieth wedding anniversary

My grandfather, a preacher's preacher, who knew "how to tell a story"

My mother, my ideal woman— smart and strong, creative and feminine

Above: *My grandfather Rochell Brown, the "Old Roman"*

Right:
My mother and a brand-new me in my first place, Due West

My father, Chaplain Charles S. H. Hunter, Jr., making sure radio star Rochester spelled my name right during an autographing session after a performance for the troops at Camp Haan, California, 1942

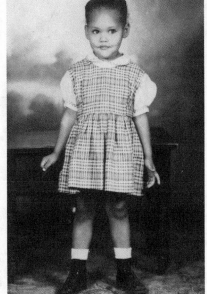

The three of us getting to know each other as a family for the first time, in Riverside, California, 1942

I was always big for my age, seen here at two years and eight months

My mother and father in a rare moment together at an Alpha Phi Alpha fraternity dance

My grandmother and I pausing at the Atlanta train station on our way back from "115th-between-Lenox-and-Fifth"

The Hunters after church in Fort Lauderdale, 1948. Back row, from left: Poppa, Johnnie (Louise's first husband), Uncle Ted, my daddy, Charles; front row, from left: Aunt Louise (my father's baby sister), Momma Hunter, my mother Althea, and me in front

One of the rare times Betty and I were separated. Here in our second-grade class picture at the Washington Street School, I'm second from the left in the back row; Betty is fourth from the right in the second row (1948)

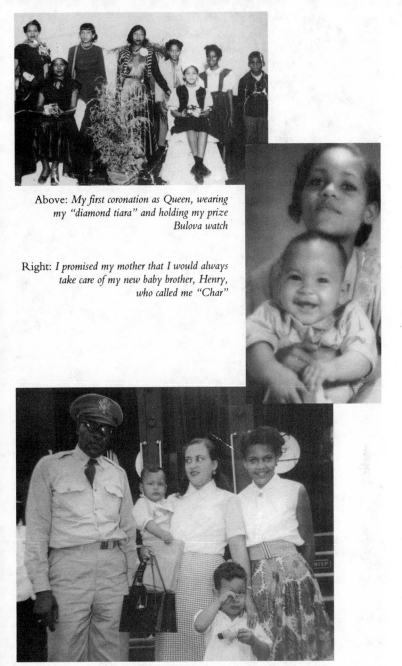

Above: *My first coronation as Queen, wearing my "diamond tiara" and holding my prize Bulova watch*

Right: *I promised my mother that I would always take care of my new baby brother, Henry, who called me "Char"*

With a smile masking a broken heart, I pose with my family—Daddy, Franklyn, Mother, and Henry—as we arrived in Alaska in 1954

Left: *For my second elementary-school graduation picture, I chose a dress that looked as unlike Alaska as possible, a light blue dotted-Swiss party dress ordered all the way from Neiman-Marcus in Texas*

Below: *Happy "un-birthday" to me—celebrated by my teachers, Rodney Delin and Fred Martin (back row, first and second from left), a member of my father's glee club, Byron Lewis (fourth from left), and friends from Ursa Major*

The National Honor Society was the club to be in, and in 1958 it included such "brains" as my good friends Wilma (fourth from left) and Carolyn (ninth from left), and me (far left)

*The campaign for student government in high school
enhanced our sense of civic responsibility,
but it was also a lot of fun*

*One of the most
exciting moments of
my high-school days
was when the Turner
High Wolverines won
the homecoming game
and co-captains James
Bolton and Hamilton
Holmes ("Hamp")
presented me with the
coveted pigskin*

Thanks to Dorothy Alexander, I had a dress truly fit for a queen

My crowning moment as Miss Turner, surrounded by my court

My mother didn't seem to mind much. She continued to go to Bethel, but I think even she was impressed with the fact that the priests and nuns from St. Paul of the Cross took such a personal interest in all of us. Father Banks was the senior and most active on our front, along with the younger Father Christian, attending our football and basketball games, sitting with us and cheering on the teams, teasing us, and generally having fun, the only white people, by the way, ever to show any interest in us at all.

On Sundays, Wilma, Carolyn, and I always went to Mass together. I had a learner's permit, and it was legal for me to drive as long as a licensed driver was with me, so when Carolyn couldn't get her parents' car, they'd come to my house and I'd drive—to Mass and anywhere else we decided to go. Usually, after Mass, we'd invade the rectory kitchen and either eat what was already prepared or fix something ourselves. Some of the nuns were almost as young as we were, as was Father Christian, whom I nicknamed Father Cookie, because his name was Kuchenbrod. They really seemed to enjoy having us around. There was one nun in particular whom I used to talk to a lot. She didn't look at all like what I had once imagined nuns would look like. She was young, petite, and pretty, with long, silky brown hair (which she kept covered at all times, although I got a glimpse of it once), and she had a sunny, sparkling personality. I used to talk to her about her being a nun and she encouraged me to think about becoming one myself. I didn't dismiss the thought out of hand.

At the end of junior year, I learned that I was losing my two soulmates. Carolyn was graduating, and Wilma announced one spring day that she was leaving, too, and would be joining Carolyn in the fall at Clark College, on early admission. I was devastated. I couldn't understand why Wilma would want to miss out on senior year. I never did understand her explanation; years later she told me that her parents had been hearing rumblings that Atlanta might finally attempt to implement the *Brown* decision in its public schools, and amid rumors that the public schools might be closed by the white power structure—a catchall term that described the broad cross section of white business and political leaders—the Longs, graduates of Clark themselves and very well connected, decided to send Wilma to Clark.

So Wilma was not there when our final year started, in the fall of 1959. But I got over it. This was my year, and nothing was going to get in the way of its being the best year I had ever had at Turner. I was starting my second year as editor of *The Green Light*, and was still an active member of all the clubs I had been in during my four years at Turner; by now I was also in the Senior Honor Society. Early in the semester, I was named (by Mrs. Evans) assistant yearbook editor. Gloria Moore was the editor. I was a little unhappy about that, but when I raised the question with Mrs. Evans, once again she gently rocked her head and sweetly pointed out that I was already editor in chief of *The Green Light* and that it might be too much for me to be yearbook editor as well. I didn't agree, but Gloria was one of the nicest people in the school and it was impossible to be angry with her, so I held my peace.

Instead, I decided that I was going after one more crown. Becoming queen at Turner was not a matter of raising money, as it had been in my previous "coronations." The Turner Homecoming Queen had to be elected in a schoolwide popularity contest. I was well known throughout the school, but so were a lot of other people, and there was no telling what variables would come into play during such a campaign. It was at times like this that I really missed Wilma, one of the few friends I had never had a fight with and whom I could rely on without question. As she used to say throughout high school, especially after some defeat or embarrassment or other, "You my hos' if you don't never win no race."

One of the major activities during the campaign was a schoolwide assembly program at which contestants would be asked to demonstrate their talents, intellect, and whatever else they had going for them in the race to be queen. Mrs. Fredericka Hurley, one of the mathematics teachers, was selected to prepare a question for each of the contestants. They ranged from "Why do you want to be Miss Turner?" to "What was the significance of 'One World'?," the question I got.

I couldn't believe my ears. What was she getting at? If I had ever heard of Wendell Willkie's "One World" attacking isolationism, it surely wasn't ringing a bell at the moment. And yet I knew that if I failed to come up with something I would be a dead would-be queen in the water. So I gambled that nobody else in the student body of some 1,500 would know, either, and said, "Well, having been born into this world and no other, I can only speak of this one." Before I could even finish the sentence, the gym was in an uproar. I was right. Nobody knew what the hell Mrs. Hurley was talking about, and my schoolmates were laughing because they assumed that I had scored one on the teacher. That was round one—a round that I won.

It was still an intense campaign, with old scores like the red pencil marks on the English papers and other arrogances committed by me or Wilma and me and/or others now being settled. Whispering in the locker room and rumors in the halls were rampant, until the final day of the campaign, the day when the entire school from grades 8 through 12 were going to cast their ballots for the 1959 Homecoming Queen.

As homeroom got underway, tension and anxiety filled the air as if it were fourth down and goal to go. I had a plan, but I had to sit on it until the very last minute. Timing was everything. As was the case every morning, the principal was droning on and on over the intercom system, repeating announcements and other items of importance (to him alone, usually). Finally, with only about three minutes to go in the homeroom period, I raised my hand and asked to be excused. Mrs. Sutton looked at me quizzically, because she, of all people, knew what was at stake and seemed concerned about my demeanor. But she wasted no time in giving me an affirmative nod. I bolted from the classroom, tore down the long hall to the stairs, bounded down one flight, and dashed toward the communications room. Principal Daniel F. Davis was just signing off, with seconds to go. I was not an unfamiliar sight in the communications room, because I was always making some announcement or other about senior activities, yearbook pictures, class ring, you name it. So he barely nodded to me as I entered, and assuming I was there to make still another senior-class announcement, he handed me the microphone.

"My dear fellow students of the greatest high school on earth," I began in my most mellifluous voice, quickly adding, "and especially our newest, proud young eighth-graders." (I did that because I knew that the eighth-graders outnumbered the seniors two to one, or thereabouts.) "In case any of you are having last-minute doubts about who should be your queen as you get ready to cast your vote this morning," I continued, "I am here now to erase any and all doubts. This is Charlayne—that's spelled C H A R L A Y N E—Charlayne Hunter is going to be your queen, with your help, and she will be a queen that will make you proud. So cast your vote for me, Charlayne, and let us be proud together."

I immediately ran back up the stairs to my homeroom to cast a ballot for myself.

Throughout the day, I faced a range of reactions to my ploy, all the way from those who congratulated me on its smooth execution to contestants who expressed their consternation in a variety of ways. But no one challenged me, because anyone else who had thought of it would have been able to do the same thing. That was the saving element for me.

At the end of the day, Mr. Davis once again took to the public-address system, starting with a few announcements. And then, with some verbal fanfare, he announced that Turner High School had a new queen. Silence. I was seated in the front row near the door in Mrs. Evans's English class. She had been undecided about the contest, because Gloria was also running. Then Mr. Davis broke the silence. "Miss Turner, for the year 1958–59, is Miss Charlayne Hunter!"

As my partisans broke out in cheering, and Mrs. Evans looked toward me, head rocking, and sweetly but softly mouthed, "Congratulations," I bolted from the room and headed up the hall to the girls' bathroom. Once inside, I bounded into a stall and locked the door. I didn't have to go to the bathroom. I just wanted to savor the moment the way I liked best of all: alone.

For me, obviously, it was the best Homecoming ever. Everybody told me that I had successfully met the annual challenge of coming up with an outfit that outdid the previous queen's, a white-leather suit that I designed and had made by a 200-pound lady who could make anything you showed her a picture of, no matter how complicated or stylish. While the leather gave her a run for her money, she not only made the suit (within hours of the football game at which I was to be presented), but also made a green leather hat to match. With that I wore green leather gloves and green spike heels that I bought at Rich's and had dyed. It was a stunning ensemble, and I tried to maintain a royal posture, despite the fact that I was still pretending to wear a size 9 and a half, triple A, and my feet were killing me.

The Turner Wolves won the game that day and co-captains James Bolton and Hamilton Holmes presented me with the game ball and sweaty wet kisses, which I thought were the sweetest on earth.

The coronation followed. Once again, I had been challenged to come up with a dress that surpassed the previous queen's. For that, my mother and I called on Dorothy Alexander, the wife of T. M. Alexander, one of Atlanta's most successful Black businessmen. She didn't have to work, but she enjoyed designing and making clothes for a select few. When we went to see her the first time, I was awed by her English Tudor–style house—the closest thing to a mansion I had ever set foot in. It sat back on a hill on Hunter Street, a long artery that extended throughout the Black southwest side. Before this stretch of elegant Black homes, there was Washington High School, the oldest Black high school in the city, and a second, newer, and thriving Black business district.

Dorothy Alexander had class, and it was apparent throughout her house, with its plush carpets, French Provincial furniture, and fancy crystal. I was wide-eyed as she led me into her sewing room to discuss the dress. She created the design, chose the fabric, and, after several fittings, presented me with the single most beautiful dress I had ever seen anywhere in my life. It was a floor-length white satin gown, with an off-the-shoulder bodice covered with rhinestones, pearls, and lace; a skirt with a frame that caused it to stand out from my body and sway gracefully as I walked; followed in the back by a long garland of hand-made white silk flowers and green leaves which dipped into a soft, graceful split that opened halfway up the dress.

As I walked down the red-carpeted gymnasium floor, people gasped at the sight. Among the queen's honor guard were Hamilton Holmes and my current but on-the-way-out boyfriend and classmate, George Smith.

If ever there was a night and an occasion and a moment to remember forever, this was it. There seemed to be no one who didn't
honor the queen, and I, in turn, celebrated the best reception among
my peers that I had ever known.

We started to focus on college sometime in the fall. Daddy Francis
conducted weekly Saturday sessions, prepping us for the exam. I later
learned that white students prepped in this way for at least two years,
but we were grateful to Mr. Long for the time and effort he expended
on us.

Earlier in the year, I had scored the highest in our school on the
Future Homemakers of Tomorrow test, and had placed in the state-
wide competition, largely, I think, on the basis of my essay. But I
hated multiple-choice tests, and all the samples we worked on in our
six-week study course were that kind. I did not look forward to the
test with great enthusiasm. When the time finally came when I was
to take the test, it was the kind of December day that matched my
spirits—cold and gray. It didn't help that the test was being given in
Decatur, one of Atlanta's whitest suburbs, at all-white Emory University, and that this would be the first time in my life I had ever set
foot on a white college campus in Georgia. I took it as an omen when
I attempted to parallel-park behind the building where the test was
being given that I backed the car into a garbage dump and bent a
fender.

The test was everything I dreaded, and worse. Nothing looked
familiar and nothing seemed to work when I tried to sort out the
math problems. I left Emory University in a sorry state.

Back at Turner, my counselors were pressing me to make some
college choices. I knew practically nothing about colleges outside the
Atlanta University complex, and as much as I loved the times I had
spent there with Wilma and Carolyn and Eleanor Walker, another
close, older friend from my neighborhood whose sister was a student
at Spelman, I wanted desperately to go to a university that had a
journalism school or, at the very least, a strong department of jour-

nalism. My counselors weren't much help, but a former student at Turner, Dorothea Brown, had gone to Wayne State University in Detroit, Michigan, and on a visit back to Turner, in a casual conversation about how much she enjoyed the place, she had told me that it also had a strong Journalism Department. I was drawn to this possibility, in part because of Mrs. Evans and her studies at the University of Michigan. I didn't have a clue what a world of difference there was between a Wayne State and a U. of M., so I proceeded to apply to Wayne, as well as to a number of small Midwestern colleges that had by now received my SAT scores, knew that I was Black (although how, I'm not quite sure), and were offering me admission, along with scholarship aid in some cases.

I studied the pictures on all the brochures, trying to imagine myself on some of these campuses. But none of them seemed anywhere near as hospitable or as beautiful as the colleges in the Atlanta University complex, with their abundant pink-and-white dogwood trees, their classic magnolias, and, of course, their beautiful students, who came in all the colors of the earth. For the experience (and for safety), I applied to several schools, including, at Mrs. Evans's suggestion, Northwestern, just outside Chicago, which had Medill, one of the most renowned schools of journalism in the country. I had managed to actually get a little bit excited about Medill and build a healthy dose of anticipation, allowing myself to fantasize about the possibility during weekends or school breaks of traveling to Chicago and visiting my mother's aunt and uncle—the one who met us at the plane on the way to Alaska—as I waited for responses to come in.

Fortunately, I had an early response from Medill. My SAT scores were not high enough for me to be considered for admission. So sorry. Oh well, I thought, who wanted to go to Evanston, Illinois, anyway?

Meanwhile, I was accepted at several of the schools that I had never heard of but that were offering me scholarships, and also at Wayne. None of the others had journalism schools or, as far as I could determine, any journalism programs. Also, even if I didn't get scholarship money from Wayne, I would still be eligible for aid from the state of Georgia, by virtue of the fact that I wanted to major in a field of study that was offered only in the white schools. In order to discourage any possibility that a Black person would even think of applying to one of those white schools, the state provided funds for Blacks to study in those fields, but at some other institution in some other state where they didn't care if Blacks went to school with whites. Many a Black in Georgia was "treated" to what probably amounted to an even better education than they would have gotten in the white state school by virtue of this segregationist policy and practice.

So, factoring in the prospect of state aid for me to study journalism anywhere but in the Georgia state system, I decided that I would look for my place at Wayne State University in Detroit, Michigan.

By 1959, the quiet rumblings of a nascent civil-rights movement were beginning to reverberate around the South, and in our "Dogwood City" as well. Several of Atlanta's young progressive Black professionals had been meeting among themselves, trying to figure out how and where to begin Atlanta's movement toward equality. They had organized themselves into a group called the Atlanta Committee for Cooperative Action, which became known by its acronym, ACCA. Among them were college professors and deans, insurance and real-estate executives, and doctors. Most of them worked for themselves or in Black institutions, but in those days, the tentacles of the white power structure were so long that almost nobody's livelihood was immune from its reach.

Some of these leaders had been involved in an earlier effort to desegregate one of the Atlanta-based colleges of the state university system—the Georgia State College of Business Administration. Jesse Hill, an ACCA member, an actuary at the Atlanta Life Insurance Company, and a member of the Education Committee of the National Association for the Advancement of Colored People, once explained to Calvin Trillin, a *Time* magazine reporter whom I eventually came to know quite well, that Georgia State had the advantage of being a city college, which eliminated the problem of travel and housing. In addition, the ACCA activists carried in their minds fresh images of the white viciousness that had tormented the nine young students who had been the first Blacks at Little Rock's Central High School in 1957. As a result, Hill told Trillin:

> In those days, people hesitated to send a seventeen-year-old kid into that hostility, and we were working mainly to get older people to try for the night school. Frankly, we did some real campaigning. We tried to get some of the people in our own office, for instance. We got three girls to apply, and we won our court case, although the judge didn't order the plaintiffs admitted. By that time, the state had investigated the girls who were applying and found some illegitimate births and that kind of thing with two, and they would have probably been turned down on so-called moral grounds. Then, the state passed a law that said nobody over twenty-one could start as an undergraduate in a Georgia college, which eliminated the third girl and ended any chance of having older people apply for Georgia State.*

What would happen if they went this way again, they wondered, convinced that if they could crack the lily-white system of higher education, then everything else would surely follow. But if they took this approach again, they could not run the risk of having someone the state could effectively challenge. They would have to find two squeaky-clean students who couldn't be challenged on moral, intellectual, or educational grounds, and the best place for that was, after all, among the seventeen-year-olds now in high school. Although not officially a part of this group, sitting in on it during one such discussion was Alfred ("Tup") Holmes, a jovial jack of many trades, who immediately volunteered his son, easily the top male senior in the entire city.

When Mr. Holmes raised the subject with Hamp at home, Hamp remembers saying that he had never given the idea any thought. After all, Morehouse was a small private, reasonably well-endowed school that smart young Black men aspired to, a school steeped in a rich

* Calvin Trillin, *An Education in Georgia* (New York: Viking Press, 1963), p. 10.

history and tradition, whose alumni assumed their place among the talented tenth all over the country with so much confidence and pride that they had inspired the saying "You can always tell a Morehouse man, but you can't tell him much." Thus, when Mr. Holmes pressed Hamp, without much enthusiasm Hamp casually responded, "Why not?"

When a small committee from ACCA came around to Turner, I listened to what they had to say, found the idea interesting, but thought the prospects remote. In the end, I had the same attitude as Hamp: "Why not?" I knew less about Georgia State than I did about Wayne, but I was willing to go and visit. So, soon after our first meeting, members of the same committee—Jesse Hill and M. Carl Holman—took us to the campus of Georgia State, in downtown Atlanta.

For me, this was a kind of lark. I had absolutely nothing to lose, and with the reputation that white schools had for having the best of everything, I really was curious to see what they had to offer in journalism training and equipment.

Hamp had also known since early high school, and maybe before, that he wanted to follow in his grandfather's footsteps and become a doctor. So his interest was in pre-med. I could always easily imagine Hamp a doctor. He had just the right stuff—from his gray matter to his demeanor. He really wanted to go to Morehouse, but he knew that the state's budget for lab and other equipment far exceeded Morehouse's, and he was excited by the prospect of getting a firsthand look at what the state had been buying all those years with our parents' tax money.

Once inside the registrar's office at Georgia State, I felt relieved. The people waiting on us were as pleasant as if this kind of thing happened all the time. It was as if they had been prepped. We asked for a catalogue of courses. No problem. Then we smiled and walked back to a kind of vestibule to look it over. I was surprised to see that it was so thin, but once I opened it, I could see why. It was light on courses. Hamp must have arrived at the same conclusion, because I could see him frowning. We both started to leave, the adults following. Out front, just beyond the doors, we didn't wait for any questions.

"They don't have anything to offer that I'm interested in," I said matter-of-factly.

"Me, either," Hamp chimed in.

At this point, the adults, for once, didn't seem to know what to do or say next. But Hamp broke the silence. "I think I would like to try over there," he said, his forefinger jabbing the air as he pointed north. I knew immediately what he meant, and so did the adults. "The university," Hamp began again. "That's where I want to go."

Before anyone else could register the concern and doubt they could barely mask, I stepped up and chimed in. "Me too," I said, with such enthusiastic finality that all anyone could say, finally, as they caught their breath, was, "Well, if that's what you want, we'll see what we can do about getting the applications."

I never knew until years later just how deeply worried the adults were over the prospect of us going to the University of Georgia. It was a wholly different proposition from Georgia State, which was not without its challenges from potentially violent racists but which was, after all, right there in Atlanta, where the men of ACCA felt they could offer us protection. Athens was seventy-five miles away, on the other side of some of the most backward, racist little towns in Georgia, and our people had few connections with anybody anywhere along the route or at its destination. But no one, throughout the long-drawn-out process, ever spoke of fear. There were published reports that a fearless Black janitor got the application blanks and catalogues for us, but actually, we sent for them by mail.

M. Carl Holman, a tall, lanky, bespectacled English professor, was teaching at Clark College. Although he was married, with three young children, he did not appear to be much older than most of his students. But we all, at least for the time being, called him Mr. Holman, the form we used for every adult we knew.

Mr. Holman was a gifted teacher who had a master's degree in fine arts from Yale and had been awarded one of the Yale Younger Poets prizes—a singular distinction for any student and most especially for one of the very few Blacks in the program. His main job for ACCA was ensuring that our applications got filled out properly, making sure that every *i* was dotted and every *t* crossed. The local

NAACP lawyer, Donald Hollowell, worked on them, too, seeing that everything was certified and sent by registered mail.

My mother, who had been managing a major Black real-estate company ever since we came back from Alaska, was totally behind the effort. If she had any concerns, she never expressed them to me. At this stage of the game, I don't think we told my father, whose most recent visit home had been solely for the purpose of presenting me at the Debutante Ball earlier in the year. Their marriage was over, and all that was missing was the legal document to that effect.

Meanwhile, by now we had our class rings, the yearbook was out, the class rankings had been announced—out of a class of 156 Hamp was number one and therefore valedictorian, and I had missed being salutatorian by one grade. Still, as number three, I had a major role in the graduation and, among other things, was awarded the English prize—a $25 check from Rich's.

Hamp and I didn't have too much time to savor graduation, because we were busy getting our University of Georgia applications ready. No one even discussed how late they were, although technically we still had time. Through Jesse Hill, the local NAACP put up the money for this phase of the process, because the whole procedure had to be carefully documented in preparation for the court test that was sure to come down the line. Within a few days, we had everything ready except for our principal's signature on the application. But by this time he was off for the summer and no one was quite sure where he was and if, in fact, he would want to be found for a move that was sure to link his name with controversy of a sort neither he nor any other Black educator in the state had ever been exposed to. He had been a fine principal, but we just didn't know where he stood on this issue.

Eventually we found him, and all that was left was to go down to the Fulton County Courthouse and be certified as residents of the state. We took our pastors along as references, and while we got the runaround, eventually we completed the process, a bit breathless but with a feeling of exhilaration. For all we knew at that point, this might be our only triumph. Meanwhile, following our submission,

ACCA members took turns patrolling in front of my house, because there were no adult men there and they were concerned about the possibility of bombing. My mother thought that this was unnecessary, that we could take care of ourselves.

The story of our plans to apply made the Atlanta papers on July 11, 1959. 2 NEGROES TRY DOORS AT ATHENS was the headline on Raleigh Bryans's front-page story in the *Atlanta Constitution*. And in it the registrar signaled the approach the university would take for the next year and a half.

Bryans wrote: "Registrar Walter N. Danner said the university is full up and already is turning down would-be freshmen. He said that because dormitories are full the only freshmen he can admit are those who are bona fide Athens residents."

Meanwhile, Hamp and I went ahead with our plans. In the fall, he would go to Morehouse and I would go to Wayne. We didn't speak for the rest of the summer or the fall before I left, but in my yearbook he had written: "Dear Charlayne. I will always remember you as one of the most outstanding persons I have known or will know. May you have only the best in the future. A friend always, Hamp."

chapter 12

Wayne State

"5050 Cass Avenue," I said to the cabdriver after I arrived in Detroit. It was supposed to be the dormitory, which I had tried to imagine during the long ride from Atlanta to Detroit. Uppermost in my mind were the images of the campuses in the Atlanta University complex, with their stately old neoclassical buildings and their long brick walkways lined with dogwood and magnolia trees. When the cabdriver stopped and announced that we had arrived at 5050 Cass, I was not ready for what I saw before me—a massive twelve-story building, larger than anything I had ever seen in Atlanta, let alone on a college campus, but not nearly as large as the disappointment welling up in me at the sight. This couldn't be the campus, I thought to myself. But I was soon to discover that this dormitory housed not only both men and women students (a unique concept in 1959) but also the main college cafeteria, faculty offices, and many of the other major offices of Wayne State University. I couldn't believe it. I was instantly engaged in beating back the wave of homesickness that was about to engulf me. It was a preoccupation that absorbed me throughout my tour of the place: the three floors for students—one for undergraduate men, one for undergraduate women, and one that was really coed, for the graduate students. On the tenth floor, I was directed to a compact two-room suite in the corner at the far end of the hall. My roommates had already arrived: two white girls from small towns in Michigan, Alpina and Dowagiac. Since this was "up North," I had thought about having two white roommates, but not a lot. They seemed curious but not hostile. It looked like a good beginning.

The freshmen were required to come in early for orientation, which would take place away from the campus, somewhere outside Detroit, on an outing called Frosh Weekend. That's where I met Kathi Fearn, a tall, slim, somewhat reserved Black girl from Washington, D.C., and the only other Black freshman there. In many ways, it was Ursa Major all over again. At Frosh Weekend, square dances and square mixers and square conversation. I remember thinking that I was glad I had grown up deprived, because there was absolutely nothing I liked about camping out.

At first glance, Wayne resembled a slightly larger version of Georgia State—a bare-bones kind of place that offered a no-frills education. Many, if not most, of the students had already been out in the workaday world or had served in the military. They did not come from college families or families that could afford to send them to college, so many of them were still working. As a result, they had a very different attitude and approach toward school. They were dead serious about making it and making every minute count, because in all probability they were paying for it themselves. In addition, most of the students who attended Wayne lived in Detroit. This was their city college, so there was no real need to provide housing. The few students who signed up to live in the few rooms that were available tended to be the younger, recent high-school graduates, who wanted to have a college experience but could afford only the price of a ticket in their own back yard.

Even though the undergraduate women were all on the same floor, it was some time before we got past our preoccupation with getting settled into college and began socializing with one another. The configuration of the floor added to the delay. It was basically a kind of horseshoe, where you emerged from the elevator into a corridor that branched off to the left and to the right. The corridors ran for several yards in opposite directions before breaking at a sharp right angle and extending another several yards. For the non-social or the antisocial, it was possible to live on one side of the dorm and almost never come in contact with anyone from the other side, except possibly during the elevator ride to the lobby. I had seen some other Black girls in the elevator, but the only one I ever saw on my side of the horseshoe was Kathi Fearn. She lived alone, although she was supposed to have a roommate, another Black girl who had shown up at the door, taken one look at the room, and announced that she was going back to Cleveland. She had never been heard from since.

As it turned out, I was the only Black person in an integrated situation. Furthermore, once I started to get to know some of the other Black girls and be invited to their rooms, it dawned on us that the "dorm" was really quite segregated. Except for Kathi and me, the right side of the corridor was all white, and without exception, the left side was all Black. When we tried to figure out how the authorities could have planned this layout so effectively, the Detroit girls realized that it was their high schools that gave them away. Even though Detroit was "up North," most of them had come from predominantly, if not entirely, Black high schools, in predominantly Black neighborhoods. In Kathi's case, she had gone to Eastern High School, in Washington, D.C., and although she was on the white side, as it were, had it not been for the sister who had gone back to Cleveland, she would have been segregated as well. The only exception was me, and we figured out that the authorities thought anybody coming from so far away had to be white and never noticed that I, too, had come from a Black school, albeit one that was segregated by law.

We were more amused than angry over the discovery, in part because the Black side of the floor was always jumping. We used to get together and fix each other's hair, and listen to music, talk about guys, make plans for dinner (the cafeteria was open only during the day to accommodate the day students; there were no meals for the live-ins; we were on our own at night), and sometimes study, although most of that was done in the library or elsewhere.

Except for my roommates and me, there was hardly any communication between the Blacks and the whites on the floor. We lived in two separate worlds.

It was at Wayne, in the "separate but equal" dorm, that I first learned that Jews were considered different from white people. Unlike in the South, where you were Black or you were white, both Black and white Northerners made those distinctions, and so did Jews. One of the few Jewish girls on the floor was a girl named Rochelle Katz, who was almost as dark as I was and whose hair was thicker and kinkier. She always used to ask us how we "fixed" our hair and did we think it would work on hers, until one day we heated up a straightening comb and waited until she had come out of the shower. "Rochelle," we called, "we've got something for you," and after she had wrapped a towel around herself we led her off to one of our rooms, sat her down, and fried her hair until it was straight. She loved it.

There were also some cultural differences between me and my Northern sisters. They found it amusing that I said "Yes, ma'am" and "No, ma'am," to all adults, and they found it downright fall-on-the-floor hilarious when, waiting for the elevator, I would ask, "Did anyone mash the button?" I also remember coming in from the scene of an accident nearby and asking if anybody had seen the wreck outside. All of a sudden, Doris Jeffries, one of the Black students from Detroit, burst out laughing. It was fully five minutes before she could stop long enough to tell me what she was laughing at.

If I had loved the freedom of changing classes in high school, I was ecstatic about the schedule of college classes. I continued the pattern of perfect attendance that I had established as far back as elementary school. I hated to miss a class—even one I didn't particularly like.

Much to my dismay, Wayne wouldn't allow any student to major until junior year, and no journalism classes were offered to freshmen. Instead, the university had the good sense to require a core curriculum of basic liberal-arts courses. There was also a foreign language requirement. Everybody I knew from Turner who had taken a foreign language other than Latin in high school had taken French. I wanted to be different, so I decided to take German instead. I had no real problems with any of my courses freshman year, except German. In class, I did extremely well. I studied and had a good German accent, and my hand was one of the few that were always up as I volunteered to answer a question, translate a passage from German to English, or vice versa. But I absolutely froze on tests.

One day, Herr Professor asked to see me in his office. "Fräulein Hunter," he began, "you unnerstond ze Churman language ferry well. Your classroom participation is excellent. But vhat is heppening to you on ze tests? Iz not so goot, correct?"

I couldn't explain what was "heppening" to me on the test, but I knew as well as he that the tests were not an accurate reflection of the German I knew. I studied and I *spracht*, and did all the things I was supposed to do; yet I froze on the test.

Herr Doktor Poster then suggested that maybe for a while I should take ze tests in his office. Just to see if it made a difference. I was stunned. Here I had expected absolutely no slack from this rigidly correct Prussian. He was going out of his way to help me. Of all the white professors, I had expected the least sympathy from him, and yet here he was making an offer that I never heard before. I accepted it, but alas, in the end, I was just not a good test-taker. I could converse *auf Deutsch* with Herr Doktor Poster about what I had done wrong and how I needed to correct it (umlaut here, accent there, verb at the end), but for some reason I couldn't function once the clock was on in a test situation. I nevertheless managed to pass first-year German with a C average and move on to the next level. German, with its guttural and umlaut sounds, was about as alien to the slow, drawling, sweet sound of the South as anything I had ever known. And while I can't say that I really liked it, what was appealing to me was that nobody would expect me, of all people, to speak German or know anything about Mozart or Rainer Maria Rilke or Friedrich von Schiller. And then there was my father, who had introduced me to Hegel. One day, I might be able to tell him more about Hegelian dialectic than he himself knew.

For all its lack of campus and charm, in time Wayne offered still another world for me. Not just the world of college, but the world of the urban North and of bohemian intellectualism. I fell in love with ideas and art, discourse and debate. And in time I even started to pay less attention to the "fine" clothes I had brought from the best stores in Atlanta and adopted a style that was more in keeping with the cost-consciousness displayed by most of the students on campus.

In fact, starting in the second semester of my freshman year, since most of the students I knew worked, I, too, got a job. It was a terrific position in the McGregor Memorial Community Conference Center, the newest and most modern structure on campus. Designed by the up-and-coming Japanese architect Minoru Yamasaki, it was a stunning ultra-modern structure, standing in stark contrast to the urban pedestrian style that surrounded it. It had many wonderful features —especially its lovely, serene rock garden. I worked behind a counter, near the front of the gallery, selling pens and pencils and other small items. Sometimes I worked the coat check. It was while I was doing this job that I learned this song:

> Don't cry, lady,
> I'll buy your goddamn violets.
> Don't cry, lady,
> I'll buy your pencils, too.
> Don't cry, lady,
> Take off those old dark glasses.
> Hello, Mother, I knew it was you.

Surrounded by art and art students, I loved McGregor's creative energy, and its atmosphere, which was somehow more open than any other place on campus. With the money I made, I bought all my clothes and other necessities for the remainder of the school year.

My roommate Lila loved my clothes and often asked to borrow items to wear. As an only girl, I never had to share, and this was a new experience for me. I wasn't sure I liked it, but I acquiesced in the face of Lila's earnest admiration. Leather was still in vogue, and I had a beige leather coat that I liked a lot, especially because, unlike most of the leather coats I had seen, this one had two huge pockets in the front. I usually wore it only to parties or to Mass, or when I wanted to feel dressed up. One evening, as I was preparing to go out with a group of friends, I reached into my closet for my leather coat and it was gone. I looked everywhere in the room for it. I couldn't imagine what had happened to it. Later, when my other roommate came in, she told me that Lila had taken it home for the weekend. I was livid. When she returned, we had a discussion about it, and that ended the clothes borrowing. The exchange, however, was not really rancorous.

Lila was like an up-North, small-town Southern girl, obliging her parents by attending college but lacking any real interest in it. She had no idea what she was going to major in, and I think she really wanted to be a nurse. She was especially naïve when it came to men. I sometimes had to run interference for her after she had blithely walked into some situation that was on the verge of being out of control. I remember once when she had started seeing a guy she had met at a dance. She knew nothing about him, and even on their first date he drank too much. She really didn't want to continue seeing him, but she didn't know how to tell him. Often, when he was in his cups, he would call. She would get so worked up over just going to the phone that we would all be miserable. So one day, when he called, I picked up the phone and, as she shook her head and gestured that she didn't want to talk to him, I said, "She's not here, and don't call her anymore!" Lila was so grateful, she hugged me.

By mid-year, I, too, was getting a lot of calls from male students, and so were some of the other girls who lived in the dorm. I think it was because we lived on campus and were easy to reach. But it really used to bug the switchboard operator. One night, she complained over the intercom. "I don't know what you're going to do," she said. "You've got two people here in the lobby." It was really none of her business. The guys were well behaved and polite, but they were Black, and we decided that what was really bothering her was just having to deal with Black guys. So my friend Kathi Fearn and I decided to teach her a lesson. We invited several guys to come to the dorm and ask for us, and we left to go to dinner before they arrived. We laughed throughout dinner thinking about her probable reaction to all those Blacks.

That was the dinner, however, where there was also a big laugh on me. We had gone to a soul-food restaurant that everybody had been talking about. There was one nice Black restaurant in Atlanta, Pascal Brothers, but going out to eat was not something Black folks in the South did. So I was still adjusting to the fact that eating out was routine; it still felt pretty special to me. My mouth was watering as the waiter recited the menu, and I was the first to order.

"I'll have a pork chop," I said, and with a display of growing worldly sophistication, I added, "Rare, please."

The waiter, a tall Black man with the air of an efficient Pullman porter (which he may have been at one time), shot me a look. "Did you say rare?" he asked.

Dismissing his tone as probably being due to the infrequency of requests for rare meat in a place whose pride lay in its capacity to cook a piece of meat to its most extreme state of doneness and still maintain the taste, I repeated my order, this time with emphasis.

"Yes," I said, somewhat arrogantly. "Rare!" "Okay," he said, somewhat indulgently. "One rare pork chop coming up."

Actually, since everybody was following my lead and feigning sophistication, it was a long time before I got the joke on myself. Fortunately, before the next time and before I contracted trichinosis, I learned better.

Because of my work at McGregor, I started getting interested in art. Whenever I had the time, I wandered over to the Detroit Institute of Art, which was within easy walking distance. If there were museums in Atlanta, they were for white people and we wouldn't have been allowed inside. So this was an awakening for me, and it was like the smell of morning coffee. I would spend hours there, usually by myself, getting acquainted with Rodin, whose *Thinker* sat, elbow positioned on knee, at the entrance, the Diego Rivera murals, ancient Egyptian artifacts, the armor of the Middle Ages. But in time the artist who interested me most was the Flemish painter Hieronymus Bosch. I was initially drawn to the unusual figures in his work—strange, monstrous creatures, weird and diabolical human figures—and I spent hours in front of the huge canvases, drifting into a world that stimulated my imagination and appreciation of the fantasy and wonder that had lived someplace inside me since the days of my Covington childhood, when I would crawl inside a comic book and disappear into the world of Wonder Woman or Nyoka, Jungle Girl. I remember once renaming myself and sharing it only with Horace and Tommy, my constant doll companions. They were to call me

Charlayne Alberta Ruth Nyoka, Queen of the Jungle and All Places. I told them that they could call me Nyoka for short. Bosch took me back to the fantasies I had known, but also propelled me forward, opening regions in my mind that I would revisit at a critical time, a few months down the road, in another place, on a cold day.

As on the dorm floor upstairs, there was a racial division on campus. It could best be observed in the dining hall during lunch. That's when you would see mostly all-white tables and mostly all-Black tables. And while the all-Black tables were clustered together and collegial, there were also divisions among them—primarily along Greek lines. The Black fraternity groupings—Alpha Phi Alpha, Omega Psi Phi, and Kappa Alpha Psi—ate at separate tables, as did the Black sororities: Delta Sigma Theta, Alpha Kappa Alpha, Sigma Gamma Rho.

Almost all the Black socializing was done around Greek activities. Freshmen could not join Greek organizations, but because Greek life was central to Black campus life, most freshmen attended "Rush Week" events where the Greek groups introduced themselves and their programs. Throughout my freshman year, I observed the women in all the sororities, and there was no question in my mind that I would eventually pledge one. The issue for me was which one. I was already familiar with Greeks from the Atlanta college community. Frats and sororities were a stable part of life on all Southern college campuses. They conferred a sense of belonging, but also established a social pecking order, although the prestige of any single group could vary from one campus to another. At Clark, where Carolyn was now a sophomore, she had pledged Delta. But I was keeping an open mind. At Wayne, the Black Greek organizations played an even more important role. On a campus with only 2,500 Blacks out of a student body of 25,000, they were a virtual necessity. It was within those organizations that Black students found respect and reinforced identity.

And it was within these groups that some small note was taken of an event on February 1, 1960. Four Black students from North Carolina A&T College sat down at a lunch counter in Greensboro, North

Carolina, and refused to move until they were served. The event made headlines all over America. The sit-in movement had begun. By the time I got home on spring break, it had reached Atlanta. And a dramatic change, which was more like a final coming of age than a transformation, had taken place in my best friends. Carolyn and Wylma (now with a γ) had stepped up to fulfill the historic mission of the talented tenth, joining with some 4,000 other students in the Atlanta University Center—the largest and most impressive group of Negro students in the country. In the simplest terms, they were the Student Movement. But in time they acquired the more impressive title of the Committee on Appeal for Human Rights. As Carolyn explained at the time, "Our plan is to end segregation once and for all over Atlanta. We're never going to shop at Rich's again until we can eat in the Magnolia Room. And that goes for everything in Atlanta that right now is closed to us." Their tactic was civil disobedience. Their philosophy was nonviolence. In fact, they required that everyone participating in a demonstration take an oath, swearing to be nonviolent.

Carolyn explained: "We had studied what happened at A&T [North Carolina], and we decided to build on that. And yet we wanted to have a movement that was an outgrowth of the historical legacy of Negro Atlanta. So we approached the problem very scientifically. We studied it, went downtown, and actually counted the numbers of seats at lunch counters. We came up with solutions, and we mapped out strategies. We were really organized. We got our hard facts from *A Second Look* [a study by a group of ACCA members, including Whitney M. Young, dean of the Atlanta University School of Social Work, and Carl Holman, which examined patterns of segregation in Atlanta], and confirmed them with the Southern Regional Council, and then we went to the students who were in the various English Department clubs and societies and asked them to draft a document reflecting the problems outlined in these reports. Then Julian Bond and I took the best parts and synthesized them into one document. That became the Committee on Appeal for Human Rights."

Carolyn also told me why and how the Atlanta students got a reputation for being the best-organized Student Movement in the country. Now, instead of who had the best sports team, there was a lot of rivalry among Black colleges as to who had the best-organized movement. "In our group," she said, "we had students who had been in the military, like Lonnie King, who became one of the major leaders, and Morris Dillard, a graduate student at Atlanta University. They brought to bear their military experience on the organization. They mapped out march routes and organized advance teams equipped with walkie-talkies, to report back to the church we were using—Rush Memorial Baptist—and to keep track of where everybody was and what everybody was doing. It was in guys like Lonnie that you could see the underlying bitterness from the contradiction that they saw of being on the front lines serving their country, and then coming home and not being able to get served at all.

"The veterans also taught us tactics for survival during nonviolent demonstrations. They taught us things like how to crouch and cover our heads with our hands in the event of being clubbed by the police; also how to fall down and pull our knees up to our stomachs in a fetal position, so that the brunt of the blows would be on the meat of our bodies, like the back and behind. One of the things we decided was that we wouldn't have any high-school student demonstrators, because we didn't think they could take the pressure and the harassment that we anticipated from the white waitresses, the white customers, and the white police."

The group's first official act as a committee was the drafting of a document outlining their grievances and their demands. Written primarily by Carolyn (Clark), Julian Bond and Morris Dillard (Morehouse), Roslyn Pope, Hershel Sullivan (Spelman), it was published in all the Atlanta newspapers except the one Black paper, the *Atlanta Daily World*, whose editor, C. A. Scott, was a conservative Republican who was opposed to direct action and wanted no part of any threats to the white establishments that advertised in his newspaper.

When I got home from Wayne on spring break, Carolyn showed me the document and told me what had happened in the wake of its publication. I thought I knew my friends, but I was now seeing a side of them that had never before been tested, and I listened in awe. Their manifesto was called "An Appeal for Human Rights," and it read as follows:

We, the students of the six affiliated institutions forming the Atlanta University Center—Clark, Morehouse, Morris Brown, and Spelman Colleges, Atlanta University, and the Interdenominational Theological Center—have joined our hearts, minds, and bodies in the cause of gaining those rights which are inherently ours as members of the human race and as citizens of these United States.

We pledge our unqualified support to those students in this nation who have recently been engaged in the significant movement to secure long awaited rights and privileges. This protest, like the bus boycott in Montgomery, has shocked many people throughout the world. Why? Because they had not quite realized the unanimity of spirit and purpose which motivated the thinking and action of the great majority of the Negro people. The students who instigate and participate in these sit-down protests are dissatisfied, not only with the existing conditions, but with the snail-like speed at which they are being ameliorated. Every normal human being wants to walk the earth with dignity and abhors any and all proscriptions placed upon him because of race or color. In essence, this is the meaning of the sit-down protests that are sweeping this nation today.

We do not intend to wait placidly for those rights which are already legally and morally ours to be meted out to us one at a time. Today's youth will not sit by submissively, while being denied all of the rights, privileges, and joys of life. We want to state clearly and unequivocally that we cannot tolerate, in a nation professing democracy and among people professing Christianity, the discriminatory conditions under which the Negro is living today in Atlanta, Georgia—supposedly one of the most progressive cities in the South.

We hold that:

1. The practice of racial segregation is not in keeping with the ideals of Democracy and Christianity.
2. Racial segregation is robbing not only the segregated but

the segregator of his human dignity. Furthermore, the propagation of racial prejudice is unfair to the generations of yet unborn.

3. In times of war, the Negro has fought and died for his country; yet he still has not been accorded first-class citizenship.

4. In spite of the fact that the Negro pays his share of taxes, he does not enjoy participation in city, county, and state government at the level where laws are enacted.

5. The social, economic, and political progress of Georgia is retarded by segregation and prejudices.

6. America is fast losing the respect of other nations by the poor example which she sets in the area of race relations.

It is unfortunate that the Negro is being forced to fight, in any way, for what is due him and is freely accorded to other Americans. It is unfortunate that even today some people should hold to the erroneous idea of racial superiority, despite the fact that the world is fast moving toward an integrated humanity.

The time has come for the people of Atlanta and Georgia to take a good look at what is really happening in this country, and to stop believing those who tell us that everything is fine and equal, and that the Negro is happy and satisfied.

It is to be regretted that there are those who still refuse to recognize the overriding supremacy of the Federal Law.

Our churches, which are ordained by God and claim to be the houses of all people, foster segregation of the races to the point of making Sunday the most segregated day of the week.

We, the students of the Atlanta University Center, are driven by past and present events to assert our feelings to the citizens of Atlanta and to the world.

We, therefore, call upon the people in authority—State, County, and City officials; all leaders in civic life—ministers, teachers, and businessmen; and all people of good will to assert themselves and abolish these injustices. We must say in all candor that we plan to use every legal and nonviolent means at our disposal to secure full citizenship rights as members of this great Democracy of ours.

On the day the document was published, March 9, 1960, Carolyn told me, she put on her best Sunday clothes, including high heels, and, along with Wylma and many of the 4,000 students of the Atlanta University Center colleges, marched through the streets of Atlanta, saying, in effect, "Our time has come."

A week later, fanning out to places of public accommodation and facilities supported by tax dollars, the students held their first sit-in. Their goal was to draw attention to their demands and to get arrested in order to make cases that would challenge the Jim Crow laws that sent us to the separate "colored" water fountains, that sent us to the separate "colored" toilets, or that kept us from eating at all. Eventually, it would include places like the Fox Theater, a movie house designed like a medieval castle. There were over one hundred stone steps winding against the outer wall leading up to the tower. That's where they made the Black folks sit. Many a time I remember going with my mother to the Fox, and while I don't remember any of the movies I saw there, I have not forgotten, and shall never forget, the stairs.

One of the main stores that we targeted was Rich's, the multistory, moderate-to-upscale department store where most of Black Atlanta shopped.

In those days, Blacks may not always have liked the treatment they got, but they had no options. In addition to all my other memories now about the subtle and not so subtle indignities Blacks suffered at Rich's, I remember once suggesting to my mother that she go to Rich's and get her hair done in the beauty salon. It was long and straight, and about all she could do with it was put it in a ponytail or a bun. I wasn't suggesting that she try to pass, I was merely telling her that she could go there and, as fair as she was, I was sure no questions would ever be asked.

My mother's reaction was typical of an attitude all over the Black community at that time. "Oh no," she said, without bitterness, "I'm not going down there and take the chance they'd find out I was a Negro and let them burn up my hair."

But something had now changed in Atlanta. And something had changed in us. We had been protected and privileged within the confines of our segregated communities. But now that we students had removed the protective covering, we could see in a new light both our past and our future. We could see that past—the slavery, the segregation, the deprivation and denial—for what it was: a system designed to keep us in our place and convince us, somehow, that it was our fault, as well as our destiny. Now, without either ambivalence or shame, we saw ourselves as the heirs to a legacy of struggle, but struggle that was, as Martin Luther King was teaching, ennobling; struggle that was enabling us to take control of our destiny. And, as a result, we did not see ourselves or the other young people demonstrating in one way or another throughout the South as heroes to be praised, celebrated, or fretted over. We were simply doing what we were born and raised to do.

While not everybody in the adult Black community was on board, the Atlanta Student Movement had spoken in terms that became the watchwords for all of us: "Ain't gonna let nobody turn me roun'."

chapter **13**

Summer of '60
and Beyond

I went back to Wayne, completed my first year, then went home again to Atlanta. Most of the students were leaving, except for a critical mass who lived there and planned to carry on the protests. For all of us the summer of '60 was like no other.

At one point, Hamilton and I had to go to the federal district court in Macon for a hearing on our applications. Our lawyers were trying to get a temporary restraining order against the university. We had been turned down repeatedly for a year, always on the basis of there not being enough room for us in the dormitories. The university never made the mistake of saying—which was the truth—that it was because we were Black. But when we appeared in court, Judge William Bootle refused to order the university to accept us, on the ground that we had not exhausted all our administrative remedies. At the same time, he ordered us to go to Athens for admissions interviews in November, and he scheduled a trial in Athens to consider a motion for a permanent injunction against the university in December.

Meanwhile, throughout the summer, I spent all my time with the students, doing whatever I could to support them. I really wanted to get arrested, too. But our lawyer, Don Hollowell, had explained that an arrest, even a "good one," was an arrest, and that for me to have an arrest record would play right into the hands of the state. They could then legitimately turn me down. Although I understood the reasons, I was still frustrated that I couldn't go to jail with my friends. The closest I ever came was one afternoon when we were having a party in the back yard of Mrs. Willie Lewis, one of our adult supporters. My mother, a friend and fellow bridge-club member of Mrs. Lewis, and some other adults were there, and although we were listening to records, dancing, and just letting off a little steam after a day of confrontation with the authorities, the group was far from rowdy or out of hand. But it was interracial. By this time, a few white students from the North had come South and were working in various Movement offices. Mrs. Lewis's house was around the corner from where I lived, and where there were still a few white families who hadn't managed to escape. One of them had obviously observed this interracial gathering and was so offended by its mere existence that he called the police. Lonnie King, one of the principal student leaders, and Julian Bond, another student leader from More-house, as well as Carolyn and others, were about to seize the moment for another confrontation with the white authorities. But Donald Hollowell, who represented all of us, didn't think this was the best time or circumstances, not least because I was there. So while they talked among themselves about how to respond to the police, I was quietly whisked out the back way. Later, with the confrontation avoided by the students, who agreed to turn down the music if the cops agreed not to come back (because they figured the whites who had called initially would continue to try to break up the party), I returned to the party. We all had a good laugh, then got back to Smokey Robinson and The Miracles and Ray Charles. In fact, Julian, who was a budding poet, was inspired by Ray Charles and the effect of his music on the Movement to write the following ditty:

> *See that girl*
> *Shake that thing.*
> *We can't all be*
> *Martin Luther King.*

None of us had lost our ability to enjoy ourselves, and we partied and dated and had as much fun as we always had had during the hot Atlanta summers. But this summer, the summer of '60, there was always something to help us keep our eyes on the prize. For example, once, during one of the sit-in demonstrations in the heart of the downtown Atlanta business district, a crowd of whites assembled and began tormenting the students. The young people sitting in wanted to scream back. But one of the leaders, Ruby Doris Smith, a small but dynamic young Spelman student whom many described as the glue of the Atlanta movement, walked the line and maintained decorum, whispering to each in his or her turn, "Don't forget why you're here."

By the end of the summer, I was torn about leaving, mostly because there was so much action in Atlanta and because I knew it was going to intensify once the colleges opened. At the same time, I was also looking forward to returning to Wayne. I was moving to a newly acquired university apartment that was much more like a traditional dormitory. By the end of freshman year, I had decided that I never wanted another roommate, but when I saw the setup at the new complex—a two-bedroom suite with a kitchenette—I decided that with the right kind of person it could work. Dorothea Brown, my Atlanta friend, now a senior, felt the same way. I liked her. A short, beautiful, nut-brown girl with a lovely wide smile, Dorothea, who at Wayne preferred Alma, her first name, was quiet, but she was also spirited and determined. I admired her because she had also made that leap over the traditional Southern options for women and Blacks and was majoring in engineering.

I also was going to make the big decision about whether to pledge, and which way. Carolyn had leaned on me a little bit, but I also knew some AKAs in Atlanta (among them my mother's best friend, Nellie Driskell), and some at Wayne whom I admired. So it was still a bit of an open question for me. When I got back, the Black students I knew had some questions about what was happening "down South," but outside of the immediate physical environment, the events all seemed remote. Even more so a few weeks into the semester, when I decided to pledge. It seems as if by this time it was a foregone conclusion that I would pledge AKA. That widely held assumption was based on the fact that I was light-skinned, and most of the light-skinned women pledged AKA. In fact, the Deltas, who ranged in color from jet black to light brown, were so convinced that I would follow the traditional color pattern of pledging that they did not invite me to their rush party. Sometime during the period, however, I asked a Delta why I hadn't been invited; she seemed surprised that I was interested. I then let it be known that I had not made up my mind and that it was, in fact, quite open. Not long after that, I received an invitation.

During the rush period, I learned that all the sororities talked about service to the community. Each had its own history of pioneers who had been involved in the political, social, and economic affairs of the country. Most of the current members were concerned about how to socially enhance the Black presence on campus. At the Delta mixer, where they presented us with sketches of outstanding Deltas, called the Hall of Fame, we were asked to introduce ourselves in verse.

> *Oopshoobedoobe,*
> *My name is Ruby . . .*

> *It won't be hard to learn,*
> *My name is Kathi Fearn . . .*

> *My name is Charlayne,*
> *And I enjoyed the Hall of Fame.*

At the end of the rush period, it might have been a tough choice, but for two major things: grades and color. It came as a shock to Blacks on campus, but I pledged Delta. In part, I think my decision flowed from the torment I had suffered on the way home from school in Covington, where my own kind showed signs of bigotry and intolerance. I also resented the whole color issue. I felt very strongly that Black people shouldn't be guilty of the very thing that Carolyn and Wylma and by now countless Black students throughout the South were fighting to overcome. It was also divisive for Blacks internally. Additionally, I was genuinely attracted to the Deltas, because they had a higher grade-point-average requirement than any of the other Greek letter organizations, male or female, Black or white. I liked that standard and that challenge.

There was something about Delta history that was unique, a history that Paula Giddings, also a soror, captured some years later in her book *In Search of Sisterhood*.

> Delta Sigma Theta [she wrote] was founded by young college women with the idea of creating social bonds or a sense of sisterhood among its members. Its primary focus has been transforming the individual . . . At the same time, however, its founding in 1913, a time of both racial and feminist ferment, also imbued it with a secondary purpose: to have an impact on the political issues of the day, notably the women's suffrage movement. By 1925, the organization made its first public pronouncement against racism and four years later created a Vigilance Committee whose purpose was to enlighten the growing membership about political and legislative issues and thus prepare them to become agents of change.[*]

I didn't see anything wrong with the other sorority women, but at that moment I saw more young women in Delta whom I wanted to emulate, like Pat Ryder, an older soror who was a mixture of urban sophistication and Southern charm which somehow managed to sustain itself through generations of migration. She had a direct counterpart in Atlanta, my neighbor Eleanor Walker's sister, Gwendolyn, now a senior at Spelman College. They represented the kind of woman I wanted to be: soft and appealing, clear-headed and strong without being strident. And I liked the fact that they seemed to have good, healthy, steady relationships with their boyfriends. The men might have been a little shaky, but they never roamed too far. Both these women married the men they dated in college, and the marriages have endured. And yet the women weren't altogether predictable. I remember that one day Pat stunned everybody in the dining hall

[*] New York: Morrow, 1988, p. 60.

when she walked in with her hair dyed a reddish bronze. Two days later, mine was, too. What I also admired about Pat was that she was so self-possessed, so poised, so in control, without being distant. She managed to get along with everybody, and it was never at the expense of anybody else.

Three other young women pledged, or became Pyramids, when I did: Joyce Whitsett, a sultry young student who earned extra money by singing with a popular Black jazz band; Shirley Settles, who was sweet and kind of schoolmarmish, and who had a beautiful operatic soprano voice; and Marcellette Gay, a tiny wisp of a girl with unusual hazel eyes and a zaniness that sometimes camouflaged her sharp, penetrating mind. She eventually dropped out of the pledge line, but she had instantly become, as she remained, my soulmate.

In order to entertain our big sisters, we used to make up songs about Deltas that we would sing to tunes that were popular at the time. For instance, to the tune of "There Goes My Baby," we made up the song "There goes a Delta . . . moving on down the line . . ." or to "That's the sound of the Men Working on the Chain Gang," by Sam Cooke, we sang, "That's the sound of the Pyramids Working for the Del-el-tas."

Because of Joyce and Shirley, the quality of our singing was high, and as the word got out that the Pyramids could sing, we started to be in demand outside our intimate circle of Big Sisters. We sang for the Big Brothers at their fraternity dances. I was the lead singer, and never started in the same key twice. Once, I sang, as a solo, practically the whole first verse of Jackie Wilson's hit "To Be Loved," but it wasn't supposed to be a solo. It took that long for my singing sorors to find the key. "The Sorors Three," as we were later called, were a big hit, and we used to say that if I hadn't had to leave there might not have been a reason for the Supremes.

Despite the fact that I had been drawn to Delta because of its high GPA requirements, the demands of pledging almost caused me to flunk out of school that semester. Instead of writing history papers, I was writing Delta songs; instead of memorizing my second-year German, I was busy memorizing the names of the founders. In the middle of all this, I had to fly back to Atlanta and go to Athens for an admissions interview, which, at the time, I thought was a going-through-the-motions waste of time. The university was wedded to intransigence.

For me, it was a pretty routine interview. But the three-man panel was rough on Hamp. They asked him things like whether he had ever been to a house of prostitution or a "tea parlor" or "beatnik places." It was so patently ridiculous to be asking Turner High School's "Mr. Clean" such questions that it came close to undoing Hamp, who reverted to the kind of stuttering that used to grip him in high school when he was under pressure or angry. Only, in this case, his speech problem fed the perception of the opposition that he had something to hide. Meanwhile, Hamp, too, had pledged at Morehouse: Alpha Phi Alpha, the fraternity my father had pledged when he was there. Fraternities and sororities were more of a way of life on Southern campuses. Joining was almost a requirement. Hamp said he chose Alpha because all the campus leaders were Alphas. "The Alphas also had the smartest guys on campus and these were the guys I wanted to be with," he recalled.

Back at Wayne, I "crossed the burning sands" with my two Pyramid sisters during a ceremony that in its own way validated and affirmed the history and struggle of Black women to take their rightful place in the leadership ranks of the campus, the community, the nation, and the world. We recited the names of women like Mary McLeod Bethune, who was a pioneer in Black education and the founder of the National Council of Negro Women, for years the umbrella of all Black women's organizations; and Mary Church Terrell, who in the twenties marched for women's suffrage and in the thirties and forties led sit-ins to desegregate public facilities in Washington, D.C.; and Osceola McCarthy Adams, a pioneering actress who also taught and directed young actors like Sidney Poitier and Harry Belafonte. All this opened for me still another chapter in the history of my people that had been shared with me in an affirming way all my life. And now it was doing something else: it was stiffening my backbone and adding yet another coat of armor for what lay ahead.

Meanwhile, Carolyn and Wylma now had their feet in the fire. On October 19, 1960 they joined the demonstration that would have the gravest and possibly most far-reaching consequences of any so far. For the first time, Martin Luther King, Jr., had been persuaded by the Atlanta students to join them in protest. That night, at his arraignment, he spoke for them all: "I cannot accept bond . . . I will stay in jail one year, or ten years."* Martin Luther King, Jr., would spend his first night in jail, and so would some thirty-five students, including Wylma and Carolyn.

From the beginning, Carolyn told me, the women were treated differently from the men. Taylor Branch reported that the men were placed in a special cell block, "in care of Negro guards who supplied them with games, books and phone messages, and [a first meal of] steak smothered in onions." Carolyn remembers the treatment of the women quite differently: "We were placed in a big, open cell with murderers, prostitutes, hardened criminals. There were not enough beds, and what beds there were were cold steel slabs. It was cold, so we slept in our clothes. We had dressed up for the demonstration, so at first the only shoes we had on were the high heels we wore when we were arrested. They were uncomfortable, so we walked around barefoot on that cold tile floor."

One of the convicts in the cell, an attractive young Black woman who had killed her husband, had some connections and she managed to get them a few amenities, like sugar for the thick black coffee that was the one thing available all day long.

For Carolyn, the determination she set out with helped her cope. For Wylma, the shock of the place sent her into a nearby rocking chair, where she spent the next four days rocking and crying. Carolyn remembers: "Wylma wanted to go home, but she knew why we were there. I think she also knew how determined I was to stay until our demands were met, no matter how long. That's what led her into that depression. Knowing that she wouldn't leave me and, knowing me, knowing that that might be years, if necessary."

But if the shock of the place made Wylma cry, it had another effect on Atlanta. Its waves jolted the city into action. As students poured out of the colleges in unprecedented numbers, the Black com-

* Taylor Branch, *Parting the Waters: America in the King Years*, 1954–63 (New York: Simon & Schuster, 1988), p. 351.

munity and the white power structure moved in an unprecedented way.

On the second day, Mr. Long, who was now a school principal, visited Carolyn and Wylma in jail. The pressure on him from all sides was enormous. Some Black teachers told him that he couldn't continue to let his children stay in jail, that it would jeopardize his job. But the pressure had been somewhat relieved by a call from the white school superintendent, Ira Jarrell, who told him, "Don't worry about your job. You're doing what any real man would do for his children." Carolyn recalled: "Daddy brought us a change of clothes and asked how we were. Then, after an awkward silence, he asked if we were going to stay. I told him, 'Of course we're going to stay; that's how we were raised. When you make a commitment, you stick to it.' At that point, he broke down and cried." Instead of going to the jail, Mrs. Long joined a group that started putting pressure on the mayor to act.

That night, the students spoke to the press. As Taylor Branch wrote:

> King spoke quietly, almost shyly, about his reasons for joining the student protest. "I had to practice what I preached," he said. He spoke proudly of the fact that his fellow prisoners included five of the six student body presidents from the Atlanta University complex, plus two "college queens" and a number of honor students. Of his own sacrifices, King mentioned only the loss to the SCLC of revenue from his scheduled speeches during the most lucrative quarter of the year . . . "I was to have been in Cleveland on Sunday," he said. "The Cleveland preachers had guaranteed the SCLC $7,000 from the event."

On Saturday a deal was struck between the mayor and the Student Liaison Committee. The students would be released and agree not to demonstrate for thirty days while the mayor helped negotiate a settlement between the students and the businessmen. But as the papers were being processed to release the students, word came that Dr.

King would not be leaving with them. A bench warrant had been issued for his arrest resulting from a May traffic violation—a misdemeanor—in DeKalb County. All the students were upset, but most were persuaded to leave . . . except for Carolyn.

She remembers: "I was all ready to go until I asked when we would be seeing Dr. King. Nobody was saying, and after a while I got suspicious. I said I wasn't leaving my cell until I saw him and he told me it was all right to go. So after a long impasse the jailers finally agreed to get him. It was the first time a man had been allowed in the women's cell block. When he got there, he sat down on the floor in the hallway and I sat down beside him. He said, 'Carolyn, it's time to go.' And I said, 'I'm not leaving without you.' He kept telling me it was going to be all right, that he was coming, too. But I didn't believe him, for some reason. Then at one point he reached out his hand to me and said, 'You just hold my hand.' So I took his hand and we walked down through the gates, and when we got to the last gate, he jerked my hand away and pushed me out. The gate clanged shut and I started screaming, 'I can't leave him in there by himself.' Then the two of us started to cry. Someone came from behind and picked me up and carried me to the bus that had come to pick us up."

Carolyn's instincts had been right. In the early hours of the following morning, Dr. King was stealthily hustled off, handcuffed and shackled, to the Reidsville State Prison, some four hours outside Atlanta, where he was to serve four months at hard labor. But the next day there came a fateful intervention. The Democratic candidate for President, John F. Kennedy, called Mrs. King, who was six months pregnant and terrified that her husband would be killed. He promised nothing but encouraged her to call him if she needed anything. It was a call that Kennedy had been reluctant to make, for fear of upsetting his conservative Southern support, and many of his supporters and staff were indeed apoplectic. But the call helped produce quick results. The following morning, when Don Hollowell appeared in court seeking bail, Dr. King was released. It was a historic turning point in the politics of the South. Led by the older "Daddy" King, who had been a staunch Republican, Black people in droves switched their allegiance from the party that freed the slaves and, in the process, many believe, caused John Kennedy to be elected President of the United States a few weeks later.

Despite this historic drama, however, the deal struck with the students didn't stick, and they were back in the streets by the time I was summoned home a week before Christmas for the trial Judge Bootle had ordered on our motion for admission to the university. My big preoccupation at that moment was to finish my testimony and get back to Wayne before the Christmas break, so that I could enjoy my first round of holiday parties as a full-fledged Delta.

chapter **14**

The Trial

I arrived in Athens, the "Classic City," on the inhospitably cold morning of December 13. The courthouse, which was also the post office, was a marble building with square columns, situated behind several stately magnolia trees. The courtroom was on the second floor. By the time I arrived, it was overflowing—mostly with Black people. But there were also white spectators present. In the morning, Blacks and whites sat together, but by the afternoon they were sitting on separate sides.

As for my own group, my mother was there, and so were Hamp's father, "Tup," and his mother, Isabel, along with Hamp. They all sat behind our lawyer's table, in the first spectators' row. The *Anderson Independent*, a newspaper from my native state, which billed itself as "South Carolina's best newspaper," reported on Hamp and me this way: "The Hunter girl and Holmes sat side by side during the hearing, behind their attorneys . . . Both the girl and Holmes are light-skinned Negroes. The girl wore a green dress. Holmes was wearing a dark business suit."

I was a little anxious, given how they had treated Hamp before, but I was excited, too. It was the biggest story in the state, if not the nation, that day, and I was at the center of it. In my head, I started composing the story as my eyes searched the courtroom for reporters.

Our legal team seemed confident. And they were prepared. The team, besides Don Hollowell, consisted of Constance Baker Motley, from the NAACP Legal Defense and Educational Fund, Inc.; Horace Ward, who relished the assignment because he had been turned down years before when he applied to the University of Georgia Law School; Vernon Jordan, a young Atlantan who had just graduated that June from Howard University Law School; and Gerald Taylor, the Morehouse College registrar, who was helping with the records search and who would be called by our lawyers as an expert witness. While I was preparing to "cross the burning sands" in Detroit, Mrs. Motley, Vernon Jordan, and Gerry Taylor had been traveling the 75 miles every day from Atlanta to Athens, searching the records of the university for evidence that would show the university was lying about why we had not been admitted. After days of fruitless searching, Vernon Jordan discovered the critical piece of evidence: a case identical to mine in which a white female student, attending a college on the same system as Wayne, had been admitted for the winter term.

In addition to asserting that there was no room, Georgia officials had also been arguing that even if they were to admit me, it would be too complicated to do so immediately because of the difficulty, they claimed, of reconciling the credits of Wayne's quarter system with Georgia's semester system. In a newfound, unexpected, and disingenuous burst of concern for me, they argued that I would lose credits in the transfer; therefore it would be best to delay my admission at least until I had completed the whole year at Wayne. "This is it," Vernon remembers saying to Mrs. Motley as he located the document. And their spirits were lifted to their highest point.

I had good relations with Don Hollowell, a tall, solidly built man who in some ways reminded me of my father. He spoke slowly and deliberately, savoring the flavor of his words; when he spoke, the sounds seemed to begin somewhere down in his diaphragm. The students were crazy about him. They used to chant, "King is our leader, Hollowell is our lawyer, and we shall not be moved."

Hollowell was always attentive to me, as he might have been to one of his own children. Was I eating properly? Getting enough sleep?

How's Brother Dabney? Things that I never heard from my father during that time. He was full of warmth and caring—not what one might have expected of a man with so much on his plate and so little in the way of financial remuneration to show for it. One day, he might be getting students out of jail; the next, he might be trying to save a Black man named Nathaniel Johnson from the electric chair. And then there was his all-important latest case, which could open the entire educational system in the state of Georgia, from the university level on down. Despite the pressures on him and his small, underpaid staff—Vernon remembers making about $35 a week, and he had a wife, Shirley, who worked at the Welfare Department, and a baby daughter, Vickee—Hollowell was always calm. I don't think I ever saw him angry.

Vernon Jordan was so close in age to the students that we treated him as if he was one of us. He had just graduated from Howard Law School, in those days, the premier place to attend if you wanted to be a civil-rights lawyer. It was the alma mater of some of the most distinguished civil-rights lawyers in the country, including Thurgood Marshall, who was now heading the NAACP Legal Defense and Educational Fund in New York City and who was overseeing our case, one of almost two hundred cases, the Inc. Fund was pursuing all over the South. As Vernon later recalled, "The Howard University Law School was the place where many of the dry runs for civil-rights cases up to that time were argued, in the moot courtroom."

Not every Black lawyer at Howard wanted to practice civil-rights law, but those like Vernon prepared to, because, as he explained it, "in those days, civil-rights law was at the cutting edge of change in the South. And the South was home, and I wanted to be home and be a part of that change." He then added, "And, of course, I wanted to join Hollowell. He was *the* civil-rights lawyer."

Earlier that summer, Vernon had taken the Georgia bar exam. While helping prepare our case, he was once in Judge Bootle's chambers, along with the State Attorney General, Eugene Cook. Cook started a conversation. As Vernon recalled, he said, "You know, you can't pass the bar this time."

Before Vernon could reply, Cook continued: "You don't show any respect. Before you could get out of law school good, you were serving the governor with papers, me with papers. Trying to be a lawyer before you were a lawyer." As Vernon struggled to maintain his composure, Cook continued, in a near-stream-of-consciousness ramble. "You know, Horace Ward made the highest score ever on the bar exam," he said, referring to the latest young lawyer to join Hollowell's firm. Ward was eager to be a part of the Georgia case because he had applied in 1950 for admission to the law school and in 1951 had been turned down for much the same "reasons" that Hamp was, some eight years later ("Evasive," "Some doubt about his truthfulness"). He then went on to Northwestern, where he graduated with honors and was named to the prestigious Order of the Coif, an academic distinction similar to Phi Beta Kappa.

At this point, Vernon remembers, he couldn't resist a question. "How did you know that?" he asked Cook. "That's supposed to be kept by the numbers, so that it can be confidential."

And Cook, smiling slyly, said, "We keep up with y'all."

Most of the time, I related to Vernon as I might to an older brother, one that I felt I was probably almost as smart as. And when he had time to think about it, which wasn't often, he responded in kind. Like the time during the trial when we were having lunch at the small Black restaurant in Athens owned by the Killian family. I wasn't hungry when the waiter, one of the Killian brothers, took the order. As usual, Vernon, who was 6 feet 5 inches tall, and rail-thin, and had been brought up by his mother, Mrs. Mary Jordan, a popular Atlanta caterer, to appreciate good food, ordered a healthy portion. When his meal came, and before he could raise his fork, I had reached for a French fry.

"That looks pretty good," I said. "You don't mind if I have a little taste?"

"Why don't we just order another one?" Vernon said, his tone a bit testy.

"Oh, that's okay," I said. "I'm not really hungry."

I believe Vernon thought I was a little spoiled, but he indulged me. I believe, too, that the few years he had on me gave him a different perspective on my needs then, and what they were likely to be in the trying months ahead.

I had a totally different relationship with Constance Baker Motley.

In fact, I was hard-pressed to call it a relationship at all. She barely acknowledged my presence—hardly what I had expected from the lawyer who had come all the way from New York to champion my cause. Almost six feet tall and solidly built, Mrs. Motley had a strong, handsome face that bespoke the heritage of a West Indian people who knew where they came from and were proud of it, a face that was rarely disturbed by smiles, and a demeanor that didn't allow for frivolous laughter. If and when she did laugh, the sound was deep, round, and resonating, and she seemed to regard it as too precious to share with just anyone. I never, for example, heard her laugh in the presence of any of the state or university officials, except as a barely masked form of sarcasm. It seemed as if this was the most important mission of her life. In fact, she often talked about the South in those days as if it were a war zone and she was fighting in a revolution. No one—be it defendant or plaintiff—was going to distract her from carrying her task to a successful conclusion.

Even though she ignored me, I didn't exactly hold it against her. I used to sit in the courtroom and watch her in action, suffering not a single state witness gladly, from the chairman of the Board of Regents to the president of the university, O. C. Aderhold.

The university, of course, continued to say that they were not discriminating against us. As Calvin Trillin later wrote in *An Education in Georgia*:

> In a state whose highest officials were declaring daily that there would be no integration, a state that had a law on the books establishing that funds would be cut off from any school that was integrated, a state whose governor had promised in his campaign that "not one, no, not one" Negro would ever attend classes with whites in Georgia, Omer Clyde Aderhold . . . had the following exchange with the state's own lawyer, B. D. Murphy:
>
> "Murphy: Now I'll ask you if, as an official of the University of Georgia for the period you have stated and as President of the University of Georgia since 1950, do you know

any policy of the University of Georgia to exclude students on account of their race or color?

"Aderhold: No, sir, I do not.

"Murphy: Have you ever had any instructions from the Chancellor of the University System or the Chairman of the Board of Regents or anybody else to exclude Negroes as applicants to the University of Georgia?

"Aderhold: I have not.

"Murphy: Have their applications, so far as you know, been considered on the same basis as the applications of white people?

"Aderhold: On exactly the same basis, as far as I know."★

Mrs. Motley's style could be deceptive, often allowing a witness to get away with one lie after another without challenging him. It was as if she would lull them into an affirmation of their own arrogance, causing them to relax as she appeared to wander aimlessly off into and around left field, until she suddenly threw a curve ball with so much skill and power that she would knock them off their chair.

It happened with the university registrar, a small, weasel-like man who appeared stooped from carrying the white man's burden.

Trillin captured it this way:

At some point in every higher-education case, Mrs. Motley, who has handled practically all such cases for the Inc. Fund, always asks the university registrar what she calls "the old clincher": Would he favor the admission of a qualified Negro to the university? The registrar, often a segregationist himself, has to answer yes, as Danner did during the Georgia trial, and face the newspaper stories the next day that begin, as the Atlanta *Journal*'s began, "The University . . . registrar has testified in Federal Court here that he favors admission of qualified Negroes to the University.†

★ Trillin, pp. 39–40.
† Ibid., p. 41.

It was during his testimony that some white spectator in the back of the room was heard to say: "Look at that poor lying bastard. He's so damn dumb he doesn't even know what just hit him."

I tried to but couldn't read Judge Bootle. He seemed not to be intimidated by, or to favor, either side. He'd just sit there, behind his black horn-rimmed glasses, seemingly at ease in his empowering black robes as he listened for evidence that could lead him to go against every tradition in his Southern upbringing and culture. Could we count on him to have the courage to uphold the law of the land, or would he be just another Southern white man?

As the week wore on, the crowd of spectators grew. Some two hundred were on hand when Hamp and I testified. On December 15 Billy Dilworth of the *Anderson Independent* reported it in a way that got the basics right, although the interpretation was clearly a reflection of the source:

> Holmes, talking in a muffled-like tone and appearing nervous at varying periods, said university officials, at an interview several weeks ago, did not ask him about traffic violations. He said he was charged with speeding at Hapeville and drew a $20 fine. He does not consider this an arrest, he said.
>
> On examination by Horace Ward, one of four attorneys, Holmes said he has never attended any racially-mixed parties, does not have any comment on the present segregation problem at New Orleans and Atlanta and has never taken part in so-called "tea house" parties in Atlanta.
>
> Holmes, of athletic build, said university officials also interviewed him about a "red light district" in Athens. Holmes said he replied he knew nothing about such a place.
>
> Holmes also denied "attending" any houses of prostitution. He did admit taking part in inter-racial cultural groups, which he described as lectures, and debates between school groups, including Emory and Ga. Tech.
>
> Earlier, Paul R. Kea, assistant registrar at the university, said Holmes "seemed to have a chip on his shoulder," in the

interview with Registrar Walter Danner, Dr. M. O. Phelps, admissions counselor, and Kea.

"He was not as cooperative as we would have liked him to have been," Kea declared. "Holmes directed answers more to the floor than to us, and answered, in many cases, in monotone, mumbling, and slouched in his chair.

"It seemed he had the attitude," Kea said, "that now, you folks have something to sell me and I am here."

The Hunter girl, in a brief appearance before the court, said she desires entry in the university because of economic factors. She said she is presently working on a newspaper in Atlanta and "wants to write about people in Georgia."

The Hunter girl seemed calm and obviously chose her words carefully.

Kea, in describing the girl in an interview with university officials, said she was "well-mannered, and answered questions forthrightly."

Our side presented "what they seemed to think [was] their prize example so far," as the Atlanta *Journal* put it. It was the case of Bebee Dobbs Brumby "of the Marietta Brumbys," as the white Southerners were inclined to say when identifying their well-to-do. (Bebee, who wanted to study journalism, had applied a year after I did and was admitted for the winter term.)

Another related piece of evidence that Vernon had discovered was a handwritten note written by the chancellor and attached to a letter asking him to use his influence to get a white girl admitted. The note read: "I have written Howard [Howard Calloway, a member of the Board of Regents] that it is my understanding that all of the dormitories for women are filled for the coming year. I have also indicated that you relied on this fact to bar the admission of a Negro girl from Atlanta . . ."

After my testimony, I asked if I could go back to Detroit. I now had a feeling that my "normal" days as a college student were about to end, and I was eager to get in as much as possible. This would be my first Christmas party as a Delta, a Big Sister, and I really didn't want to miss it.

My lawyers said it was fine for me to go, but when they asked the counsel for the state, the answer was no. I was as furious as I think Hamp had been about the way he had been treated during the examination. And while they had been much gentler with me, I now felt they were getting back at me. After court adjourned for the day, I lapsed into a funk so strong it was casting a separate shadow from my own. I walked to the car and slumped down in the back seat, funk in tow. A few minutes later, Mrs. Motley slid into the car beside me. The first thing she did was take off her shoes. She had a problem with water retention, and during the long periods in the courtroom when she was examining or cross-examining a witness, and refusing to diminish her power and authority by sitting down, her legs would swell so much that her ankles would disappear and her feet would look as if they were about to spill over the sides of her shoes. When she got in the car, I hadn't expected her to say anything, so I was startled when she spoke.

"I know how you feel," she said in a voice more tender than I had ever heard from her before.

"You do?" I said in disbelief.

"Oh yes," she said warmly. "My husband and 8-year-old son, Joel, are back in New York, and I had hoped to be able to get away early so we could have a long weekend. I have to be away from them so much." Then she paused, as if she were contemplating the faces of her loved ones, and she frowned. "Those bastards!"

I instantly forgave every slight. Here was this woman who was systematically making mincemeat of all of "those bastards," now empathizing with the crushed feelings of a nineteen-year-old in a way so tender as to be almost unimaginable. I was so moved by this moment of connection that I almost got over my funk, except that I didn't want to abandon the mood that we were now so intimately sharing.

On Saturday, I returned to the stand briefly to testify that I was not taking any courses at Wayne that I couldn't get credit for if I didn't continue with them in the second semester. Then Judge Bootle gave our lawyers five days to submit their briefs, and the state five days after that. He set a deadline of January 4, by which time he said he wanted to have everything in his hands.

I flew back to Detroit just long enough to pack for the holidays and attend one party. Back home, the student boycott of the Atlanta stores, with its slogan "Wear old clothes for dignity," had already significantly hurt retail sales and was now affecting Christmas shopping.

Bobby Dabney, who had graduated from Tuskegee Institute the year I graduated from Turner, and had been commissioned in the air force as a second lieutenant, was home on leave from Hempstead Air Force Base in New York. He had rediscovered me the year I graduated, and we had been developing a relationship through the mail. We spent a lot of time with each other over the holidays, discussing, among other things, whether we had a future together. The papers had been full of stories about the trial, and everywhere I went people wanted to discuss the case. One night Bobby raised the issue of my career aspirations, which were now familiar to everybody who read the newspaper, listened to the radio, or watched television.

"How serious are you about this reporter business?" he asked.

"Very," I answered. "It's the only thing I've wanted to do since ninth grade."

"Well, can you imagine if we get married and I've been on the base all day, and you've been at the newspaper all day. Do you think I'd be interested in hearing about all of that?"

I was so taken aback by the question that I had to think about my response for a minute. Had I heard what I thought I heard?

I said, "Well, I would hope so."

Then he said, "Well, I'm not so sure."

Remembering Zora Neale Hurston's Janie, I felt something inside me fall off the shelf, and I had to go inside and look around to see what it was.

On Bobby's final night home, we went to Mass and came home late. I was driving, so I dropped him off first. We sat talking in his driveway for a few minutes, and I brought up the thing he had said and tried to tell him how it had affected me. He said I had misunderstood. What he was trying to say was that he didn't know anything about the newspaper business and that it would be hard for him to discuss it.

I responded by telling him that he could learn more if he read more newspapers and magazines and books. He then promised me he would, and asked me to continue to think about our spending our life together. At that moment, he was very tender and appealing. We kissed good night, and he got out of the car.

I lived just a few blocks away, and was home only a few minutes before the phone rang. I was startled, because everyone knew that my mother didn't allow calls that late. When I answered, it was Bobby. I thought he was calling to make sure that I got in all right, but before I could be pleased at the thought, he said, "Two white men just left my house. They approached me as soon as you drove off and said they wanted to ask me some questions."

My heart started pounding hard. Who were these men? What did they want? Was there any danger?

I told Bobby to sit tight, that I would call Donald Hollowell immediately.

I awoke him out of a deep sleep, but he was immediately alert. He listened as I outlined the conversation I'd just had, and then asked for Bobby's phone number. "I think I'll just have a little conversation with the brother," he said. "Don't worry. It's unfortunate for him, but this is what we've got to expect. Now, you get some sleep. And don't worry."

I was worried but reassured. Hollowell had that effect. Within no time I was asleep.

We never did figure out exactly who the men were, but Hollowell thought they might have been Georgia investigators. We never heard any more of it, and they never again attempted to see Bobby.

When I left for Wayne a few days later, no one was making any predictions about what Judge Bootle was going to do. Back on campus, it was business as usual—until Friday, the end of my first week back. An article I wrote shortly after for a new Black magazine, *The Urbanite*, captured the moment as I lived it:

So it was on that afternoon of January 6, 1961, when I rushed into the dormitory at Wayne, grabbed my mail and ran up to my room on the second floor, my only concern was getting into something comfortable before going to a sorority meeting at five o'clock.

I had not been in my room ten minutes before I was called to answer the phone out in the hall. Expecting to hear one of my friends on the other end, I was surprised to hear, instead, an unfamiliar voice saying, "Congratulations!"

"For what?" I asked, completely in the dark.

The woman on the other end identified herself as a reporter for a New York newspaper. She told me that news had just come over the wires that Federal Judge Bootle had ordered Hamp and me admitted to the University of Georgia.

By the time she managed to read the entire release to me, both of us were between laughter and tears. My caller brought both of us back to reality by pointing out that she had a story to write.

From that moment on there was no possibility of a moment of calm and quiet in which I could think about what was ahead. Downstairs the switchboard operator was soon swamped by calls. I grew even more confused as reporters seemed to be arriving by the carload.

In a way it was a relief to break away and rush off to a sorority meeting. I arrived, bubbling over with elation, and began eagerly sharing the long-awaited news with my Delta sisters. But I found [some of] their reaction[s] rather puzzling. Instead of sharing in my jubilation, they became quiet and solemn.

I remember walking over to one of the several Pats in the room, throwing my arms around her, and asking her why she was so solemn. "This is so great!"

Pat, barely able to contain her emotions, reached to wipe a tear from the corner of her eye and said, "I'm afraid of what they might do to you."

It was a thought that had never crossed my mind, so I

held her even closer and now, a little teary-voiced myself, said, "Don't worry, Pat. It's going to be all right."

It was not until thirty-six hours later, as I sat on the plane to Atlanta, that I began to realize what Pat had already seen. As I looked around the plane, wishing for someone with whom I could share my happiness, all the faces I saw were cold and unfamiliar. Gradually I began to realize what I had left behind, and what might lie ahead.

chapter 15

UGA: The Beginning

I arrived at the Atlanta airport on Sunday and was greeted by a lively throng: my mother, grandmother, and brothers; Attorney Hollowell; Father Banks; lots of reporters and photographers. I was wearing one of my favorite new acquisitions, which I had purchased with the money I had earned at Wayne, a fake-fur leopard jacket, and I was carrying my talisman, a stuffed dog named Snooky. My aging grandmother grabbed us both with a hug that belied her increasing frailty. Everybody was very excited and happy. All over the airport, I could see people reading newspapers that carried headlines about the decision and its immediate aftermath: STATE ASKS U.S. JUDGE TO STAY NEGRO ENTRY. NEGRO BOY REGISTERS AT ATHENS. UNIVERSITY, STUDENT LEADERS PRESS FOR ORDER ON CAMPUS.

I could see in the eyes and on the faces of Black skycaps and porters, maids and janitors, not the shiftless, diffident "*niggah, naggah, raggah taggah*," but the same prideful brightness that I saw emanating from my own family as one after the other recognized me as I walked through the airport. *Our time has come.*

It was a heady but humbling experience—one that I would go through many times in the coming years, saying of them and people like them, as my father had said of God to me, "If you are with Him, you are Power." They imbued me with their power through the light in their eyes and the smiles on the faces, the light that would keep fear in its place and confidence in mine.

I had been disappointed when I learned, before I left Wayne, that Hamp had already gone to the campus on Saturday morning. But as Donald Hollowell explained, the Attorney General had dispatched himself to Macon to request that Judge Bootle grant a stay of his order "to allow [the State] more time to prepare an answer" to the integration order, or, as one paper called it, the "mix" suit. In addition to Attorney Hollowell, Hamp had been accompanied by his father, the Reverend Samuel Williams, the pastor of the Friendship Baptist Church in Atlanta and president of the vigorous NAACP Atlanta chapter, and Julian Bond, in his capacity as reporter for the *Atlanta Inquirer*, an upstart new newspaper that grew out of the movement.

They caught the registrar's office by surprise as they entered and laid a copy of the court order on Walter Danner's desk. After securing the registration papers, Hamp and the others left, with Hamp promising to return Monday morning. Later, President O. C. Aderhold told reporters, "If he shows up with all the credentials required by the court, then I think Mr. Danner will be required to register him."

That day, the university was relatively quiet, although some students burned crosses and, at the entrance to the campus, hung a Black effigy, which they called "Hamilton Holmes." Calvin Trillin, then a reporter for *Time*, had arrived on campus Saturday, and later wrote about a "sorry demonstration" he had witnessed that night. He described it this way: "Twenty or so students wanted to burn a cross made of two-by-fours, but, owing to lack of kerosene and a lack of experience in the art, they were unable to get it ablaze."

Some students, however, were successful in another location and even one white journalism student, Marcia Powell, told me later that it was a frightening, almost unbelievable spectacle. The dean of students, Joe Williams, met with campus leaders, including fraternity and sorority heads, presumably in an effort to head off trouble. He later revealed that he had a "plant" among the fraternity brothers who kept him apprised of the real attitudes inside the fraternity houses. Later, there were reports of Klan members visiting some frat houses and urging members to revolt against the desegregation order.

There was also great fear at the university, from the president on down, that Governor Ernest Vandiver would attempt to honor his campaign promise of closing down the university by letting "not one, no, not one" Negro student ever to attend classes with whites. President Aderhold issued a statement expressing the "firm belief" that the university would continue its century and a half of service to "the people of this state without interruption." And a group of students began organizing a petition drive to that effect. One eighteen-year-old student from Macon was quoted in the combined Sunday *Atlanta Journal-Constitution*: "I don't want them to close the school. I had rather that [integration] just happened than to close the school."

If there was one symbol of pride that personified the aspirations of white Georgians of every class and stripe, it was the 176-year-old state university, or, as Georgia liked to claim, on a technicality, the oldest state-chartered university in the nation. To be sure, Georgia was not Yale, the elite institution that inspired its charter and much of its early architecture—the explanation for the fact that many of the buildings on campus have what Trillin called "a blocky, New England look." But it was the place where the sons of Georgia's majority—small-town farmers and businessmen—passed on their traditions and sense of place, not only in Georgia but in the universe, which also tended to be Georgia.

It was through such critical institutions that white privilege and power were nurtured and preserved. The governor of Georgia was an alumnus, and so was U.S. Senator Richard B. Russell, along with members of the Board of Regents and the state legislature. Georgia was the place where the good ol' boys cemented their relations with other good ol' boys, and where they found wives among the good ol' girls, most of whom had come there for that purpose. But on that Saturday the governor was telling Georgians that Judge Bootles's ruling had put the university in jeopardy of closing, and that if Hamp and I entered a fund cutoff would go into effect because of the provision in the state law that said, "No further funds shall be used or expended on an integrated school."

On Sunday, we had a reunion at my house. It was decided that we would go to the campus early Monday morning, in part because there were no hotels for Blacks in Athens, and even if we could find a Black home courageous enough to take us in, we had no security. We weren't afraid, but we weren't crazy. Throughout the weekend, the entire state was caught up in the fast-moving developments that had now placed Georgia in a historic spotlight, white sons and daughters facing their most apocalyptic moment since Sherman marched to the sea, Black sons and daughters their most liberating moment since the Emancipation Proclamation.

It was with a heady sense of history that we started out for Athens early Monday, just as the sun was rising on a cold Georgia morning. My mother, Vernon Jordan, and I were in one car, and Hamp and his father in another. We had no security, and no plan for what we would do in the event that we were attacked on the way or after we got there, despite the history of white violence on this route. No, this was the morning when I thought about how I was going to take my first steps onto the campus as if I knew my place, only this time, for the first time, it would be I who would be defining my place on *my* terms, on territory that was their pride but was now mine, too.

I found myself thinking about Gwen Walker and how she glided so regally across the Spelman campus, in a cool, confident stride that said, "I love myself, and even if you don't love me, you will respect that which I love above myself." That's how I would walk onto the campus at Georgia, loving myself a lot and demanding respect.

It was on the way to Athens that my mother recalled for me her first memory of the University of Georgia, and the fate of the niece of the white woman who had been so evil to my grandmother. It wasn't as if my mother took any pleasure in the awful event of the niece's untimely death all those years ago, but it seemed just one of the many ways that a Black mother of Georgia could put into context the awesome step that her child was about to take.

I didn't know what to expect as we pulled up to the entrance to the campus and saw a large crowd milling about the arch. We got out of the car, and with Vernon Jordan leading the way, we mounted the steps and walked onto the campus. The crowd, noisy and boisterous but not threatening, was all white, and turned easily into a blur on my visual screen. We walked through the crowd, unhurried but with purposeful strides. The university did not have a security force and hadn't made any provisions even for temporary protection on this potentially troublesome occasion. As the crude dissents of some of the louder students found their way to my ears—"Nigger, go home" and "There goes the nigger"—I thought of them as just that: the crude dissents of people not sophisticated enough to "throw some big words on them," as I used to do on the way home from E. R. Carter. And while I felt that they were more of an amusing nuisance than anything else, the pace that Vernon and I had set proved too much for my mother, who was several inches shorter than either of us. At one point halfway between the registrar's office and the Journalism Building—a five-minute walk at most—she called out, "Slow down. My legs are not as long as yours."

Even with the distraction caused by the crowds I was struck by the quiet majesty of the beautiful old white building, with its two towering Roman columns, which housed the Henry W. Grady School of Journalism. That remarkable façade did not relate to anything inside; still, I looked forward to its seedy, unpretentious interior, which I imagined would be rather like some old Southern newspaper office.

I was met at the door by George Abney, a member of the journalism faculty, a gentle, balding man of medium height and weight who always seemed to be on the verge of being embarrassed about something. As I got to know him later on, I came to realize that that was just a manifestation of his shy nature. Despite his apparent nervousness, he was friendly and almost warm. He looked me straight in the eye when he talked to me, and I liked that. As we discussed my schedule, it sounded almost like a routine student conference, but for the presence of my mother, my lawyer, and a horde of newspeople outside clamoring to get in. In fact, although we were unaware of it at the time, a local radio reporter had been peering through the mail slot and recording for broadcast later that night an "on the scene" report.

Everything was going smoothly, when we suddenly heard a loud cheer rise from the crowd. We had no idea what provoked it, until seconds later when the phone rang. George Abney listened without expression and a lot of "Uh-huhs," then hung up. He told us he had just been informed that Judge Bootle had granted the state's request to halt the registration. The disappointment was obviously evident, as, from over the transom, one of the students who had a clear view of Vernon yelled out, "The nigger lawyer ain't smiling no more."

It was a devastating blow. We had come so far, and now this. Wasting no time, we gathered up our things and headed for the car, saying nothing and trying to put on our best faces. Once in the car, we discussed our options. Ray Ware, a local Black businessman who had been gracious and helpful during the trial, lived a few blocks away, over a funeral home in an old two-story wooden building. So we drove to his house, where we found him and wife, Lulu, eager to help.

Vernon got on the phone and learned that Mrs. Motley and Attorney Hollowell were already on their way to the Court of Appeals in Atlanta with a request to lift the stay. Marcia Powell, the perky nineteen-year-old white sophomore from Columbus, who had introduced herself as a reporter for the campus newspaper, *The Red and Black*, and who seemed to understand that this was no ordinary campus assignment, had somehow managed to latch on to us and was now scribbling furiously. Years later, she shared her notes of that moment. They read:

> A little after 2 p.m. two newspapermen and I arrived at the apartment where Hamilton and Charlyne [sic] were resting and awaiting the decision of Judge Tuttle . . . We sat watching TV, several other white pple there—rptr from the *Banner* and another student . . . Charlyne was sleeping when we arrived . . . looked completely exhausted . . . Hamilton and I talked for a while, he said he was pre-med & wanted to specialize in surgery; rest just general conversation . . . His lawyer asked me where I was from, etc. I let them know my position on the issue . . . [around] 3:30 p.m. the phone rang & Hamilton answered, then called the lawyer, who listened for several seconds. Hamilton woke Charlyne and we & her mother waited for the lawyer, Vernon George [sic] to give us the decision of the judge . . . He hung up and said that the judge had thrown out Bootle's ruling . . . "We're in," was Hamilton's reaction . . . His father, Alfred, said, "Well,

I'm happy now. I've been awfully disappointed, but now I'm jubilant . . . About that time everyone seemed to come in & prepare to go to the university . . . Charlyne said when asked her feeling: "I'm just anxious to begin classes." I had been chatting with Mrs. Hunter, passing time, until the news came. Watching bulletin on TV, she said: "God is good, isn't He?"

Judge Elbert Tuttle's "hard-hitting" decision generated the head-line TUTTLE BOOTS BOOTLE. Judge Bootle had said his stay was solely for the purpose of allowing the state to "test the correctness" of his integration order, but Judge Tuttle declared that "the quickest dis-position that can be made of this case, so far as granting these plaintiffs their right to an education in a state institution—as the trial court has clearly found that they are entitled to—is the best solution not only for them but for all others concerned."

As to the argument that the state faced a possible fund cutoff, Tuttle said that the courts cannot fail "to prevent a continued denial" of constitutional rights simply because granting relief "will produce difficult or unpopular results." White sons of Georgia, affronted by one of their own, lashed out at Tuttle. Lieutenant Governor Garland Byrd called the ruling "a political decision," and, echoing a wide-spread sentiment among white Southerners everywhere, said that the decision indicated that Tuttle "apparently has no regard for the general welfare of our educational institutions and further demonstrates an inclination to impose the harshness of the full force and effect of the U.S. government on the people of his native state." The Attorney General announced that he would fly to Washington to appeal to another Southerner, Supreme Court Justice Hugo Black.

The Atlanta papers profiled Tuttle, Byrd, and Black as the "Trio Deciding School's Fate," pointing out that Black, a former Ku Klux Klanner, was feared by both liberals and conservatives, who pointed to his record as a New Deal liberal senator from Alabama; Tuttle was a native Californian, a vigorous long-time Republican, and trustee of three of the Black colleges in Atlanta; and Bootle, a long-time Re-publican and former law-school dean. Both Bootle and Tuttle were appointed to the bench by President Eisenhower, who in 1957 had ordered federal troops in to protect the "Little Rock Nine," the Black children who were integrating Little Rock's Central High School. This week, coincidentally, was Eisenhower's last as President. He never spoke on the matter. (A good many Blacks in the South still maintained allegiance to the "party of Lincoln," despite the Kennedy victory, and these actions by Republican judges helped solidify that allegiance.)

At that moment, we all loved Judge Tuttle and, with warmth for him in our hearts, rushed back to the university to complete our registration. To sign up for our classes, we had to actually go to each of the various departments, which were situated all over the vast, sprawling, hilly campus. The crowds followed us everywhere we went—especially me, for some reason. There was always speculation about why they followed me and not Hamp, but I didn't and don't have a clue, because while the officials were more willing to admit me than Hamilton, this display seemed to suggest that perhaps they thought I would be the more easily frightened.

The closest we came that day to an incident that could have turned ugly was when we got into a car belonging to William Tate, the dean of men, to drive to Ag Hill, the part of the campus where agriculture and sciences were taught, and where all the dormitories were situated. Dean Tate was a bear of a man, with a rather odd shape. He was burly and broad on top, and his body increasingly narrowed below the waist and toward his feet. He was easy to caricature because he was so much like a caricature in the flesh. The gruff old dean had spent most of his life at Georgia, dating back to the beginning of his own student days in 1920. Years after this particular day, he told me that he and President Aderhold "felt that integration was inevitable; it would come. But we felt . . . that the longer we could delay it, the less possibility there was of violence." However Tate felt at the time, his stoic countenance obscured it. Later he told Calvin Trillin that his philosophy during that first week was merely "to keep some of the boys who feel strongly from making fools of themselves."

As we got into the car, Tate had his first big opportunity. We were a tight fit, and at first, the students thought this was funny; then, as they moved in closer to peer into the car, some of them started to rock the vehicle. It was a very tense moment—but only a moment—before Tate hurled himself out of the driver's seat and started grabbing at the students closest to him. He was known for snatching up ID cards, and this whirling-dervish act did the trick. While not dispersing, the crowd pulled back far enough to allow the car to pass and, except for a few "nigger thises" and "nigger thats," we proceeded without any more interference.

We returned to Atlanta that night with plans to come back to Athens for classes the following morning—amid rumors that the school was going to be closed for a "holiday" session, the governor calling it "the saddest duty of my life."

Meanwhile, the campus was in turmoil, with the mood changing often, depending on what was leaking out about plans to close the university. The students pressed President Aderhold, whose inconclusive statements led some to call out, "O.C., can you say?"

In Washington, the appeal was passed to the full Supreme Court, which declined to hear it. Students responded by hoisting Confederate flags, exploding firecrackers, and roaming up and down the streets of Athens chanting and blowing horns. Later that day, Hamp and I returned for classes and went our separate ways, he to the home of the Black restaurant owners, the Killians, who had rented him a room in their house, and I to Center Myers Hall, the central dorm of three adjoining buildings called North and South Myers. Had we been admitted as freshmen, Hamp would have had to stay on campus, too, but now the on-campus requirement applied only to women.

I was met at the entrance to Center Myers by a charming, grandmotherly woman with thinning gray hair and a case of low-slung post-middle-age spread. Greeting me kindly and without self-consciousness, she introduced herself as Mrs. Minnie Porter and welcomed me to Center Myers. I introduced my mother. We chatted for a few minutes; then she led us across the huge, unadorned center lobby, furnished with chairs and low tables where the young women "received company" and up two steps to a narrower corridor. A few more feet beyond, on the left, Mrs. Porter stopped and opened the door onto a two-room suite. As I stepped inside, I quickly eyeballed the spacious room, seeing a kitchenette to my left, an adjoining room to my right with a twin bed, and off the room in which I was standing, a full bathroom. Not bad, I thought; it could have been a lot worse.

The suite, she explained, had been the offices of the Women's

Student Government Association, but they had been moved elsewhere to make room for me. The fiction of no-room-in-the-inn was
still being maintained, although I didn't get the feeling that Mrs.
Porter really cared one way or the other. During the course of the
conversation, I learned that there were no other students living on
the first floor. Since we hadn't known what to expect, I had packed
only a few clothes in a small suitcase, which I now placed on the
floor in the bedroom off to the right. Mrs. Porter showed me the
phone buzzer, explaining that I would have to come out of the room
and into the hallway booth to receive any calls.

It had been a long day and we had come a long way, and while
I wasn't sure how I would feel after my mother and Don Hollowell
left, I knew that it wouldn't help matters if I delayed their departure. At that point, however, no provisions had been made for me
to eat. Whether I would be allowed in the cafeteria was still an open
question, one that nobody wanted to pursue at that moment. So,
after I deposited my things, we went off to Killian's and ate an early
dinner.

I was back before dark. My mother and I hugged each other, and
if she was worried she never let me know. I said goodbye and went
into my room to await my first night as a student at the University
of Georgia.

Within a few minutes, there came a knock on my door. A few
of the girls wanted to say hello. Somewhat shyly, they introduced
themselves, and I invited them in. They looked around and com-
mented on the spaciousness of the suite, and on the fact that I had a
full bathroom. Upstairs, they told me, they had only showers. And
no cooking facilities. They didn't stay long, and soon I was alone
and thinking about what my life was going to be like in the coming
days.

Outside, a crowd was gathering as the early winter darkness fell.
Dean Joe Williams had advised me to keep my blinds drawn for the
time being, but I could plainly hear the noise outside.

> *Two, four, six, eight,*
> *We don't want to integrate . . .*

Eight, six, four, two,
We don't want no jigaboo.

I was too tired at this point even to be tempted to look out the window. I reached into the suitcase, which was still where I had set it down, and took out a pair of pajamas. Within a few minutes, I had drifted off to sleep, to the strains of those peculiar Southern lullabies.

On Wednesday morning, Hamp and I sat down in our first classes at the University of Georgia. Although nearly two hundred years of segregation had just officially died, in my classroom in Meigs Hall, at least it was a quiet death. No words were spoken to mark the moment, although a psychology class on human behavior might have been a good place for it. In a way, though, this was a relief to me, because at that point I just wanted to get on with being a student as quickly as possible. I thought that the worst was over. Sometime near the end of the class, I wrote in the margin of my notebook, "Boring."

When I left Meigs that morning, accompanied by a university official, I caught sight of Calvin Trillin. I really liked him, and so did Hamp and Carl Holman, who always called him Trilling. He was known as "Bud," and he had a way of interviewing that was unobtrusive, that made you feel he really cared. I think it was because he listened more than he talked. A lot of the white reporters seemed always to be trying to convince me that they weren't "like the rest of them," that they weren't bigots or, in a kind of cathartic confession, that they once had been but were getting over it. Then they'd want to tell you their theories and solutions and give you advice on what you should do and how you should act. Then, too, there was the egregious incident in which a CBS reporter, Robert Shackney, or his cameraman—there's always been a dispute over which it was but no question that it was a CBS employee—who had arrived late to a demonstration that had taken place as I walked by, and not to be outdone by the other networks, organized a group of students to reenact the incident long after I had left. But even against lesser sensation-mongering, Trillin stood out in my book. And he was all over the place; every time I looked up, even in the middle of a rambunctious crowd, he never seemed far from my side.

I had had only a few conversations with Trillin, but I trusted him instinctively. We developed such a good rapport that in no time he was telling me what a dumb idea it was to major in journalism. An English major from Yale, Trillin, whenever he had an opening, pressed me to switch my major to English. But I wouldn't hear of it.

My first journalism course, Ethics, was taught by the dean, John Drewry, the epitome of the aging Southern gentleman, courtly, portly, and deliberate in speech. The one thing no one discriminated about was gossip about the dean, and within short order I had found out about his peccadilloes, one of which had led his wife to shoot him in the behind—an image that defied even my vivid imagination.

I was a little taken aback by his announcement that he was about to call the roll, a practice I thought I had left back in grade school, but given the lingering antebellum attitude toward women on the campus and the immature behavior of many of its students, I soon realized that it made all the sense in the world.

It was about 2 p.m. when a college official brought me back to my ground-floor room at Center Myers. I did an interview with newspaperwomen in which I was asked if I was excited during the hours preceding my first class.

I responded, "The only thing that excites me is the night before a German exam."

I also was upbeat about the reception I had received throughout the day both in class and at the dorm.

I said I felt that it seemed to me that one of the big problems in this situation was that "a lot of people don't know about other people. And a part of a lot of this is that people don't know enough about one another."

I added, "The best way to find out is to ask questions."

I was asked a lot of questions, which ranged all over the lot, including what I was planning to do for the weekend ("Go home and get some more clothes") and for the coming summer (". . . thinking about going to Africa," a trip the Deltas were offering for the best essay on "Why I Want to Go to Africa," which I was sure I would win).

Early that night, on the NBC network news, Chet Huntley praised the governor, the university, and the students for their behavior, which, he said, "has made this whole country feel good." His comments proved premature.

Outside the door there were crowds. At one point, I got a phone call. It was Bud Trillin calling—to see how I was holding up, I suspect—but asking me instead if I wanted him to bring me a pastrami sandwich.

I captured the rest of the events of that fateful day in an article I wrote soon after for *The Urbanite*. The new Black entry into the magazine world was published by Byron Lewis, the former private in my father's glee club in Alaska, who was now out of the army and living in New York. I wrote:

> The lobby of the dormitory was almost empty, but after I had gone to my room many of the girls came down as they had the day before—to welcome, observe, inspect. Mrs. Porter, the housemother, came down and told the girls not to stay too long because I was tired. She had advised me earlier that it would be best to have my dinner in my room that night. This, again, seemed only a normal precaution, considering the circumstances.
>
> It began getting dark around six o'clock. After the last of the girls had gone, everything became amazingly quiet inside the dorm. I picked up a book and tried to study, but then firecrackers began popping outside, as they had the night before. I decided there was nothing to do but go to bed, despite the racket outside. Mrs. Porter came in again to see if I had eaten and to ask how I was feeling. She suggested that I keep the blinds closed and stay away from the windows. "We expect some trouble," she said.
>
> Later, as I went into the hall for a drink of water, I caught a glimpse of the faculty members the students had nicknamed "The Baby-Sitting Crew," because they had volunteered to patrol the building. It seemed to me the group was larger

than it had been the night before. I returned to my room. After a while, the noise outside gradually grew larger and uglier. Though I did not know it at the time, a hotly disputed last-minute defeat of the basketball team at the hands of Georgia Tech had helped create anything but a mood of sweet reasonableness in the crowd that had marched from the gym to the dormitory. Reading or sleeping was out of the question. I was in the first room of the duplex apartment. Suddenly there was a loud crash in the bedroom. Not stopping to think, I rushed in, only to be stopped in my tracks by another crash, as a Coca-Cola bottle followed the brick that had ripped through the window a moment before. Jagged splinters of window glass and fragments of the bottle had spattered across my dress, slippers, and the skirts and blouses that I had not yet had time to unpack.

Strangely, I was not at all afraid at this moment. Instead, I found myself thinking, as I stood there in the midst of the wreckage, So this is how it is.

At this time, I did not know that all the students had been told by the riot planners to turn off the lights in their rooms when it got dark. With the rest of the building in darkness, the three brightly lit windows of my apartment must have made an inviting target for the mob out on the lawn.

I heard the dean's voice in the hall and called out to him, but he didn't hear me. I met a campus patrolman in the hall and told him what had happened. As he went into my room to investigate, I continued down the hall to a counselor's office a couple of doors away. There in the darkness I went to the window and looked out. All I could see was a moving mass—not a face that could be recognized as belonging to a separate person. Even the voices seemed to run together in one confusion of shouts and jeers.

Turning from the window, I saw that the partition between the counselor's office and the lobby was open. The crashing of the glass and the screams of one girl on the floor above, who had been struck by a brick as she looked out her window, had brought most of the girls into the lobby. Some of them passed back and forth, looking to see how I had reacted to all of this.

I realized that it was nearing time for the eleven o'clock news and that my mother in Atlanta would be waiting up for it. I called her and told her that I was all right. Though I knew she could hear the noise in the background, she seemed relatively calm. But I could not get her to promise that she would go to bed at once, without waiting to look at the television news program.

After I hung up, [Paula Leiter], one of the most genuine persons it has been my good luck to meet came down and began talking to me. Though it was clear that she herself was nervous, she did all she could under the circumstances to take my mind off what was going on. This was anything but easy, since by now the hostility from outside was being echoed by some of the girls inside the dorm. Perhaps it was partially out of hysteria, or partially because the girl upstairs had been hurt. At any rate, a group of girls began tramping in a continuous circle, yelling insults first at me and then at the schoolmate who had come in to befriend me.

It was hard to sit there and listen to some of the things that were said about me without being able to answer. I was told I was about to become "a Black martyr, getting fifty dollars a day for this from the NAACP"—a piece of news that would have considerably surprised my family.

The city police outside, after having waited in vain for the state patrol, finally resorted to tear gas. The gas fumes began seeping into the dorm, and the girls were told to change the linen on their beds. This prompted deliberately loud offers of a dime or a quarter to Charlayne for changing the sheets of these same residents who professed to believe that I was already being paid at a rate of over six dollars an hour, if figured on the basis of an eight-hour day.

My new friend was beginning to get drowsy, though she tried not to show it, and I suggested that she go to bed, assuring her that I would be all right. After she had left, I wondered how many people, myself included, would have had the courage to do what she had done.

Mrs. Porter came in, looking worn-out from the ordeal of trying to console over 150 overwrought girls. She gave me an orange. "It's a sweet orange," she said. "You might enjoy it."

Mrs. Porter left as I began peeling the orange. Before I had finished, she was back again. This time, she was serious and unsmiling. Slowly and sympathetically, she told me that the dean had said I would have to leave. I was to be taken to Atlanta, so that I would be safe. I don't think I heard the rest of what she said. I suddenly felt totally sick and miserable. All I could think was: I've failed, I've failed. I began to cry and, hard as I tried, I couldn't stop. Mrs. Porter patted me on the arm and told me not to cry and not to worry. "Everything will be all right," she said. Needless to say, I could not really believe this.

I packed quickly, not even bothering to remove the pieces of glass from my suitcase. Dean Williams came to my room and repeated what Mrs. Porter had said. Feeling empty inside, I followed him out of the room, stopping only to pick up my Madonna from the table beside the bed. Afterward, it bothered me to think that people looking at the newspaper pictures would mistakenly think I was crying because of fear, but at that moment I was too sick to care.

The girls were all quiet now. They were huddled together in the lobby as I went by. A few of them started to hiss, but they were immediately shushed into silence by the others. The state troopers had finally arrived. (It was after midnight.) As we came out into the chilly night air, I saw the gray patrol cars parked at the curb. The husky, red-faced troopers in their gray uniforms and broad-rimmed hats were impassive and coolly official in speech and manner. We stopped to pick up the Dean of Women at her residence. I remember saying something about being sorry to inconvenience her at that hour, to which she answered that she couldn't sleep from worrying about what was going on. When we arrived at the house at which Hamp was living, he was on the phone talking to Attorney Hollowell in Atlanta. (Until the call from Hollowell came, he had been asleep, unaware of what was happening a mile away.)

Hamp wanted to drive his car home. I tried at first to reason with him, telling him I thought it was dangerous; that he could be more easily isolated, even if there were patrolmen in front of and behind him; we didn't know how much we could trust them. "They could just pick you off," I said. But Hamp loved that car, which his grandfather had given him when he got into Georgia, and he was not about to leave it. I knew that Hamp didn't like scenes, but I was desperate. So somewhere between reality and drama, I found a zone of hysteria that was persuasive. I had my hands on his shoulders and was shaking him frantically and screaming, "You've got to go in the car with me . . . You can't drive . . . You've got to come with me!" Finally, somewhat embarrassed by this performance, which he couldn't quite decipher, he gave in.

As we sped along the often bumpy highway toward home, Hamp and I had little to say. Neither of us could get used to the idea that we had been "suspended." Yet what could we say or do about it? I remember almost nothing of the trip itself. Before I knew it, we were in Atlanta, turning into my block and pulling up in front of the porch where a local Black man had stood so many months ago telling me that I should give up the idea of trying to go to the University of Georgia. The news of our coming home had preceded us, and a few close friends had gathered at the house. Most reassuring of all, my mother, her hair all done up in braids, came out with open arms to welcome both Hamp and me and to take some of the sting out of our forced homecoming.

No one I knew slept much that night. Wylma and Carolyn had sat glued to the television set, waiting for a call or some kind of word. But, of course, I had no time to call. Events were moving too fast.

At my house, reporters and supporters mingled in what for me was a very surrealistic moment. Hollowell talked about the plan to go to Macon the next day to file a motion to get us readmitted, and there was some talk about whether we would go back immediately or get some rest, at least through the weekend. A lot would depend on what Judge Bootle said.

Finally, sometime in the wee hours of the morning, the only person left at our house was Carl Holman. By this time he had become, if not the guru to me that he was to the Student Movement, something close to that. Whenever I needed to talk to an adult on whom I could count not to be judgmental but to give me advice that I could trust without qualification, the person I went to was M. Carl, as the students who were closest to him called him, or "Mo," for Moses, as those who knew him going back to his younger days in St. Louis called him. Like Elsie Evans before him, Carl came close to my idea of an educated person—quick-witted, sharp-tongued (when necessary). He not only was well-read but retained everything he had ever read and could quote with ease (though never pedantically) from Shakespeare, Marx, Gandhi, Faulkner, Du Bois, the Bible, you name it. While most of us treated him as if he were married to the Movement, Carl, in fact, had an actual family. His wife, Mariella, taught high-school French and had an appealing sassiness that complemented and sometimes checkmated Carl's sharp wit. They had three children: Kerry, Karen, and Kent, all under ten at the time. And then there were all of us.

Carl was the guiding light of the *Inquirer*, which had evolved from the early days of the Movement, when the students made use of leaflets to inform the community of their activities, local support being an important element of their efforts. The leaflets took the form of a newsletter entitled *The Student Movement and You*, and every Sunday, Julian Bond, Mary Ann Smith and her sister, Ruby Doris, and a handful of others would fan out to the churches and, as worshippers entered or emerged, hand them a leaflet. Each Sunday, Julian recalled, they would hand out between 50,000 and 75,000 leaflets.

At the same time, James Gibson, who was home from the army and taking a break before going back to graduate school at Temple

University, was working at the Welfare Department. As his younger brothers, John and Ben, students at Morehouse, told him what was going on with the students, he soon got the idea of sharing this information with other Black workers at the Welfare Department. Using sheets of carbon paper, Jim typed summaries of the information piped from John and Ben. Workers surreptitiously began funneling contributions for the students' bail fund through Jim. "I used to put the money in a brown paper bag and deliver it to the switchboard operator at Atlanta Life," Jim recalled. "Then, one day, the switchboard operator told me Jesse Hill wanted to meet me. When he came down, he told me he wanted me to meet Julian Bond and Whitney Young. Shortly after that meeting, we combined all our efforts and became the Publicity Committee for the Students. Jesse Hill and others arranged for Black realtors to withhold their advertising from the *Atlanta World*, which was refusing to report on the students' boycott, and with the first $300 they collected from the realtors to place their ads with the students, the *Inquirer* was born.

In many ways Carl, who was well over six feet and had a kind of gangly walk, was like the typical bespectacled, absentminded professor. For example, he would begin boiling eggs on the stove, then go off to work on an editorial. Once, we were all working in his basement, where the *Inquirer* was produced, when we were stunned by what sounded like shots being fired. Since that was totally within the realm of possibility, we headed upstairs somewhat uneasily, only to find out that the water had boiled out of the pot and the eggs had exploded all over the ceiling. But there was nothing typical about this forty-two-year-old "Young Turk." If, as the students used to say, "King is our leader, Hollowell is our lawyer, and we shall not be moved," Carl was surely their philosopher-king, who inspired them with his clarifying vision, both in his crusading editorials, in which he wrote under the pen name Vox, and in the endless strategy sessions among the students and all the various adult camps.

From the first day, Carl treated my journalistic aspirations with dead seriousness, and helped nurture and encourage them every step of the way.

"Char," he said now, in my empty living room, calling me by

the name used by my family and closest friends, "you're not going to like this, but you're going to have to abandon your precious bedroom tonight and sleep in the back."

"But why, Vox?" I asked.

"Well, it's just a precaution, in case we get some visitors of the unwanted kind."

Although he never said it, there was a lot of concern over the fact that there were no grown men in my house—just my younger brothers, my mother, and my grandmother. The two women had been taking care of us and each other and the house for so long that they never would have given the situation a second thought. But in this case, the gentle giant, though still gentle, was talking like a warrior.

My mother didn't say anything, just quietly left the room. A few minutes later she reappeared. "Here," she said as she walked up to Carl. "You may be needing this."

"Yikes!" Carl yelped, lurching back and throwing his hands up in the air. "What's that?"

"It's an old German Lüger that Charlayne's daddy brought home from the war. But it works and it's fully loaded."

That sent Carl into further paroxysms. "No," he said, with a half-groaning, gravelly laugh. "You better hang on to that. It'd be just my luck to open those blinds and wing a policeman."

Earlier in the evening, there had been considerable police activity outside. My ten-year-old brother, Henry, told me that earlier that night he had slipped out onto our screened-in front porch and, crawling around on his hands and knees, had witnessed an incident in which a white man drove up into our driveway. As the man was getting out of his car, he was set upon by several white men wearing suits and stingy brim hats, one of the identifying symbols of the FBI. The man did some fast talking, and they let him continue up to our door. It turned out to be Father Banks, who had seen what was happening on television and had come to offer support. But now, as Carl prepared to bed down for the night in the most vulnerable spot in the house, we couldn't be sure if the good guys were really good guys and if they were still out there.

. . .

There were no incidents that night, and early the next morning a rather sleepy-eyed Vox ambled out of our house and went home to his family. Throughout the day, reporters dropped in or called. Sometimes, it all resembled a wake. As they interviewed me about my reaction to the riot, I interviewed them about the same thing. Although I was yet to take the course, I was practicing basic Journalism 101: Who, what, when, where, and why?

I learned that there had been a lot of to-ing and fro-ing about whether to cancel the basketball game. Everyone knew that such a blood-feud event would be intense in the best of times, and it was a mild understatement to say that these were not the best of times. In fact, one student was quoted after the game as saying, "We got beat by Georgia Tech and we got beat by the niggers." In addition, the plan for the evening's post-game activities was so well known that one of the main activities around campus was getting a date to the riot. Also, Klansmen had been spotted in the crowd, including the Grand Kleagle from Atlanta, Calvin Craig. And it was known that several Klansmen had visited some of the fraternity houses during the day. The papers were reporting that six Klansmen had been arrested and accused of disorderly conduct. They were all released on $205 bond.

This information was disturbing, but I think there were two things that disturbed me more than any of the others. One was that the riot was being organized by students from the law school, possibly during a meeting of the Demosthenian, a campus literary society. During an earlier meeting, one of the ardent segregationists had predicted that we would "receive the same greeting Autherine Lucy had gotten at the University of Alabama." Lucy, the first Black woman to enter the University of Alabama, had been expelled from there five years before.

It was this core group that was believed to have been encouraged with phone calls from top officials of the state and other "big names in state politics." John Pennington and Gordon Roberts, two well-plugged-in reporters I got to know during the crisis, wrote on Sunday: "Judging from the wild disregard for law and order, and the open flouting of city police and university officials, the demonstrators must have had reason to believe that they could raise the roof with impunity."

One of the names most often mentioned was Peter Zack Geer, executive secretary to the governor, who in fact issued a statement saying, "The students of the university have demonstrated that Georgia youth are possessed with the character and courage not to submit to dictatorship and tyranny."

The other piece of what I considered really bad news was that "at the height of the mob action," after at least ten windows in my dorm had been smashed by bottles and bricks, Joe Williams, the Dean of Students, who later led me out through tear gas, had called for help from the State Patrol, whose headquarters was only five minutes away, and they had never arrived during the riot. They did come eventually to take Hamp and me back to Atlanta. Upon learning that bit of news, I felt a total vindication for my histrionics of the night before.

When reporters asked me about the riot, I first tried to correct their mistaken assumption that I had been crying because I was afraid. "I was crying because I was very much disturbed, disappointed and hurt that I had been suspended," I said.

When asked if I would go back, I said, "I would go back if given the chance, whatever it entails."

No one had ever told us what to say or what not to say, from the very beginning of the process. We did know that Autherine Lucy was expelled from the University of Alabama when critical remarks were made by her Inc. Fund lawyers over her suspension "for her own safety" during a riot the previous day. She never went back. Our attorneys had simply told us to be careful not to give the Georgia officials the kind of bogus excuse they used against Autherine. But other than that, we had not been coached. And generally we spoke our minds.

While I continued to be upbeat, saying that the ugliness was far outweighed in my mind by "the friends I made who impressed me as being really sincere," Hamp was less sanguine. "I'll go back with an open mind," he said, but added, "I don't think anything could compensate for what happened Wednesday night."

Meanwhile, Attorneys Hollowell and Motley made it to Macon

and asked Judge Bootle orally for an immediate reversal of the suspension. Bootle refused to entertain the plea, and ruled instead on another motion before the court that struck down the state law that would have cut off funds to any state institution that desegregated. In Georgia newspapers, it was called "A Killing Blow to Ga. School Segregation Laws." It wasn't the victory our attorneys had gone after, but it was a victory nonetheless.

One day later, however, on Friday afternoon, our attorneys had again made the trip back to Macon and stood, once again, before Judge Bootle. After giving the university time to readmit us voluntarily, and following a discussion about whether rules would be bent or changed to allow me to live off campus, Judge Bootle issued his next-to-last ruling in the case of *Holmes et al. v. Danner*. He ordered the university to admit us no later than 8 a.m., Monday morning.

chapter **16**

Almost Quiet Time

The "wake" now over, I spent the rest of the weekend emotionally and psychologically preparing to return to the campus. Carolyn and Wylma took me to their house to help me "get away from it all" for a little while. As soon as the front door closed, we heard Mrs. Long calling from the basement, where she and Mr. Long spent most of their time. "Y'all come on down here," she said. We headed for the basement; at the bottom of the stairs Mrs. Long leaped toward me and threw her arms around me. "Oh, my child," she said, close to tears. "You are safe. I wasn't going to rest until I could lay eyes on you myself." And then, gently pushing me away from her but not letting me go completely, she asked, "You all right?"

"Course she's all right," Wylma chimed in before I could speak. "You see her here, don't you?"

Wylma, Carolyn, and I weren't sentimental with each other; we had our own ways, I think, of reinforcing each other. They also seemed to have new levels of insight into the mechanics of survival, and they instinctively understood the need for striking a delicate balance between too much and too little coddling. They wanted to make sure that my suit of armor remained intact, because they seemed to know that one way or another I was going to have to get up and put it on, if not for the rest of my life, certainly for the time being.

The visit was the perfect respite.

On Sunday, we all went to Mass. In confession, I felt bad that I had no sins to ask forgiveness for. I had been a little too busy to get tempted. Instead, I talked about the strength I had gathered from the Madonna and from the support of my family and friends. And I asked Father Banks, who clearly knew it was me, to pray for my strength on my return. He assured me that the Holy Father was with me, and so was he. Wylma had a saucier confession—she always did—and Carolyn's was bland, as usual. Thus absolved, we took communion together.

Even though it was not exactly a routine day in our lives, we still had our usual run of the church, and after warm goodbyes, I returned home feeling strong and ready for my trip back to Athens the next morning. The only thing that caused me some brief anxiety was the news that came over the radio, later in the day, that a man carrying a gun had walked into the Center Myers dorm asking for me. When a night watchman attempted to question him, the man "whipped out a pistol," took the guard's gun, and disappeared. I immediately got on the phone to Donald Hollowell.

"You heard about the man they found in my dorm?" I asked in a tone slightly more insistent than usual.

Remaining calm, Attorney Hollowell answered that he had.

"You taking care of it?" was my second and last question about the matter, and when Hollowell assured me that it was being "dealt with," I let it go. I had to.

The only hitch on our return came as we were driving back to Athens. A radio reporter who had interviewed us earlier that morning, with the understanding that he not divulge the time or the route we were taking back to the university, came on the airwaves. Attorney Hollowell adjusted the volume so that we could all hear what we thought was going to be an interview about our mood as we prepared to try again. Instead, the reporter led with the news that we were heading back even as the broadcast was in progress, and then went on to estimate where we probably were at that moment.

I could tell that Hollowell was as furious as I was. Fortunately, nothing happened, but the experience taught us a lesson about trusting reporters we didn't know.

Once back on campus, I found the place quietly recovering, as if from a hangover. Nobody seemed to feel good, but everybody was doing the best he could, under the circumstances—except for the Kappa Alphas, who had lowered their Confederate flag again. It had flown at half-mast the previous Wednesday, when Hamp and I started classes.

Hamp and I went our separate ways—but with armed plainclothes government escorts. We both were a little uncomfortable with them, I, for one, feeling that they made us stand out at a time when we needed to try to blend in.

The efforts made by campus leaders and others over the weekend seemed to be paying off. Some fifty of them had met and had urged each person in attendance to contact five others and pass the word to stay out of potential trouble areas, not to drive past the Center Myers dorm on Lumpkin Street, and, if any of them felt inclined, to write one or both of us a friendly note. They also drafted a handwritten flyer, which they distributed in the fraternity and sorority houses. It read:

> . . . If I were in the situation Hamilton Holmes and Charlayne Hunter are in, I think I'd want to be treated the same as others are treated—no better, no worse . . . I wouldn't want people following me around curiously, or staring at me as though I were an exhibit. I'd hope that people wouldn't debase themselves by showing their antagonism in mean and violent ways, although I would realize that many feel opposition toward me. I wouldn't expect everyone to welcome me or like me, but I would hope that they would be civil even in their dislike. I'd be thankful for kind actions by students, a casual greeting, a word or a wave of the hand.

Meanwhile, the university had announced that any student "attending or taking part" in future riots or demonstrations would be suspended or expelled from school. And as we were returning to classes on Monday, the FBI was conducting an investigation into the cause of the riots and a Clarke County grand jury was continuing a similar investigation it had begun over the weekend. Already, eighteen male students had left the university, including ten who were suspended, three who refused to attend school with Negroes, and five others who "wanted to drop out until the crisis was over," according to the *Atlanta Journal-Constitution*. Two students had publicly admitted taking part in the riot, and the gun-toting intruder in my dorm was arrested and recommitted to the insane asylum.

My second class was in Western Civilization, at LaConte Hall. My professor, Dr. Lothar Tresp, a handsome German with a heavy accent, had been personally selected by the chairman of the department to take me into his class. Married to an Athens native, Dr. Tresp attributed his own racial sensitivity to growing up in Nazi Germany—an experience that, he said, "certainly left some scars. I was just a boy, but I still remember the so-called Kristallnacht. Of course, my family was properly in bed when it happened, but the next morning when we went to school the son of the local *Kreisleiter*, the political boss of the county, a fairly important office, was not in school. The excuse was that he had been watching the mob setting fire to the synagogue. And this sort of appalled us."

Dr. Tresp had been among the majority of faculty members to sign a petition deploring the violence and calling for our return to the campus. Most, if not all, of them were "very leery of what politicians of the state might do to us if we associated ourselves with this kind of action," Tresp recalled many years later. "Nobody was really sure that this might not become a witch-hunt of sorts. So people took their jobs, in a sense, in hand and offered them up on the altar of the moment." Dr. Tresp was an assistant professor at the time, without tenure, and he was encouraged to act by his wife, Lucy, whose family had lived in Georgia since before the Civil War.

Dr. Tresp prepared his class before I arrived by giving an hour lecture, followed by a "heated discussion." He said, "I remember one student speaking up and saying, 'Why would you go in a man's locker room and take a shower when there is a Black person in another stall there taking a shower?' I said, 'Well, why not? If he is healthy and doesn't have any communicable diseases, I wouldn't care at all.' And the student almost exploded. Things of this nature were discussed, but I felt that the important thing was to bring the question up and to give some opportunity for discussion, so that they would become a little bit acclimated to the idea of having a Black person with them, and that it wouldn't hurt them at all."

I had already met Dr. Tresp on my late registration rounds, before coming to his class that day. He had made a seating chart for the class, and when he met me he showed me the chart and told me, "Pick any empty space that's available." When I arrived, however, someone was in my seat.

As class started, Dr. Tresp said, "Oh, I see we have a new student." Everyone, including me, thought he was talking about me, but ignoring me, he walked down the aisle and stood in front of the young woman in "my" seat. "What's your name?" he asked her, and she identified herself.

"Are you a new student?"

"No," she said, adding that she was just auditing the course.

"Well, if you're auditing the course, you must have an ID card. May I see that?"

The student didn't have an ID card, so Dr. Tresp asked her courteously to leave.

Then it became known that she was a reporter for the *Atlanta Journal-Constitution* and just wanted to observe the class. As she was being evicted, everybody in the class, including me, roared.

It was a great icebreaker and tension reliever, except for one student who bolted from the class in tears. She later told Dr. Tresp that her parents were "adamant segregationalists," and he reasoned that she "just couldn't stomach the internal pressures." Later, however, in the unavoidable routine of seeing me every day, of having to confront a flesh-and-blood person rather than the imaginary dark demon in her mind, she made the adjustment, and we became friends.

I was very interested in history, and found Dr. Tresp a compelling teacher. But while the campus was essentially quiet, this was not the case in my dorm. There, for roughly a week, girls on the second floor above my room would take turns pounding the floor for hours at a time. Eventually, I would go to sleep, but that, plus all the other tensions of either real or anticipated problems, kept me awake late into the night and sometimes till early morning. By the time I got to Dr. Tresp's class, most days, the lack of sleep had caught up with me and I would find myself fighting drowsiness without much success. The pages of my notebook, in addition to my history notes, also contained a lot of lines that just squiggled off the page as I dozed off while trying to write.

Dr. Tresp never acted as if he noticed, and I passed the course, albeit without distinction.

During the week, I had talked with Carl Holman several times, and he was encouraging me to write a piece for the upcoming edition of the *Inquirer*, summing up my first week back. The editors held the front page until I could get home with the copy Friday night. The article ran the next day, with the headline CHARLAYNE FINDS FRIENDS AT U OF GA, beginning over a picture of prominent Atlanta Democrats as they "entrain for Washington and the inauguration of John F. Kennedy." The white papers, of course, carried the story of Kennedy's inauguration, his speech marking "an end as well as a beginning, signifying renewal as well as change," and calling on his fellow Americans to "ask not what your country can do for you—ask what you can do for your country." Black papers had celebrated his historic choice of Robert Weaver as the head of the U.S. Housing and Finance Agency and the first Black member of a presidential Cabinet.

My fellow citizens of Atlanta, especially those from my community, had done a lot for us in our "new beginning," and in my article I wanted to let them know that their support had not been in vain.

The story was captioned "Exclusive to the *Atlanta Inquirer*," by Charlayne Hunter, Staff Reporter, and datelined Athens, Ga.

It read:

> I can only hope things will continue as they have been for Hamp (Hamilton Holmes) and me since our return. We want nothing so much as to forget what happened on the night we were taken from Athens and to become, as much as possible, just two more busy students among over 7,500 here on this huge University of Georgia campus.
>
> On my first night back, I received flowers, accompanied by a card which said, "Welcome to the classic city." Mean-

while, a flood of letters, telegrams, postcards, and gifts from all parts of the world—including Brazil, France, and Australia—convinces us that there are more kind and sympathetic people than we had ever dreamed of. Doctors, housewives, students, teachers—all offer prayers and encouragement.

Moving about the campus from class to class, it has been a relief to see the crowds grow smaller and smaller. The newsmen no longer shower us with questions from every direction. Gradually it's becoming very much like a silent movie—the expressions and actions are there, but no sound.

A few of the friends I felt I had perhaps made proved my intuition not far wrong. Those friends were here when I returned. They were as steadfast as before, as steadfast as Hamp and I feel in the rightness of what we are doing.

Classes? They have progressed at what seems to be a normal pace. Oh, yes, because of the time lost I am behind. But as I talk to each of my professors "behind" does not seem an impossibly long way off.

My room is almost as I left it a week ago. The cottage cheese had to be thrown out. But the instant coffee and lots of sugar were still waiting in the cupboard.

Just now on my bed are pages and pages of history notes loaned to me by "a classmate." An open psychology book means that Psych is next on the agenda. A syllabus from the Journalism class reminds me that a quiz has been announced for that course.

Along the corridors of the dorm there are whispers, "She's back." But nothing more is said. The housemother at Center Myers is a sweet and charming lady who always "looks out for her girls." And, indeed, this gracious lady excludes no one as she carries out her role.

Now we are walking to classes alone, with no officers accompanying us. An occasional "Hi" from other students, along with the calmness in the brisk campus air, helps to ease whatever tension I might feel.

Finally, as I approached LaConte Hall today, on my way

to my next class, the bell rang, I suddenly had the familiar feeling of rushing to get inside the classroom, and by the time I had dashed in and sat down I felt even more "normal" than ever before.

The University of Georgia is beginning to seem more and more like "my" school and I think both Hamp and I are developing a sense of pride in being a part of it.

I sincerely hope and trust that nothing will change this.

Meanwhile, there were all kinds of dramas unfolding. Some of the students who had visited me and checked out my quarters before the riot were now complaining about being "discriminated against," because my bath and kitchen facilities were superior to theirs (no tubs, no kitchens, period). At the same time, I had so many visitors I had a hard time studying. Sometimes those visits turned out to be revealing surprises, including one from two girls from the adjoining dorm who dropped by just "to chat for a minute." One of them, Sue Floge, said she had come to the university "to have a good time and find a husband." We had a good laugh about that, and did not see each other again for years, and then under circumstances that we never could have foreseen at the time. (At different times, we ended up being married to the same man.)

There was also a delegation of girls who identified themselves as Jewish students. They said they felt bad about how I had been treated, and that because Jews had a history of persecution, too, they could in some small way understand how I must be feeling. I tucked this encounter away, because it was one I wanted to revisit at another, less intense time.

Another night in that first "aftermath" week, as I described it in the *Urbanite* article,

there was a knock at the door and a tall, blond, rather attractive girl came in with a bag of groceries in her arms. "Hi," she said, smiling. "Let's cook dinner. I'm starved."

Whatever sadness I [was feeling at the moment] was forgotten as we made a tossed salad. I began washing the lettuce, and she and another girl who had come along began slicing tomatoes and all sorts of vegetables that go to make up a tossed salad. We fried hamburgers, too.

Dishes washed, food eaten, company gone, I was alone again. A little sad, a little lonely.

The things that had made dormitory life bearable at Wayne—my special bedspread, my curtains, my record player—had gradually been moved to my rooms at Center Myers. Hamp and I went home every Friday after our last class. Sometimes I hitched a ride with him in his now reclaimed Opel; at other times, when our schedules didn't coincide, I would take a bus from the still-segregated tiny Athens bus station to Atlanta, where my mother would meet me and take me home. All that semester, Hamp and I would return together early Monday morning, in time for our nine o'clock classes.

My Delta sorors from Tau chapter at Wayne and from chapters all over the United States were flooding me with letters, and so was the Grand Chapter, under the auspices of the current president, Jeanne Noble, a professor of education at Columbia University. Dr. Noble told me she took great pride in the fact that when I had been asked about my sources of strength I had been quoted in *The New York Times* citing the Delta oath: "I will not shrink from undertaking what seems wise and good because handicaps or obstacles confront me; but striving to preserve a calm mind with a courageous spirit, barring bitterness from my heart, I will strive all the more earnestly to reach the goal." Dr. Noble also sent telegrams to the Dean of Women demanding that she personally intervene to take care of me.

Then I got a letter from Bobby Dabney.

Dearest Charlayne,
I can imagine how uncomfortable and inconvenient things are about now. Stay with it and good luck.
Everywhere I look, I see you. Hold your head up when you walk.

On the same day, I got another letter from Jim Gibson, at Temple in Philadelphia, who by now was working his way into my head, if not my heart.

Dear Char,
Naturally I wish there was something I could do, but so does the rest of the U.S. . . . Won't say much, could only add to the hubbub. Rest, enjoy yourself, cry, laugh—the works; your course is well set and you know better how to steer when left alone . . .

Yours,
Jim

At the end of the day, that was, finally, what I was—alone—except for the voices, the voices of my grandmother reciting the Twenty-third Psalm: "Yea, though I walk through the valley of the shadow of death, I will fear no evil; for thou are with me," and of Nina Simone and Her Friends, who soothed and comforted me with "He's Got the Whole World in His Hands" and "Try a Little Tenderness."

chapter 17

New Realities

If memories of the Old South lingered, along with most of its traditions, as the winter weeks went by and headed for spring there was also, if not yet a New Beginning, at least a new reality. None of the public schools anywhere in the South was desegregated, and every case the NAACP took on was challenged by massive resistance, fomented by those who were still fighting what they liked to call the long arm of judicial tyranny stretching down from Washington. And yet a new mood and a new energy among the South's "sons of Ham" were beginning to usher in changes so swift and sweeping that minds, if not hearts, were starting to accept the inevitability of desegregation. Even in the retrograde state of Mississippi, Negro students from Jackson State College staged their first sit-in, and were undeterred by the fact that applauding Black spectators were attacked with clubs, guns, and police dogs.

Meanwhile, Georgia had abandoned its massive-resistance laws, which had been designed to keep schools segregated "for a thousand years." Court-ordered desegregation of public schools would begin in the fall of 1961. Also, the Student Movement triumphed. In exchange for an end to the sit-ins and other demonstrations, merchants agreed to desegregate their lunch counters and other facilities after the schools were desegregated in the fall. A tired but jubilant Mayor William B. Hartsfield proclaimed March "Shop Downtown Atlanta Month," and spoke the words that gave rise to Atlanta's becoming known as the "City Too Busy to Hate." At the University of Georgia, holdouts had assumed a fall-back position: "You can't legislate morality." But that was all right with us. We weren't there because we wanted them to love us. We were there because we were entitled to get the education that our parents' taxes paid for as citizens of the state of Georgia.

As the winter of discontent gave way to a somewhat more hopeful spring, our spirits remained high. On weekends, when we went home, I often kept going—on speaking trips as far away as New York or as close by as some small Georgia town where the local NAACP branch wanted to see in the flesh what its dollar memberships from its hardworking rank and file had helped make possible. Hamp also traveled some, as when we went to St. Louis to receive the John B. Russwurm Award, named for the pioneering Black editor who established *Freedom's Journal*, the first Negro newspaper in America. But Hamp didn't enjoy public speaking as much as I did. For me, it was like a lifeline to a different world. And the incredible affirmation that I found everywhere I went always helped me through the cold spells, which, despite the thaw, still blew through from time to time. One day, as I sat in front of my mirror in my bedroom at school, I looked up and realized as I saw myself that I had not uttered a human sound in several days. I had gotten up, gone to class, sat down, taken notes, gotten up again, gone back to my room and studied, and gone to sleep. When I calculated how long it had been, I remember being mildly surprised and smiling to myself. I really was the right one to desegregate the University of Georgia, because I had no problem being alone. In fact, I had always relished my solitude. Except that up to now it had always been by choice.

At times, the "Queen" in me, the Turner High yearbook's "Most Popular," the Honor Society president and Delta soror missed all that activity and attention. I think I was most aware of how far out of my usual place I was when some of the white students who came to my room were those who may have been well-meaning but who also had nothing else to do. They were either the outcasts or the wall-flowers of their world, the girls who never got asked out either by other girls or by guys. We had little in common, because I had always been involved, but now they were making assumptions about me and expecting me to be grateful for their company. But if I was resentful—and I think I was on occasion—I tried never to let it show, in spite of the fact that there were times when I would have preferred to be alone, and occasionally I did not answer the door. It was at these times that I learned a lot about tolerance, which would serve me well in the days and years to come.

One of the trips that helped my spirits the most was when I flew to New York to receive an award from the Black Business and Professional Women's Organization. Jeanne Noble, who always seemed to know where I was and what I was doing, had arranged for me to stay with her. I really admired and respected Dr. Noble. Not only was she quite beautiful, with a perfectly shaped oval face, olive skin, and jet-black hair, which she wore in a soft, short "bob," but unlike a lot of women college professors who seemed to want to play down their femininity, Dr. Noble always wore the most beautiful, graceful clothes. And she was a gifted, lyrical speaker. She was a very popular national president.

The people honoring me had asked her what she thought I would like as a token of their appreciation. Always plugged in through the young women in the sorority, she suggested that they give me a gift certificate to Bloomingdale's, saying, "What young woman, even a pioneer, wouldn't enjoy a shopping spree at Bloomingdale's?" Well, she was dead right. I lost myself completely in the store's abundant racks, concentrating on the sale items so that I could double the value of my gift certificate.

But that wasn't the high point of the weekend. After shopping, I took a cab, as she had instructed me, and directed the driver to Morningside Heights, to an apartment near the Columbia University campus which she shared with another professor. Dr. Noble was already there, and told me to come in and freshen up, because we were going to have dinner and go "somewhere" for dessert.

"Somewhere" turned out to be 300 West End Avenue. When we got off the elevator and rang the bell, I still didn't have a clue what was up. But then the door opened and, standing in front of us, in a pink-cotton shirt and black pedal pushers, was the single most beautiful woman I had ever seen. Although I could scarcely believe it, I knew immediately it was Lena Horne. "Hey, y'all," she said, flashing a smile so bright and wide that it came out into the hall and wrapped itself around us.

I looked at Dr. Noble, who was beaming at what she had pulled off, and the two of us walked inside. Lena then threw her arms around me, saying how proud she was of me. I, for once, didn't know what to say.

Miss Horne led us into the living room, where she introduced her husband, the pianist Lennie Hayton, a charming white-haired man with a goatee. We chatted for a few minutes, I trying to sound as sophisticated as possible. Then Lena, as she insisted I call her after several "Miss Horne's," stood up. I almost fell off my chair when she announced that she was going into the kitchen to "fix" dessert.

I thought, This isn't possible. Lena Horne fixing dessert with her own hands, and serving it to me! But by the time she reentered the room, bearing plates of strawberry shortcake drowning in whipped cream, I had recovered enough to dig in with a passion.

In spite of all that, the real dessert was yet to come. Soon we were joined by Lena's son by her first marriage, Teddy, who was tall, caramel-colored, with hazel eyes, and one of the most gorgeous men I had ever seen. He, like his mother, was totally down-to-earth and easy to talk to. After a while, Dr. Noble rose to go, informing me that Teddy would be bringing me along later. I then learned that it had been arranged for Teddy to take me to Birdland, where I would soon hear my first live big band. Had Teddy not been so nice and easy to be with, I could easily have been overwhelmed by it all. But he played it cool, in the vernacular of the day, and so did I.

It was late when we got back to Morningside Heights, but instead of going right in we walked along the sloping hill that overlooked a sweeping expanse of rooftops that Teddy identified as Harlem. It had been a long time since "115th-Between-Lenox-and-Fifth," but I still remembered it warmly, as I would this day and night.

Despite the fact that the university was now officially desegregated, there was some confusion in the administration's minds over just how much was required under the court order. Trouble arose when I pressed the issue of eating in the cafeteria. I believed I had a right to eat there, and I was also having stomach problems, which my Atlanta doctor, Clinton Warner, thought might be related to my somewhat less than assiduous eating schedule. Some nights, when I was bent over double, Mrs. Porter would bring me a cup of hot tea and toast, and sometimes the advice that maybe a laxative might help. I still went over to the Killians' from time to time, but that was getting to be an effort, especially since a lot of the time Hamp was off playing basketball with some of the local brothers around dinnertime.

Since Hamp ate all his meals at the Killians' and had no interest in the matter when I raised it with him, I was the only one who had pressed the issue of the cafeteria with my weary and overburdened lawyer, who I thought was pursuing this secondary push for desegregation with less vigor.

Finally, he took the matter before Judge Bootle, and Bootle ruled that the desegregation order included all the university facilities, including the swimming pool. For my part, he could have left that out, since I had no interest in swimming, especially as I was not yet liberated enough to feel comfortable wearing my hair in its "natural" state. In fact, I didn't want to take *any* physical education, although it was required. I had already been excused from modern dance, because some of the students had objected to my being in the class. Once that happened, I thought I had a plan that would meet my objective without giving in to their racism. Using the old "rabbit in the briar patch" ploy, I selected swimming as my first choice and bowling as my second. I knew that concern had already been expressed by some of the students who didn't want to have to get in the water with the "nigger," and I also knew that the bowling alley used by the university belonged to the town of Athens and that the desegregation order didn't extend to town facilities. The result: no phys. ed. that quarter, although I eventually did end up taking archery and, when the girls had gotten a little more used to the idea that I was there to stay, tennis.

The same day Bootle ruled on the facilities, I walked the short distance from my dorm to the dining hall, and as the word spread and all eyes focused on me, I held my plate for one of the Black cooks to fill with food of the South that transcended race—spareribs, rutabagas, butter beans, and cornbread.

I walked over to an empty table and took a seat. But soon I was joined by a familiar face. Marcia Powell had been there at every critical stage of my desegregation of the university, and once again she was on the scene. I had come to recognize in Marcia some of the same qualities that I had seen in Bud Trillin—she was a human being who didn't see any conflict between her basic humanity and her capacity to be a good journalist. For some journalists, objectivity required distance. But Marcia had already learned that fairness was a far more desirable and attainable tenet of journalism, and she was doing her best to ensure it in my case. As a result, she was able to have an exclusive experience, getting a taste not only of the food but of the lingering meanness of some of those who were eating it. Indeed, that first meal in the cafeteria found Marcia more an object of scorn than me, as the white-girl traitor who gave them no alternative but to call her, openly and loudly, "nigger lover."

If she heard their words, I was never to know. We talked about the story of my eating in the cafeteria for the first time as if it were a thing apart, simply as two nineteen-year-old aspiring journalists who took themselves very seriously. Marcia and I would remain friends until she graduated, a year ahead of me, and beyond. And she was one of the people who would help me create and sustain some of the spirit that most college students take for granted but that I had to work at every remaining day of my college life.

Since 1954, the month of May has held a special place in the annals of civil-rights history. May 17, 1954, was the day the Supreme Court handed down the *Brown* decision, outlawing the concept of separate but equal. But the month of May 1961 seemed to have more than its share of stunning events and developments. On the day that astronaut Alan Shepard returned from his epic trip into space, which helped America partially redeem the pride it had lost to the Russians when they launched the first man into space, Robert F. Kennedy made a historic trip. He was to be the Law Day speaker at the invitation of the University of Georgia Law School.

Anticipation had been building in the state and on campus, and it had been mostly negative. Georgia's top politicians, fearing a "bombshell" speech on civil rights, boycotted the talk, and while the governor's assistant Griffin Bell, who more than a decade later was to be Jimmy Carter's Attorney General, was there, Bell failed to introduce Kennedy as scheduled. Within a few short months of assuming office, John F. Kennedy had already captured the nation's attention like no other President in recent memory, and so had his brother, the Attorney General. Young people, whether they liked the Kennedys or not, were captivated by their bold, take-control style, and I was no exception. I also dug Jackie—her confident sense of her own style, coupled with her impressive substance. I hadn't paid a lot of attention to Mamie Eisenhower; neither Eisenhower, in fact, had made much of an impression, except when the President sent troops into Little Rock. That had grabbed me in a visceral way, even as young and as preoccupied as I was with being young. But this was the first presidential election in which I was old enough to vote, and voting was serious business for us young Black people in the South. I had even thought ahead and obtained an absentee ballot, because I was going to be at Wayne in Detroit on Election Day. Part of what had been embedded in our consciousness was that voting was a right so precious that white people, in some places in Georgia, were still trying to keep the franchise exclusively their own. It emanated from our homes, from our pulpits, and from teachers like Mrs. Sutton and Miss Bradley. It was one of our rites of passage. Turning sixteen meant being able to get a driver's license. Turning eighteen meant being able to vote. On Election Day, after we voted, we got a little flag that said, I VOTED, HAVE YOU? and we attached it to our blouses or sweaters and wore it the entire day so that everybody would know we had carried out our duties as citizens. I think that's one of the reasons young Black students were able to get so passionately involved in the Movement. They had always been good citizens, and that enabled them to focus with a rare clarity of vision on their duty as citizens now: to see to it that the American South lived up to its citizenship responsibilities. They would teach by example, and it would be important enough for them to put their lives on the line, their bodies at the front. Capturing this feeling, we all now sang with gusto another Movement song: " . . . and before I'll be a slave, I'll be buried in my grave. And go home to my Lord to be free."

The battle over where we could go and what we could do on campus was still being waged, in spite of what Judge Bootle had said. But there was no question in my mind that I was going to see and hear Bobby Kennedy that day, and I convinced Hamp to go, too. I recall thinking of the irony of where the invitation to the Attorney General had come from, given the role of law students in the riot outside my dorm. I made my way to the auditorium, which was spilling over by the time I got there. Still, I managed to find a seat where I had a clear view of the dais and the podium where Kennedy would speak. Only polite applause greeted the introduction.

As the speech got under way, I could feel the tension rising, including my own. I was still not sure about how much in control these people were of themselves. Kennedy allowed as to how this was his first formal speech since taking office three months ago. He then moved on to display some of the already legendary Kennedy humor. "They have told me that when you speak in Georgia you should try to tie yourself to Georgia and the South," he said, "and, even better, claim some Georgia kinfolk. There are a lot of Kennedys here in Georgia, but as far as I can tell I have no relatives here and no direct ties to Georgia, except one. This state gave my brother the biggest-percentage majority of any state in the union, and in this last election that was better than even kinfolk."

I laughed, and so did more than a few other people, although it was not the kind of raucous political belly laughter that Georgians are capable of and prone to.

Then he went on: "We know that we cannot live together without rules which tell us what is right and what is wrong, what is permitted and what is prohibited. We know that it is the law which enables men to live together, that creates order out of chaos. We know that law is the glue that holds our civilization together. And we know that if one man's rights are denied, the rights of all are endangered. In our country the courts have a most important role in safeguarding these rights. The decisions of the courts, however, much as we might disagree with them, in the final analysis must be followed and respected. If we disagree with a court decision and thereafter irresponsibly assail the court and defy its rulings, we challenge the foundations of our society . . ." He went on to say that "respect for the law—in essence, that is the meaning of Law Day—and every day must be Law Day or else our society will collapse."

Kennedy talked about the challenge of international Communism—the defining context of the Cold War era in which we were living—and about organized crime. And then he entered the real danger zone—civil rights, which Southerners unabashedly viewed as a "comminist conspiracy." He started out by saying that "Southerners have a respect for candor and plain talk. They certainly don't like hypocrisy," and he proceeded to lay some candor on them.

He pointed out that "50 percent of the countries in the United Nations are not white; that around the world, in Africa, South America, and Asia, people whose skins are a different color from ours are on the move to gain their measure of freedom and liberty," and he continued: "From the Congo to Cuba, from South Vietnam to Algiers, in India, Brazil, and Iran, men and women and children are straightening their backs and listening—to the evil promises of Communist tyranny and the honorable promises of Anglo-American liberty. And those people will decide not only their future but how the cause of freedom fares in the world . . ."

I was thinking to myself at this moment, This is a helluva speech, and wondering how much he had been told about the University of Georgia "situation," if, indeed, he even knew our names. I vaguely heard, "In the worldwide struggle, the graduation at this university . . ." and then I heard words that almost knocked me off my seat: ". . . of Charlayne Hunter and Hamilton Holmes will without question aid and assist the fight against Communism, political infiltration, and guerrilla warfare."

From this point on, I sat there in a mild state of shock. What did he just *say*? I kept asking myself. Did I hear him right? Did he really say that our graduation was going to assist in the defeat of Communism? guerrilla warfare? And what was that other thing? Earlier, I had told myself that I would be content just to get into the auditorium and hear him speak; now I knew that before the day was over I was going to have to meet this man and shake his hand and let him know that I was the one he said was going to help defeat Communism.

The speech drew a standing ovation, although there was clear evidence of dissent. Some lawyers did not applaud, including one who had represented the state on many segregation cases. But I tried to make up for all those who were sitting on their hands. My hands were burning I was clapping so long and so hard.

As the crowd started to move, Dr. James Popovich, a friendly professor, came up to me and asked me what I thought of the speech. When I told him, he asked me if I wanted to meet the Attorney General. When I said yes, he said he would help me get over to the Continuing Education Building, where the Law Day Committee was holding a reception.

At CE, as it was known, it was hard to tell that there had been anyone who didn't believe the speech deserved the standing ovation that it got. Kennedy was surrounded by lawyers and would-be lawyers, all of whom were white, of course. But I waded right through the crowd, leaving my escort behind, and all of a sudden the waters seemed to part, and there, standing in the middle of the lobby, it seemed, were only two people, the Attorney General and me. I stuck my hand out confidently, but before I could introduce myself, he said, "You must be Charlayne Hunter. It's nice to meet you, and congratulations."

"It's nice to meet you," I said, and added, "And congratulations to you, too." I later learned that he had earlier asked to meet me.

Between the brother and the wife, the Kennedys so far had earned my precious vote. Two down and one to go.

Within the month, in Alabama, the Kennedy brothers would face the most serious test so far of their commitment to civil rights, devised by the Congress of Racial Equality (CORE). In December, the courts had outlawed segregation in buses and terminals serving interstate travelers. So the plan was that groups of Blacks and whites would board buses headed South. Whites would sit in the back of the bus and Blacks would sit in the front, which was illegal across the Mason-Dixon line. They would refuse to move if ordered, and at rest stops would use the white toilets and restaurants. CORE was counting on Southern law enforcement to act against the Freedom Riders, which would force the federal government to uphold the new law.

Thirteen riders boarded the bus on May 4 in Washington, D.C. Led by CORE executive director James Farmer, they included Student Movement veterans John Lewis and Diane Nash, both from Fisk University and the Nashville sit-ins, and James Peck, a forty-six-year-old white man who had been on an earlier Freedom Ride in 1947.

Ten days later, the riders were set upon by mobs in Anniston, Alabama, and Birmingham. One bus was firebombed; fortunately, its riders escaped. The others were not so lucky. There were reports that the police knew of the pending attack and stayed away on purpose. In the melee, one man was beaten so badly he was paralyzed for life. The Governor of Alabama told reporters after the attack: "When you go somewhere looking for trouble, you usually find it."

I remember looking at the picture of the burning bus on the front page of the newspaper the next day and thinking, It's really getting bad. It occurred to me that somebody could be killed. And yet, as I was thinking about it, I was also mentally preparing to deal with the news of such an eventuality. I knew that the students out there on the firing line were prepared to deal with that reality. None of them wanted to die, but they had said, and I believed them, that they were willing to die, if necessary, for their freedom. It went with the territory.

By now, there was never a dull moment on the civil-rights front, as my mother would say, and while the bigots on campus may have snoozed, they never slept. I could always count on some kind of ripple whenever there was any development in civil rights anywhere in the South. Whenever the Freedom Rides were in the news, for example, I braced myself and waited for some voice, from out behind a rock or a tree, to call out, "Freedom Rider," as I passed. Frankly, I rather liked the association.

Without any idea of what lies ahead, Hamp reacts to news of Judge Bootle's historic decision paving the way for him and me to become the first two Black students to enter the University of Georgia, January 6, 1961 (AP/WIDE WORLD PHOTOS)

My grandmother greeting me at the Atlanta airport as I arrived from Detroit hours after the court ruling

At the airport meeting, Attorney Donald Hollowell inspired our optimism with his confident assurance that victory was in easy reach

Our lawyers, Constance Baker Motley and Donald Hollowell, made a formidable team because of their skills and their dedicated belief that they had right on their side

Led by my mother and Horace Ward, and followed by "Tup" Holmes and Vernon Jordan, Hamp and I take our first steps onto the campus and into history
(AP/WIDE WORLD PHOTOS)

As students called out "Nigger, go home" and a variety of other unoriginal taunts, I found myself more bemused than angry or upset (AP/WIDE WORLD PHOTOS)

As we focused our attention elsewhere during registration, a boisterous crowd advanced on Dean William Tate's car, but the Dean routed them and prevailed (AP/WIDE WORLD PHOTOS)

In downtown Athens, about a half mile from my dormitory, along a street that abuts the campus, white students demonstrate against the desegregation order and our presence on campus (AP/WIDE WORLD PHOTOS)

Above: After completing my first "boring" class at the University of Georgia, I feel a sense of triumph and elation as I answer questions from the throng of reporters outside Meigs Hall (AP/WIDE WORLD PHOTOS)

Right: The forces of mass resistance picket the state capitol, protesting the desegregation order (AP/WIDE WORLD PHOTOS)

Leaving a class in the journalism building, I try to ignore the students, as well as the "escorts" who are there to protect me from them (ATLANTA JOURNAL AND CONSTITUTION)

Above: *The first two nights I stayed on campus, I was serenaded by students chanting words I had a hard time relating to myself* (AP/WIDE WORLD PHOTOS)

Right: *Tear gas was used outside my dormitory to disperse rioting students and "others" during my second night on campus* (AP/WIDE WORLD PHOTOS)

Following the riot, as I was led from my dorm by Deans Tate and Williams, after being suspended "for [my] own safety," I was so angry I was having a hard time maintaining my composure (AP/WIDE WORLD PHOTOS)

As we left campus in the patrol car, a statue of the Madonna provided my only solace when the unfairness and finality of it all hit me and I burst into angry tears (AP/WIDE WORLD PHOTOS)

After one of the worst night rides of my life, it was a relief to be back home, greeted by the waiting arms of my mother (DON UHRBROCK, *LIFE* MAGAZINE)

The man who came to my dorm looking for me, with a loaded gun, was captured and recommitted to the insane asylum (AP/WIDE WORLD PHOTOS)

JET

JUNE 22, 1961

**TEN BIGGEST
LIES ABOUT
FREEDOM RIDERS**

**Summer
Job Outlook
For Students**

CHARLAYNE HUNTER:
Pretty U. of Ga. coed
has summer job with
white Louisville paper

*Support for us was demonstrated in many ways, including this cover story about my
summer internship at the previously all-white* Louisville Times *in the June 22, 1961,
issue of* Jet, *the Black news bible*

On my first trip to Washington, D.C., I visited the Labor Department, where the Secretary, Arthur J. Goldberg, presented me with a $500 scholarship in recognition of my work in civil rights (AP/WIDE WORLD PHOTOS)

Graduation Day, 1963. Only Hamp and I could really appreciate the special sweetness of this final moment of our unique history together (AP/WIDE WORLD PHOTOS)

My mother had also bought me a car. The university officials had been adamant in prohibiting me from joining in the hitchhiking down from Ag Hill, where my dorm was located, the routine means of transport for girls without cars to the main campus. The man who had come to my dorm with the gun was now safely tucked away in a mental hospital, but no one was sure how many other nuts—certifiable or otherwise—were out there. For me, hitchhiking was dangerous, and whether the university officials really cared or just wanted to protect themselves from liability, they pressed the point. So, considering the stomach problems I was having, plus everything else, the car seemed a necessity.

Of course, all the students who were predisposed to believe that I was on a retainer from the NAACP (if they only knew!) assumed that the car was also bought by the NAACP. It not only wasn't but by now I was no longer a legal dependent of my father, and so it represented no minor strain on my mother's budget to have to buy a second car. We chose a stick shift because it was cheaper. The only problem was that I didn't know how to use a clutch. So the weekend we bought the car I had two days to learn how to drive it before making the 75-mile trek back to Athens.

My driving lesson was one of the few things that created any real tension between my mother and me. She went around the block a few times to show me how to do it, but finally gave up and called our neighbor down the street, Mr. Powell, who taught Driver's Ed at Washington High School. I got the concept after a while; it was the execution that was suffering. So I practiced all weekend—not enough, as it turned out—before I left for Athens. But my lack of skill didn't stop me. So early Monday morning, I pulled out of Mozley Place, my new car lurching and bucking like a bronco.

Both Hamp and I had problems with our cars. Once, in the more isolated Ag campus parking lot, students let the air out of all four of his tires. On another occasion, he had parked his car on a hill in front of the notoriously racist Kappa Alpha house—the ones who used to lower their Confederate flag to half-mast when we first came to the university. (Hamp, in fact, used to say he didn't understand how they could care so much about that flag, inasmuch as they left it outside in all kinds of weather.) It was late afternoon when he parked the car, and after locking it, he walked across the street to the German-language lab. By the time he returned, it was close to twilight, but he could see that his car had been blocked in front, on the back and on the sides.

"I looked up and I could see them all in the window; the look on their faces told me they knew 'they had the nigger,'" Hamp later recalled. "Then I saw that the car in front of me was open. I got in and knocked it out of gear and let it roll down the hill a bit. As I was getting out, I looked back up the hill and about thirty guys were coming out of the KA house. One called to me, a little guy: 'Hey, boy. Is that your car you just got out of?' 'No,' I answered. 'Well, what were you doing in it?' I said. 'Look, man, I don't want any trouble, I just want to leave. I'm tired.'

"The KA walked toward me, leaving his buddies behind. I was getting angry and, quite frankly, a little scared. What could I do? There were thirty of them. So I walked around to my glove compartment and reached in and got my flashlight and put it in the pocket of my London Fog. Then I turned around. The little guy who had been advancing on me was now backing up the hill. I said, 'Look, man, if you guys want trouble, you're going to get it. I'm leaving.' Then I let them see the bulge. They backed off and I stood there. I had only been back at my house five minutes when Dean Tate called and asked me if I had a gun.

"'Dean, do I have to tell you that?' End of conversation. But the word went out that I had a gun, and I never had another problem."

As for me, nobody ever confronted me; I would just get out of a class and find a tire flat, or, on one occasion, someone had taken a sharp object and scratched NIGGER on the driver's door. On the weekend, I got a paint job in Atlanta, and that never happened again.

Somehow, we made it through the first year completely intact. Hamp's grades were phenomenal; with courses in physics, zoology, psychology, etc., he had nothing lower than a B-plus. My grades were all over the place, from the D-plus I got from dozing in History to an A in the dean's Ethics class. By this time, I also had an offer to intern at the Louisville *Times*, the afternoon paper belonging to the Bingham family. The *Times* and the morning paper, the Louisville *Courier Journal*, in those days were considered bastions of liberalism, although there were no Negroes on the staff, and hardly any coverage of Black life in general—a matter taken entirely for granted. The letter to me came from the editor, Norman Isaacs. I was not aware at the time I took the job that I would be the first Negro ever to be hired. I discussed the prospect with Carl, because I really wanted to work on the *Inquirer* that summer. He encouraged me to go to Louisville and check it out, arguing that the experience of working on a "real" daily newspaper would make me even more valuable to the *Inquirer*, and that I would have plenty of time to make my contribution to the paper after I got back. Before making a decision, I flew to Louisville.

Norman Isaacs looked almost exactly like my idea of a managing editor, yet he was anything but crusty, which was part of the image I had. Instead, he was warm and persuasive. He had also taken the liberty (or the pains) to get in touch with a prominent Negro doctor and his wife about a place for me to stay. They had no children, were familiar with my case, and had already agreed by the time I was taken over to meet them.

John and Murray Walls were a classy-looking couple, on the other side of middle age, with a lovely, well-appointed house. They were on a first-name basis with Isaacs and seemed genuinely excited about the whole venture. They showed me a nice room on the second floor across from their bedroom which would be mine. I decided to come.

My eleven-year-old brother, Henry, drove up with me. He was accustomed to this, because he used to get out of school on Fridays in Atlanta, go straight to the bus station, and board a bus for Athens. From the bus station in Athens, he would walk the few blocks to the Killian restaurant, where they would feed him, and he would wait for me to finish classes so that I would have some company on the drive to Atlanta. (My baby brother, Franklyn, would come sometimes, too.) In Louisville, he stayed overnight, and I sent him back on the train.

I had no idea what the tensions were that my presence unleashed in the news room. The outrage over the paper hiring a Black person is captured in Susan E. Tifft and Alex S. Jones's book on the Binghams,

The Patriarch: "When the executive editor Jimmy Pope heard that Hunter was coming, he put up such a fuss that Mark Etheridge, the paper's publisher, was forced to fire him."★

I had a real hands-on summer at the paper. Many of the reporters were slightly older than I was and took me under their wing and taught me some of the rules of the game of being a reporter, not the least of which being how to consume several glasses of beer at lunchtime and be clever enough to fake it through the rest of the afternoon undetected. I didn't really drink at that time, and didn't much like the taste of beer, so I usually ended up also faking it during the instruction period. Two women reporters, Connie Courteau and Barbara Carlson, took a special interest in me, although everyone seemed to be trying to make me feel as much at home as possible.

There were two summer interns. Basically what we were supposed to do was keep ourselves occupied with busy work. Actually, one of the better intern assignments was collecting material for advance obits. The other intern, Betsy Trout, got relieved of that assignment early on, when she called a prominent businessman and, after being asked the purpose of her call, told him she was writing his obituary.

I didn't see much of my fellow intern after that, but I was determined not to spend my summer doing research on obits or anything else that kept me from getting out into the field. I wanted to be a reporter, and I wanted to get on with it as soon as possible. So far, I had not tried out for the campus newspaper, *The Red and Black*, essentially because I had had as much on my plate as I could handle the previous two semesters. But I was dying to try my hand at it, so I went into the morgue and found a service the paper subscribed to that provided ideas for features. I thought that with a little improvisation a couple of them had some potential, so I went to the editor and asked him if I could take a crack at them. One was about a renaissance in art among amateur painters, and the other was about a home for delinquent girls. Both ended up as prominent features, with pictures, in the paper.

I had one really traumatic experience. Now that they knew I liked

★ New York: Summit Books, 1991, p. 220.

to go out, the editors sent me to cover the retirement luncheon of a veteran Black teacher. When I returned, I sat down at the typewriter and banged out a story of several hundred words that began, "Both happy and sad, Mrs. So-and-so said goodbye today to X years of teaching," and went on to talk about her background and some of her experiences. When the story came back from the editor, it had been chopped down to one paragraph under a picture of the teacher. I went off.

"It's just because she's a Negro, isn't it?" I shouted to the editor, Leonard "Lefty" Lefkow. "That wouldn't have happened if she had been white."

Then Lefty went off.

"How could you accuse me of racism, for Chrissakes?" he said. "I'm Jewish."

"I don't know about all that. I just know this wouldn't have happened if she were white."

At this point, both of us were so overwrought that he stormed out one door into the big newsroom and I stormed out another. We both ended up on the street on opposite sides of the building, only to round a corner and spot the other advancing. We both turned on our heels and retreated back the way we had come.

Later that day, after I had calmed down and returned to my desk, the senior political reporter, a tall, rather arrogant guy named Richard Harwood, who rarely ever had anything to say, came over and asked me what had happened. As I was telling him, he walked over to the huge round wastebasket where all discarded carbons were thrown and fished out the carbon of my story. He read it without comment, then came and sat down on the edge of my desk. "This is a piece of shit," he said unceremoniously. "What kind of a sophomoric cliché lead is this, 'Both happy and sad . . .'? Didn't she say anything, do anything that you could describe?" For the next fifteen minutes or so I got an earful of good instruction from a guy who was, if not necessarily well loved, well respected in the business.

The next weekend, I was invited to Lefty's house for dinner. As I complimented his wife on the roast, Lefty, who had not spoken of the incident between us since it happened, said, "It's the same one you would have had last week if you hadn't pissed me off."

After two months, when I was preparing to leave, Norman Isaacs let me know to my delight that I would be welcome back the next summer, and probably as a reporter when I graduated.

Back in Atlanta, I took everything I had learned at the *Times* and applied it to my work at the *Inquirer*, which had just been written up in *Time* as the "Loud Voice in Atlanta." The article said in part:

> The Atlanta *Inquirer*, a Negro weekly, is neither a good newspaper nor a financial success. The paper has the same 15,000 circulation that it started with eleven months ago, and a full-time staff of only three. It is often badly written, amateurish, and narrow in its approach. As far as the *Inquirer* is concerned, the only important stories are those involving the Negro's aggressive pursuit of equality. But in this electric sector of human endeavor, the *Inquirer* is giving lessons to newspapers all over the South.*

By this time, the paper was raking muck to a fare-thee-well, scooping the "real" Atlanta papers on a regular basis. It wasn't that the stories weren't there for any inquisitive mind to see, it was that the white papers weren't looking. The *Inquirer* managed to expose in stark relief the emptiness of the *Atlanta Constitution*'s slogan that it "covers Dixie like the dew." It seemed as if in their minds not even the dew fell on Negroes and their communities.

By the time I got back, the paper had not only its regular cadre of student reporters like Julian Bond and John Gibson, Jim's younger, wilder brother, but also the services of some of the reporters who worked for the Atlanta *Daily World* owner, C. A. Scott. Some of them were frustrated at the way C.A. felt about the Student Movement and how he not only refused to cover it but aggressively opposed it, as when he directed his staff to join him in crossing their picket line to shop at the A&P. So they moonlighted for the *Inquirer* for professional and personal satisfaction. One of those was Paul Delaney,

* *Time*, June 30, 1961.

a recent graduate of Ohio State's School of Journalism, who had a wife and child and couldn't afford to work, as we did, for love. So Paul told the *Inquirer* he would freelance, and when he turned in his first piece, probably a rewrite of a sanitized piece he had done for the *World*, he told Julian to pick a nom de plume.

"Any suggestions?" asked Julian, who was talented but moved to industry only when there was no other choice.

"Naw," Delaney replied. "Just pick something that is as far away from my own name as you can get."

When the paper came out the next day, Paul's article was prominently displayed, but he almost had heart failure when he saw the nom de plume Julian had given him: P. Delano Lane. Oddly enough, even though almost everyone else figured out who it was, C.A. never did.

Meanwhile, I was assigned to the school story. My first piece was a report on how Negro students from overcrowded David T. Howard High School were having to pass near-empty white schools to attend classes in hot, airless, quonset-hut-type structures on an unpaved, dusty, red-clay lot in the middle of nowhere.

I was impressed with myself, because not only had I put in a call to the superintendent of schools for a comment but she had got on the phone and given it to me herself. The *Inquirer*'s power was growing, and Ira Jarrell was nobody's fool.

Although the students had accomplished their main goal, the fever of freedom and equality was still burning inside them every day as they took up new challenges or managed old ones. There had been stresses and strains in the old-line Black leadership, but most of that was in the past. Everywhere any of us went we found gratitude expressed in ways that kept us inspired. For example, a lot of planning and strategy sessions took place in Atlanta's new Black pride, an eating establishment owned by five brothers. Pascal Brothers Restaurant was the first really high-class place where Negroes could go when they were dressed up, and have a really good time after church or during the week. It had two dining rooms and the best fried chicken ever cooked in a pan.

Wylma was working there over the summer as a waitress, earning some money for her last year in school. Hunter Street, on the west side of town, was now a serious competitor to Auburn Avenue. Hollowell's office, the NAACP, and the *Inquirer* all were contributing to the new dynamism of Hunter Street, which was also where my mother worked. And everybody, sooner or later, passed through Pascal's. The restaurant was popular with the students not only because it was central but because during the sit-ins the Pascal brothers used to send food to the jail. The brothers were essentially self-made men, and one day James, the first among equals, a tall, light-skinned man with a soft, gentle manner, approached Carl Holman with a question. He said he had been following the Movement and listening to what the students were saying, and he realized that something was going on that was bothering him.

"There's this white vendor who comes in here all the time," James Pascal began. "And he always says, 'Hi, Jim, how you doing?' and I always say, 'Hi, how you doing?' I don't ever call him anything. Now, I've been hearing you-all talk about freedom and dignity and respect. And I've been wondering about that white man."

Mr. Holman remembered that at this point his mind leaped forward, and he was formulating an answer to the question he thought Mr. Pascal was going to raise, when he heard the conclusion of the question: "Do you think I should ask him to call me James?"

One day when I was having lunch, James Pascal saw me. He came over to my table and started to tell me how much he admired what I was doing at Georgia, and told me that if there ever was anything he could do for me, just let me know.

"Well, Mr. Pascal," I began, in jest, "there are a lot of nights down there when all I can think about is a chicken sandwich from Pascal's."

"Well, Miss Hunter," he said with characteristic deference, "any time of day or night that you even *think* you want a Pascal's chicken sandwich, you just call me and it'll be there as fast as we can drive to your dorm."

Similarly, one day I was walking up Auburn Avenue when the person I was with suddenly said, "There's Martin Luther King." In all this time, I had never met Dr. King. When he was demonstrating with the students, I was in Detroit, and since I had been back, the growing demands from his SCLC work had kept him out of Atlanta more than he was in. So I was very excited at this moment.

Hurrying up to the little knot of people surrounding him, I called out, "Dr. King, I'm Charlayne Hunter, and I just wanted to—"

Before I could finish my sentence, Dr. King had grabbed my hand and, pumping it energetically, said, "Oh, my dear, I'm so proud to meet you. You are doing such a magnificent job down there." He went on to talk about the importance of education to our people and why this case was so important in the struggle. Education, he said, was the key to our freedom, and then he generously thanked me again and wished me success.

I never got to finish my sentence, which would have been to tell him how proud of him I was, and how inspired I was by his leadership. But maybe he knew, or could see it in my eyes, which were now misty with tears.

chapter **18**

Bosch Breakthrough

No other Black students joined us in the fall, the beginning of our first full year. During the summer, Mary Frances Early, a music teacher from Atlanta, had transferred her graduate work from the University of Michigan, and the university officials put her in "my" space for the summer session. But when the summer term ended, she went back to Atlanta. And when I got back, my room was just as I had left it, and so was the university.

Hamp and I were beginning to change a little bit, however, possibly because we had gone our separate ways over the summer and possibly because each of us had, in Atlanta, separate cheering squads who related to us the way partisans of Washington High related to partisans of Turner. The third possibility is that each of us had developed different ideas about how we wanted to approach the next year and a half at Georgia. Hamp felt all along that he had something to prove at Georgia, that he wanted to show whites that they were wrong in their attitude that Blacks were inferior. He knew he had the equipment to do it. Hamp was a naturally brilliant student, one who was assiduous and who got it the first time he read it. He also had a very scientific, orderly mind—a real asset in the field he was pursuing. He still had no desire to get involved in anything beyond his studies. He also despaired of his encounters with the students, most of whom refused to acknowledge his presence with even as much as a routine "Hello." Whatever else Hamp was, he was a Southerner, the kind of human being who said "Good morning" even to strangers, making them feel they were connected to some unified whole. When Southerners who were a different color violated that tradition, it was almost more than he could bear.

We talked about why he felt I had been admitted and he had been rejected before the court order, and he said he thought it was because of the white Southern male's historic fear of the Black male, the fear that he would at some point "mess with" white women, one way or another, and, maybe even deeper than that, a fear of turnabout as fair play. "I was even more qualified than you," he said, asking rhetorically, "What else could have explained their behavior?" He eventually got over that hurt, but it would take many years.

There were also times during the year that Hamp found it hard to explain or accept my behavior. I had made a few friends now—Marcia Powell, Joan Zitselman, a graduate student in the Journalism Department, and some students from the Newman Club, a Catholic group. I had come to the realization that this was the only college experience I was ever going to have, and while I wanted to do well in my classes, I didn't feel I had to prove anything to anybody. I wanted to get the most out of everything, and I decided that the way to do that was to get personally involved. As for my performance, my brain, and my instincts, every aspect of my being had a hard time absorbing absolutes, the hard-and-fast principles of physical and biological science and mathematics. In Atlanta, Carl had put me in touch with Dr. C. B. Dansby, a legendary professor at Morehouse, who had volunteered to help me with math on weekends. The gentle tutoring helped a bit, and I was both awed by and grateful to "Pop" Dansby, as everyone called him. Maybe it was because my best form of expression was the written word and I had a hard time boiling down the plethora of words that spelled out these expansive concepts into simple ideas that you could identify by checking the boxes marked a, b, c, d, or e (all of the above), or f (none of the above).

When I did poorly on exams in those areas, Hamp accused me

of not studying hard enough. There were times when I thought, Well, maybe in some things I am inferior, but it has nothing to do with race or gender. For example, my mother was the mathematician in our family and was not only an excellent bookkeeper, often doing sums in her head, but also a "counter," a person who fills idle moments counting things visible to the eye that repeat, like the myriad lily pads on an Al Loving painting. I ended up on academic probation at the end of my junior year because I decided to take all my remaining science requirements the same term just to get them over with. Hamp used to come to my place to help me study, but we'd usually end up having arguments—especially when he would state an absolute principle of science and I would tell him that I refused to accept absolutes.

"But there are always buts," I remember saying to him.

"You have to accept absolutes in science; otherwise you won't be able to pass these tests," Hamp said, mildly exasperated.

"Well, I'm not going to, so I guess I won't," I responded defiantly.

The fact that Hamp always scored the highest on most tests in all his classes may have convinced the white students that he was not inferior, but it also caused them to dislike him all the more, since his grades raised a normally modest curve to a level that was beyond the reach of many of them.

On the other hand, a strange phenomenon occurred in my classes when I got a D or flunked with the other students. There was such a feeling of relief that I hadn't pulled a Hamilton Holmes on them that mutual commiseration ensued, and so did real communication.

Not that I didn't have some good grades. I even made dean's list one semester. And I always maintained a B-plus average in my major, even though Trillin thought some of the courses were for sissies. That didn't stop him from responding to my request, called in collect to him at *Time* headquarters in New York, for some of *Time*'s advertising brochures and related materials for a project I was doing for my Advertising class. I developed an ad campaign to market *Time* on Mars. I got an A-plus on the project and an A in the course.

I, too, thought there were too many journalism requirements— like makeup and typography and the magazine. But the Communications Law course was excellent, except for the fact that the professor hadn't updated his now-yellowed notes to include Alaska statehood. I also did really well in courses that challenged my imagination, like Greek Classical Culture. And in those, if I didn't set the curve, I made the mark my way.

For example, I was taking Greek Classical Culture one term, and the professor, Dr. Best, asked us to write a paper describing the shield the god Hephaestus made for Achilles at the request of his mother, Thetis, as he was going to war. I thought it was a dumb assignment, because Homer spent five pages describing it in the *Iliad*. But until I got the paper done, I thought of almost nothing else. That was generally my pattern. If something got my attention, it tended to be to the exclusion of everything else. I carried that paper around in my head, writing it for days, before I finally sat down one night and banged it out on a portable electric typewriter my mother's boss, the realtor Bob Wilson, had given me. Sometime after I had turned the paper in, and had really forgotten all about it, the professor walked into class. It was a class in which no one had spoken to me since it started, but I had become oblivious to that kind of treatment. I was sitting in my seat and had just popped a piece of Mary Jane candy in my mouth when I heard the professor calling my name. As was the case with most of my professors, I had no idea where he stood on the desegregation issue. But now I decided that he was about to take me publicly to task for eating in class, thereby revealing that he had been a racist-in-waiting, just lying in the cut for the perfect moment to embarrass me. The whole class came to attention and fell silent in anticipation.

"Yes, Dr. Best?" I answered, swallowing the Mary Jane whole.

"So you think Achilles' shield looked like a painting by Hieronymus Bosch, do you?"

At this point, there were only two people in the room who knew what he was talking about, and one was me; you could see it on the faces of everybody else in the room. Now I was convinced that the professor was about to humiliate me—only worse than if it had been about the Mary Jane. He was going to humiliate my mind.

"Well, Miss Hunter," he said, "I don't know where you came across Hieronymus Bosch, but this is the best paper I've read in a long time."

There was a palpable change in the atmosphere in the room, and while Dr. Best moved on immediately to the topic of the day, at the end of the class I was surrounded by students wanting to know where I got the idea for the paper and how I'd done it and what was I going to do next. And who, by the way, was that guy he mentioned, Botch something or other.

Dr. Best was cordial, but some of the professors were more than cordial. Two English professors in particular went out of their way to visit me in the early, uncertain days, and continued beyond those uncomfortable times when it was hard to find words that didn't seem false or forced. Both invited me to their homes. Dorothy McCullough and Frances Wallis were friends on the English Department faculty, exceptions to Trillin's characterization of the English Department as "still reflecting the influence of the Southern Agrarians, a group of Vanderbilt University English professors and writers who believed for a while in the twenties that everything would be all right in the South if the cultured benevolence that they attached to plantation days could just be brought back."*

I would see the two professors together at first, but eventually, since Miss Wallis lived in an apartment building across the street from Center Myers, I saw more of her. Both of them provided a different kind of respite for me, talking about writers and poetry. I loved Robert Frost—especially the poem he had recently written, "The Gift Outright," for the Kennedy inauguration ("The land was ours before we were the land's . . ."), and I had just discovered Yevgeny Yevtushenko. But Miss Wallis, who had a wonderfully wry sense of humor and a kind of loving disdain for many of her less-than-serious English students, was also a Catholic, so we talked a lot about religion, too.

Miss Wallis reminded me a lot of Miss Sutton, in that teaching was her life and she did it with a committed passion. More than any other professor at Georgia, Miss Wallis came closest to being a real confidante, someone whom I could complain to about the food, the faculty, or fickle friends. Like Carl Holman, she could help you arrive at a solution on your own, without being judgmental.

* Trillin, pp. 168–9.

A couple of other professors also invited me to their home for dinner. One was a young artist, Joe Schwartz. His wife, Jean, had attended the trial every day. I liked the Schwartzes—especially because they didn't feel bound to the school's sillier rules or traditions. Joe had helped organize the Faculty Resolution, and at the trial Jean had been friendly and reassuring to my mother without knowing exactly who she was. My mother had mentioned this to me and described the woman as a professor's wife who was prematurely gray. I put it all together that night. Also, at dinner, they offered me a martini. Drinking was strictly against the rules for university students, and for a moment the thought crossed my mind that maybe I was being set up, but it quickly vanished. I drank the martini, but then spent the rest of the night throwing up. Martinis and I have never mixed.

I didn't hold that against Joe. When he sent word through a mutual friend that he wanted to do my portrait, I agreed right away and spent many delightful hours sitting in his studio. We talked about art and all the things that I used to talk about back in the old days at Wayne. In fact, when I was deciding what outfit I wanted to be immortalized in, I picked a well-worn, oversized maroon crew-neck sweater. Back to bohemia.

Hamp and I were often invited to functions at Westminster House, where the director, the Reverend Corky King, had formed Students for Constructive Action. They used to have sessions on Sunday night where they would try to promote a full and frank exchange of views, but I soon got turned off. As I told Trillin, "They kept making statements that started with 'you people.' There was a lot of Cause talk that I don't believe in, and I just never felt I could be a human being over there. I told them I get tired of causes, and they were shocked." I think Hamp gave it a shot, but in the end he gave up on it, too.

I spent a lot of time at the Newman Club, the Catholic organization that had its quarters in one of the old houses on Lumpkin Street, a stone's throw from my dorm. One semester, when they were having an election, a hefty food-technology student from Hempstead, Long Island, who was running for secretary, approached me and asked if I would be his campaign manager. I told him I thought

I would be a good campaign manager, but I wondered if he had considered the possibility that I might also be a liability. Tony assured me that he had, and had come out just where he was: he wanted me to manage his campaign. I went into action, although Tony didn't have any outstanding arguments for why he should be secretary. So my approach was to talk generally about the principles of Newmanism and somehow at the end attach Tony to them like a postage stamp.

Still uncertain about where everybody's head was on my presence generally and my participation specifically, I nevertheless took a deep breath, got up before the group, and made my case. Tony won the election and vowed to be my friend for life. From time to time, he'd drop by Center Myers or stop in the dining hall and we'd make small talk. Sometimes he'd make a smart remark to somebody who shot us a look. And sometimes I thought he was being unnecessarily provocative. But when I'd speak to him about it, he'd talk about not being able to understand these white Southerners and their attitudes. It was difficult to understand this kind of thing, when you came from up North. I kept trying to explain it to him.

During the course of this, I was called into the dean's office and grilled about whether I was dating any white boys. I couldn't believe it. Who could she possibly be talking about? The relationship I had with Tony was far from romantic. But I had learned a valuable lesson: they were watching everything.

One day, Tony dropped by at the dorm. I could tell immediately that something was wrong, because he looked like a big old teddy bear, and when he was sad his big old shoulders fell, rounded and droopy. He started out by talking about where he had come from, and how as an Italian he had been raised not to think ill of any race or group. Then he went on to say that the guys in the dorm were not like that. They were all from the South and had a different viewpoint. They were putting a lot of pressure on him to stop talking to me. It was getting to him, he said, because the threats were escalating. It would be different if there were other guys like him, but he was the only one.

Later, I found a note from him on my car with an apology for not being able to see me anymore. As I told Trillin afterward, "I saw him later and told him I thought the note was childish. Maybe that wasn't fair; I couldn't really blame him. But I just didn't have any sympathy for people who ask for trouble and then can't take it."

A couple of times during that first full year at Georgia, I invited a date from Atlanta to come down for an event. Once, when the guy—a student at Morehouse—agreed to come, the university refused to allow it. Another time, I invited a reporter from the *Atlanta World*, who had been asking me out in Atlanta, to come down for a football game. He said he'd get back to me, but I never heard from him again.

Whenever I went home, and to a dance or some other public function, I was always a center of attention. I didn't know anybody who wasn't proud of what I was doing—even the Hamp partisans —but that kind of constant, hovering, excuse-me-I-know-you're-dancing-but-I-just-wanted-to-say kind of attention was perhaps more than anyone could reasonably expect a healthy twenty- or twenty-one-year-old male to deal with.

After a while, I got tired of making the trek to Atlanta every weekend, and eventually hardly went at all, unless I had a speaking engagement or had to fly somewhere. I still spent a lot of time alone, but I had enough friends now that it was by choice. I never went for days anymore without talking to someone. On the other hand, I don't think Hamp ever spent a weekend in Athens. Friday afternoon, he hit the road and was gone for the whole weekend.

But in times of crisis Hamp and I always came together. Throughout the year, I was in and out of the infirmary with continuing stomach problems. Whenever I was admitted, it seems Hamp was always the first person in my room, wanting to know what was wrong and asking if I needed anything. By this time, his grandfather, a wiry old gentleman who looked a lot younger than his seventy-seven years, was on a campaign to get Hamp and me involved with each other romantically. Once old Doc Holmes called me and told me he'd get me any kind of car I wanted if Hamp and I got married. But we were just too different. Still, in spite of our disagreements, I had come to truly love Hamp, as I did my brothers, Henry and Franklyn. Our relationship was very special, and I never developed another like it, even with the desegregation pioneers who followed us. For example, one night I was summoned to the phone in my dormitory. When I got to the phone, the voice on the other end said, "Hi! It's James."

"James who?" I asked.

"James Meredith."

A few days earlier, James Meredith had had to be escorted by federal marshals into Ole Miss, in an atmosphere of small-scale warfare, the worst case of mob action in a school-desegregation case so far, and one that would sorely test the new Kennedy Administration's mettle. Mississippi Governor Ross Barnett, like Georgia's Vandiver, had his holdout slogan: "Never, no never." And as violence escalated on Ole Miss's campus on Sunday night, September 30, the state troopers left the scene and uncontrollable rioting erupted. One French reporter was killed, shot in the back.

I had seen much of this on television, and had felt mild reverberations at Georgia. So when this voice on the other end claimed to be James Meredith, I thought it was just another crank. But for some reason I didn't hang up.

"Who is this, really?" I implored on the telephone.

"It's really me, James Meredith."

At a loss at this point, I said, "Prove it."

Meredith said, "Hold on and listen."

I then heard in the background noises that were familiar—the popping of firecrackers, and possibly bullets—and through the cacophony of sound, I could make out, "Two, four, six, eight."

A confident Meredith returned to the phone. "Convinced now?" he asked, with about as much humor as I ever heard from him.

"Oh my goodness," I blurted out. "It *is* you. How are you?"

Meredith told me he was fine, and was calling just to touch base with a fellow traveler. We had never met, and I was touched by this gesture. For him, the noise outside would be uglier and go on longer, and under my breath, as I hung up, asking him to stay in touch, I said a little prayer. I was well aware of the possibility that he could be killed. He survived, and we met for the first time a little over a year later, when even in Mississippi Blacks had a new place.

In the spring semester, Mary Frances Early returned and was assigned to my room. She was nice, but I resented what the university was doing. For the most part, as a graduate student in music, Mary Frances and I didn't run into each other on the campus much. In the suite, she was quiet, and we got along just fine.

At the end of the spring term, I didn't need to wait for my grades to know that I was going to be on academic probation. By the time they arrived, I had already considered the options: summer school or not graduate on time. As tough a choice as it was, I was determined to graduate with Hamp. So I took a deep breath and got ready for a new adventure in Athens.

chapter **19**

"An Idle Gift"

The hot, sultry Athens summer brought an unexpected gift: the evoc-
ative sights, sounds, and smells of my small-town childhood, the
almost overpowering sweet smell of honeysuckle and banana shrub
seducing buzzing bumblebees and yellow jackets; the screeching cries
of crickets emanating from every shrub and bush; clouds of black
starlings producing shadows wherever they flew over the dusty red-
clay haze. This was the part of the South that I loved, that made me
happy to be a Southerner, that left me unaffected by the seamier side,
which would deny I could have pride in anything but Aunt Jemima.
I was also taking courses that I really enjoyed and, with the exception
of the Classical Culture of Rome, that seemed more appropriate for
a summer session: the History of Journalism and Radio/TV.

One day, I was having a sandwich in the coffee shop at the
Continuing Education Center, the building where I had met Robert
Kennedy, and the one that housed the state's public television station.
The gifts of summer also made CE a more hospitable place, situated
as it was next to a lawn of flowering hedge bushes and giant oak
trees. At one point, I was approached by a guy, blond and slender,
dressed in army khaki trousers and a short-sleeved white shirt. Smil-

ing, he asked me if he could join me for lunch. I didn't have any idea where this guy had come from, but he seemed harmless enough, so I said, "Sure." He told me that his name was Walter Stovall and that he was in the Journalism School, too, revealing that he knew something about who I was. He said he was from Douglas, a small south Georgia town, and was fresh from the army and two years in Paris. Somehow I found the image of him in Paris rather amusing, since he spoke with such a heavy Southern accent. I was also mildly amused that this son of the Deep South spoke of the University of Georgia with something bordering on disdain.

From time to time during the rest of the summer, I would run into Walter, and when I did, we would usually end up talking. I remember once asking him to say something in French, partly to be amused, only to hear out of his mouth a language so beautifully accented that it contained not a trace of roots in the "whites only" South that went back nearly three hundred years. It seemed to transform him, too, causing me to let down just a little of the guard I always maintained in that environment. Hmmm, I thought, here's somebody different.

Meanwhile, I was having a ball with an assignment for the Classical Culture of Rome. I had to write a paper, and I had decided to write about Juvenal, the vitriolic Roman satirist, but à la Hieronymus Bosch, I decided to use him to draw a comparison between the ancient society of Rome and the present. It would be a paper that would allow me to write about many of the poets and authors I had been discovering and discussing with Miss Wallis, like Lawrence Ferlinghetti, the poet of the current "Beat Generation"; Allen Drury, author of the recent Pulitzer Prize-winning book *Advise and Consent*; Tennessee Williams; and the Black author Willard Motley, whose book *Knock on Any Door* was nowhere in the Georgia library but had been given to me by Carl Holman.

After quoting lengthy passages from those authors, strung together with brief lines of connective tissue, I produced a thirteen-page paper, ending with these words:

> Is this not enough? Or shall the writer continue? She thinks
> not, for as Juvenal's words appear on these pages alongside

the writers of the present day, in their discussions of satire, homosexuality, the vileness of the city, the poor people, women, and avarice, it almost seems as if either one or the other has transcended time and the society of Ancient Rome become the society in which we now live, and they are one.

When the professor returned the paper to me at the end of the summer, she wrote: "A large part of this paper consists of quotations, but I am giving you A because of its originality and your initiative in finding the material. Written report A, Oral report A, Average A."

Back in Atlanta, I eagerly showed the paper to my mentor, Mr. Holman, who promptly said he thought I had gotten away with murder.

When the fall term of my senior year opened, I was not only still in the freshman dorm, I now had two freshmen roommates, energetic seventeen-year-old Black girls from Atlanta: Alice Henderson and Kerry Rushin. They were joined at Georgia that year by Mattie Jo Arnold, a graduate student (and fellow Turner High-ite) who was living off campus; Mary Blackwell, a freshman from Athens who lived at home; and Harold Black, a freshman who lived in a men's dorm. I thought it was great that some of the awful stigma Blacks had attached to Georgia since "that night" was starting, however slowly, to erode, as evidenced by the presence of this handful of students. But I was furious with the university for continuing to deny me my rightful place this year in a dorm for seniors. Every now and then, I think, I took it out on "the girls," as we all called them— especially when I was trying to study in my room and they were engaged in a marathon giggling session next door or were listening to music at a decibel level that I had outgrown. But although they didn't have to contend with the same degree of resentment that Hamp and I had faced our first year, they were still extremely vulnerable, and I was conscious of their fragility, so I would sometimes share with them how I dealt with some of the same situations they were now encountering and listen whenever one or the other or both of my roommates had a problem. Suddenly I had two little sisters, and I felt responsible for them. They didn't have a car, so I used to drive them to and from class, or to town occasionally to eat at Killian's. If I wasn't around, they'd call Hamp, and he'd fetch them and bring them back.

This was the semester I also decided to take my advisor's suggestion and get some experience working on the student newspaper, *The Red and Black*. I wasn't sure how I would be received, since there were still only a handful of students in the J School that I had had more than casual conversation with. Also, I didn't want to work on the editorial side, because, as I later told Trillin, "I would have had to go out and talk to a lot of people I didn't want to talk to. I had already had the problem in one of my journalism reporting classes of not being able to get any of the practical experience the other students got by covering events or the courts and other things that took place in still very much segregated Athens. But I had seen Tom Johnson, the business manager, around, and while I didn't know where he stood on the "issue," either, he seemed like a nice enough kind of guy, so I offered myself to his section, and for a while I worked with him, making up page dummies and doing other such work. I told the story of my short unhappy life with *The Red and Black* to Trillin:

"We usually worked Tuesday nights, making up the ad dummy for the editorial people to fill the next night. But one Wednesday night, when we went to the weekly criticism, the editor asked everybody to stay, because they were short of people. Tommy had left for some reason. I stayed, but I just sat there. They went around asking everybody if he could print. Nobody could, so I finally said I could print, just because I wanted something to do. I got through with the printing, and the editor kept asking people to do things, but he would never ask me. So I just left. I never went back."* It wasn't my place.

Early in the fall term, I ran into Walter Stovall again. He was standing in a long registration line snaking glacially into a building. I was glad to see a familiar and friendly white face. "Walter!" I yelled,

* Trillin, p. 78.

breaking into a run. We threw our arms around each other, and as we enthusiastically exchanged pleasantries, we noticed after a few minutes that the line had parted on either side of us by a space of ten yards and everybody was staring at us with expressions of extreme shock.

Maybe that's part of the reason we continued to see each other; aside from enjoying each other's company, we enjoyed our small act of defiance. In the ensuing weeks, we met often for coffee at the Co-op, a cramped, dark, pine-paneled room with booths, down a small hill from the J School. I'm pretty sure I saw Walter wince one day when we filed down the serving line and he ordered a coffee with cream and one of the Black attendants shouted, "One high yellow."

We also shared our first crisis. For seven days in October, the Cold War once again invaded our little north Georgia world as President Kennedy and Nikita Khrushchev duked it out verbally over the U.S. discovery of secretly installed Soviet missiles in Cuba. Stuck on the mirror of the dresser in Walter's room was the telegram from his draft board giving notice that he might be recalled to the service of his country at any moment.

"I know about your French, but how's your Spanish?" I thought of saying to help relieve the tension. But Walter's now sober demeanor caused me to think better of it. In fact, he was more attuned to the crisis than most students, especially since he had recently returned from Europe, where he had been almost close enough to touch the Berlin Wall that had just gone up, a defining symbol in the East-West Cold War competition. Attuned as I was to his sensitivity and concern, rather than making a quip, I let him borrow my tiny portable radio, which, more than me, was his constant companion until Khrushchev blinked, recalling the Soviet missile-bearing ships bound for Cuba and agreeing to dismantle the arsenal on the ground.

Being a journalism major, I probably would have had more than a passing interest in that crisis, but as a result of Walter's near-intimate connection, I got a wider glimpse, a more worldly look. Without my realizing it at first, we were developing a bond that was taking me places I'd never been before. And it was exciting, a staple of anyone truly serious about becoming a reporter. In the cafeteria, occasionally at Killian's, and on long rides, often with Joan Zitselman, in the dazzling Southern autumn countryside, through Walter I began to get a glimpse of the white world of the South that I had never seen, one that had its share of deprivation, too. Before Walter left Douglas, for example, the environment he described was a stultifying society that in its own way kept most whites in their place—self-centered, socially homogeneous puritans, whose worldview was restricted to the Protestant Church on Sunday and a limited range of weekday activities that included running small businesses or farming, regular bridge parties, the occasional round of golf at the country club, and Friday-night football.

Everybody wrapped himself in the Confederate flag but the Black citizens, who washed and ironed it. Except for their value as manual labor, they were hardly regarded at all, unless they were characters, like Coot Morris, the strongest man in town, who in his younger days was reputed to have been able to lift a Ford engine under each arm. The few Blacks who managed to get their way did so because of a shrewd understanding of the relationship between erstwhile master and erstwhile slave. Like Faulkner's Dilsey, they endured.

Walter also provided a window into small-town white public education: it was designed to teach you to read, write, and do your sums, and prepare you to go to a non-threatening, non-challenging place like the University of Georgia, where you would be educated to take your place in that little world, thrive in it, and see to it that it continued in perpetuity just as it was. Walter said that, unlike me, he had never heard of the College Boards until he sat down to take them, and thought he was competing for a scholarship whose sponsors included Sears, Roebuck. When he invited me to the first football game I ever attended at the university, he explained to me that for people back home as well as in Athens, football was close to a religious experience. At Georgia, loyalty to the football team was evidence of loyalty to the university.

Hamp hadn't been to a game before, either, so we called him up. Walter recruited Joan Zitselman, who had a minor crush on him, and the four of us took our seats in the student section on the thirty-yard line a few rows down from the band. The only time anybody looked our way was when we were the only ones to remain seated when the band played "Dixie." Of course, we were also the only ones looking at the other group not standing: the Black citizens of Athens who had come to the game and still had to sit in the segregated section known as the "crows' nest." I think the only one of us who really enjoyed the game was Walter. Tech won in a romp, and he was as out-of-place in the Georgia section as Hamp and I, because he was a Tech fan.

If there had been anything other than study that Hamp had wanted to do at Georgia, it was play football. When he broached the subject early on, shortly after we were admitted, the dean told him it wasn't a good idea, that it was entirely possible that someone from either the other team or his own might try to kill him. It was widely known that Hamp had wanted to play football, and there had been equally strong opposition from whites. But Georgia had been on a long losing streak, and one Georgia alumnus had been heard to say of the stocky, athletic-looking Hamp, "The more I look at that nigger, the whiter he gets."

As the fall wore on, Walter and I spent more and more time together, taking long drives in the countryside or making dinner in his apartment on fraternity row. I had become an avid J. D. Salinger fan, and he was a fan of Stephen Vincent Benet. I read aloud from *Franny and Zooey*, and he from *John Brown's Body*. We laughed at the strange differences in our college careers, I having had to go to court to get my education; he having flunked out of two or three places, starting with Vanderbilt, before arriving at Georgia, where he was now on the dean's list.

What I found increasingly appealing about this strange guy was that he had a sense of honor that was as deep and old-fashioned as his manners. To him, being unfair was dishonorable, and he saw clearly that segregation was, above all, unfair. Every now and then, I thought about the emotional and physical danger zone I was entering, and about the other relationships I had in other places. But I was also feeling the weight of two years of being a symbol, and Walter was there within reach, treating me like a desirable human being. Somehow, I said to myself, it will all get sorted out; I'm just too tired right now to care.

When the Christmas holidays rolled around, I gave Walter a copy of *John Brown's Body*, inscribed "From a Brown Girl Bearing an Idle Gift," after one of the verses we both loved. Then we went our separate ways—but not for long.

In Atlanta, where the long days of implementing the agreements were proving less exciting than the days of challenge and confrontation, a sense of ennui had set in. Carolyn had been married to a dashing young army lieutenant, who had whisked her off to Hawaii, from where she was writing letters to Wylma and me about the moonlight walks on the beach she was enjoying as part of an extended honeymoon. Wylma was working on her master's degree in Education. Other weary veterans of the Atlanta Movement Wars had taken refuge in fellowships or other vehicles that removed them from the struggle, some temporarily, others permanently.

Some of those who remained took part in the last gathering of its kind I was to attend in Atlanta: the Emancipation Proclamation Services at Union Baptist Church. It was one of the galvanizing events of the year for Black people, and I had been asked to introduce the speaker, Donald Hollowell. While it was an emotionally moving day, I decided when it was over that it was the last civil-rights event I was going to participate in for a long time. Not only was I tired, I was frustrated. Walter had come to visit, and some of my friends were wildly disapproving. I found the things they said to be racially insensitive and totally at odds with the Movement position articulated by Dr. King: that people should be judged not by the color of their skin but by the content of their character. Besides, wasn't anybody concerned with my personal happiness? How much of a sacrifice was I supposed to make? And who was in a position to judge?

That was how it had been for a while, even unrelated to Walter. People like Carl Holman and Attorney Hollowell and Wylma and her family continued to act as buffers between me and any of the pro-Hamp critics. Carl also tried his best to see that the promises of financial support made by organizations and members of the community were kept. I was no longer eligible for support from my father, but I hated having to beg, and when Carl took me one day to see Johnnie Yancey, a prominent Black Atlanta woman who was in a position to help, when she started to ask me what I needed, I couldn't bear to tell her.

To be sure, some groups did come through, like the Elks, which paid the $83-a-term tuition for a year, and the Deltas, who also paid room and tuition for a term. I once got to go to Washington, where then–Secretary of Labor Arthur Goldberg presented me with a $500 check from the United Packinghouse Workers, the first annual Russell Bull Scholarship grant, established to honor the late union pioneer. But these amounts, however much appreciated, fell far short of what I needed to help defray my accumulated expenses of some $1,500. Of course, my mother was doing the best she could and never once complained of the strain she was under.

While I sometimes earned a few dollars when I spoke somewhere, I was also growing weary of traveling. I just wanted to finish this last year and live for a while in blissful obscurity, preparing myself for the next phase of the struggle; for what I now regarded as a near-sacred calling—providing the kind of information that would help people understand one another as human beings, acknowledging but affirming their differences, in the hope that never again would a Black child of the South have to cross the kind of burning sands that Hamp and I had at Georgia, to take our rightful place. My experience at the center of the news, along with my work on the *Inquirer* and at the Louisville *Times*, had transformed my Brenda Starr fantasy. Journalism might be as exciting, as mysterious, and as much fun as it was in the comics, but it also had the awesome power to help change things. By now, the Movement had endowed me with a sense of mission that was bigger than myself, and I felt I had to lose my public self in order to find my place in that new world where other people's lives would be the focal point, no matter their color or status in life. If I were going to be known to the world, I wanted it to be through the efforts of my ability, rather than through something that but for the time and the place should have been an ordinary, routine occurrence. I wanted to be famous one day, but not simply for going to college.

Sometime in the spring, Trillin arrived to interview us about our two and a half years for a book he was writing. He had spoken to me once on the phone about it. While I wasn't all that enthusiastic about reliving the experience, because it was Bud, I agreed to do it. We discussed the idea on a trip I made to New York to talk with the editor of *The New Yorker*, William Shawn. His office had gotten in touch with me and asked if I would be interested in coming to the city to discuss the possibility of employment. I loved *The New Yorker*, not least because I thought of it, in part, as Salinger's magazine. That's where I first read "Franny" and also "Zooey," and I had just spent a whole term devouring everything else that Salinger had written. In New York, I met with Leo Hofeller, the personnel editor, and then Mr. Shawn, who was the gentlest, most soft-spoken man I had ever encountered. It was hard to imagine him as the genius who had molded and shaped some of the world's best writers, because he didn't exhibit any of the gruff cynicism that I had heard in Journalism School was another hallmark of a good editor.

A lot of our conversation revolved around his questions about how I had survived the two and a half years at Georgia, rather than how I might fit in at a place like *The New Yorker*. At the time, I was unaware that there were no Blacks on the staff, but Mr. Shawn's caring questions and responses put me totally at ease, and when I was offered a job later by Mr. Hofeller, I had no hesitation at all about taking it. He explained that I would be hired to do no more and no less than all the other young graduates from schools like Vassar and Bryn Mawr. They started out as editorial assistants but could go anywhere their ambition, talent, and energy could take them. Because of Mr. Shawn's interest, the meetings lasted much longer than I had anticipated, and after I had been there a while Bud called to make sure I hadn't gotten lost. I was a little embarrassed that I had received a personal phone call, so I quickly explained who he was and told them about his project. As Bud was about to depart for Athens, he dropped me a note that said something to the effect that "as fate would have it" Shawn had gotten in touch with him after I left through Gerald Jonas, a budding poet and an old friend of Trillin's at *The New Yorker*, and he was going to be doing the book first as a series of pieces for *The New Yorker*, where he had just been hired.

I was happy to see Trillin; less happy to answer all his questions. But I tried to, as fully as I could. Still, I wasn't in the best of moods. As an act of love and of defiance, Walter and I had decided to spend the rest of our lives together, not as concubine and master, but as every segregationist's nightmare, husband and wife—only we couldn't tell anybody yet, because such marriages were illegal in the state and also unacceptable at the university. Walter had already been summoned to the dean's office, where he had been grilled about our relationship. Dean Tate's message, which took several hours to deliver, was this: He was as sympathetic to the plight and aspirations of Black folks as anybody in the world ("I was asked one time to speak at a nig' funeral," Walter told me he said. "You know, they don't ask just any white man to speak at a nig' funeral"), but he was deeply concerned that public knowledge of our courtship might touch off an "incident" (read "riot") at graduation. "What I'm saying," Dean Tate said, "is don't rock the boat."

I got the same treatment from the Dean of Women. But it was too late. We would show them, and all the hypocrites in the world, how we lived by our beliefs and didn't just pay them lip service.

Still, the incident added to my concern about whether I would ever be able to establish an identity as anything other than a symbol. Whereas Hamp had wanted to show "them" that he was as good as they were, I now desperately wanted to be esteemed for the abilities I now felt confident about, rather than for some moment in history when I felt I had done no more than countless other Black students would have done, given the chance. One history professor in particular was really getting on my nerves, because all he ever talked about was the role he and the faculty played in the "desegregation crisis." Clearly it was the high point of his life, but was it going to be the high point of mine? His life was half over; mine was just beginning.

Yet, as usual, the community that had above all nurtured me and helped me stay on my course somehow beckoned me at this critical moment and helped me put it all, once again, in perspective. The help came by way of a favor to Vernon Jordan. After much pleading from him, I accepted a speaking engagement for the NAACP in Tampa, Florida. My father, whom I had not seen during the two and a half years I had been at Georgia, had just retired from the army after twenty years. He was now pastoring a church in Tampa.

A cast of what seemed like thousands had been lined up for the event: the NAACP's regional conference, including Hamp, James Meredith, and Harvey Gantt, who desegregated Clemson College in South Carolina in 1963. But in the end, the other people had previous commitments, and only Meredith and I showed up.

My father didn't come to the airport, and it wasn't until several hours later, when we arrived at the gym where the event was being held, that we met. When he saw me, his face lit up and he rushed toward me, grabbing me up into his arms. "Baby," he said, "you look just great." Before I could say much of anything, he had proudly begun introducing me all around: "This is my daughter, Charlayne." He didn't have to say it; the pride was as much in his voice as when I looked from him to my grandfather, who was also there, and saw the power of the genes in the "Hunter mouth."

Although I think I was hurt that there had been so much distance between my father and me, and I blamed him for it, I also believed in the genuineness of his pride in me and in his delight in my presence there, even if I was in his eyes simply an extension of himself. In spite of everything, I felt good about it. My father was a man whose ministry was to people who needed him. In his mind, I think, he must have long ago decided that he had given me all he could, and that the rest was up to me.

By the time the evening was over, I had been humbled and renewed the way I always was when I attended such gatherings. For me they were always the best antidote for cynicism and despair, the best reservoir of inspiration and hope. I found that spark, once again, in the faces of people like the man who had been the NAACP secretary in the remote little town of Live Oak, Florida, a place still so notorious for its white racism that, the NAACP executive secretary Ruby Hurley said, "you want to get out before nightfall." This was a big moment for him, and he walked up to the front of the room and handed Mrs. Hurley his contribution—fifteen dollars.

I also heard it in the young voices of the gospel choir, which brought me to the point of tears as they sang "I've Been 'Buked and I Been Scorned." Those words now carried a deep, abiding message for me, and although I had been hearing them all my life, it was as if I was listening to their message for the first time.

I been 'buked an' I been scorned,
Chillun, I been 'buked an' I been scorned,
Chillun, I been 'buked an' I been scorned,
I been talked 'bout sure as you're born.

Ain't gon' lay my 'ligion down,
Ain't gon' lay my 'ligion down,
Ain't gon' lay my 'ligion down,
CHILLUN.
Ain't gonna lay my 'ligion down.

By this time, preparations for graduation were already under way. We had taken pictures for the yearbook and I had declined to order a school ring. Invitations had been ordered, received, and mailed. I don't recall how many I sent, but my mother and I tried to include everybody who had played a meaningful role in my life, let alone my two years at Georgia. I even sent one to my eighth-grade teachers, Fred Martin and Rodney Delin in Alaska, and just hoped that someone would forward it, wherever they were. (They were still in Alaska, I later learned, where they had decided to homestead after retirement.)

Hamilton Holmes was on his way to making history all over again. He had been elected to Phi Beta Kappa and had already been accepted at the all-white Emory Medical School—another first.

By the time June 1, 1963, came, it already had the feel of an anticlimax. But if that was how I felt, my feeling was certainly not shared by the Black people from Atlanta who joined my mother, my grandmother, my brothers, Henry and Franklyn; Hamp's parents and brothers; Donald Hollowell and his wife, Louise; Mrs. Hurley from Turner; all dressed in their Sunday-go-to-meeting best, in a caravan the likes of which had never been seen passing through Lawrenceville, Da-*cu*-la, and all the other white enclaves on the road to Athens.

By this time, my grandmother had begun to experience the effects of old age in a way that sometimes taxed my mother, but also joyfully, as she sometimes fantasied herself as the little girl Frances, calling after her beloved mother, Ellen Wilson, or as the wife of Rochell, calling lovingly to him. Sometimes she'd attempt to speak and her words would come out garbled. Often when that would happen, she could hear it with the lucid part of herself and she would say, "Did you hear that stupid thing I just said?" and laugh as heartily as she had in the best of times. The first time I remember its happening, everybody else froze in place. But I joined in the laughter, and soon, with great relief, did everyone else.

Grandmother's being in this condition also meant that my brothers, especially Franklyn, got less attention. I was still her favorite grandchild, but with me gone most of the time, she turned her attention to Franklyn, who, unlike Henry, had not started school when my mother began working full-time. She adored him and he her, but her traveling days were over, and so, while he had the benefit of her love, he never had the benefit of her adventurous spirit.

I think both the boys suffered somewhat as a result of so much family energy being devoted to my needs during those two and a half years. It would take each of them a bit longer to find their place, as it would others of their generation, like the Holman children, who for a while could react only to what had registered in their young consciousness—the horror of "that night," which they had seen on television and had sacrificed their father to, the incidents they heard me describe to their mother and father as we sat so often talking in their living room, the worry they saw on the faces of their parents and heard in their voices when I was no longer in their presence. For them, it was too early yet to calculate the worth of it all. That would take years, after Kerry, Karen, and Kent had become Kwasi, Kinshasha, and Kwame in their generation's search for their place. Still, whatever invisible wounds or scars my brothers bore, not from each other, but from the experience of being "the brothers of," were not visible that day as they made their way to the graduation. They clearly loved their big sister.

Also joining the caravan, once it reached the giant football stadium where the ceremony was being held, was my father and his fiancée, Ollie, a pleasant young woman who was a classmate of Carolyn's at Clark and had graduated from college two years ahead of me. She, too, was a Delta. It was the first time we had met, and although I later realized that she was a strong woman of substance, who idolized my father and patiently and assiduously took care of him when he began to suffer some of the lasting debilitating effects of his emphysema, attributed in part to his cigar smoking but also to long periods of exposure to the bitter Korean winters during his war service, she seemed to be shy and just a little nervous. My mother greeted her warmly, and she in turn addressed my mother as "Miss Althea."

Because the campus had never fully come around, I was a little anxious about what might happen when our names were called out for our diplomas. But by the time it happened, the only sounds to be heard were the cheers and applause emanating from our families and close friends. No one else seemed to notice, and I remember thinking to myself, This is how it ought to be, as I sat there in my place.

chapter **20**

In Our Place

Twenty-five years later, I returned to the site of my graduation, this time as the first Black person to deliver the graduation address in the school's now 203-year history. Under the stewardship of Charles Knapp, a former official in the Administration of former President and fellow Georgian Jimmy Carter, the university now had a chair in honor of Hamp and me, where once a year a distinguished lecturer was invited to speak on some issue related to civil rights or race relations. The first speaker in the series had been Vernon Jordan, now one of the country's most successful corporate attorneys.

Once again, a caravan made the journey from Atlanta, where Hamilton Holmes was a prominent orthopedic surgeon and lecturer at Emory University, soon to become medical director of Grady Memorial Hospital. He was also a member of the distinguished Georgia Foundation—similar to a Board of Trustees—of the University of Georgia. His son, Chip, was a freshman at Georgia at the time, trying hard to establish his own identity, not as "the son of . . ." In the audience were many of the professors who had taught one or both of us, as well as Judge Bootle, whom I had called personally and invited to attend. After all these years, I thought it was time to say thank you. If I had one regret, it was that my grandmother Frances Wilson Layson Brown Jones and my father, Charles Shepard Henry Hunter, Jr., were not there. But I could feel their spirit, as I did those of all my forebears, who I believed were now in the heavenly mansions of their Father's house, in their final place.

"IN OUR PLACE"
Address by Charlayne Hunter-Gault
to the 1988 graduating class
University of Georgia
Athens, Georgia
June 11, 1988

President Knapp, members of the faculty and administration, family, loved ones, and lovers of the Class of 1988—and most especially the Class of 1988—"hello again." It's good to be back home again. In a place that I have always thought of as "our place."

It is probably the case that twenty-five years ago today some of your parents were sitting in this place, waiting, like you, to hurry and get this ceremony over with so that you could get on with your newly credentialed life. That some of them, probably like some of you, were anxious up until two days ago about whether you would in fact be credentialed today. And that like some of you, twenty-five years hence, won't remember who the graduation speaker was, let alone what was said. With all due respect, I had to have my own memory jogged about that. And once I did, by rereading the graduation address by the late Senator Richard Russell, I knew that what I had to talk about today was memory . . .

For me, in my time and place twenty-five years ago, it would be the memory of many things. Of things taught: Dr. Charles Kopp's lecture on how "We Learn from History That We Do Not Learn from History," or from some history class or other, Santayana's admonition that "those who cannot remember the past are condemned to repeat it."

Part of what I remember of the past of a mere twenty-five years ago was that the day I sat in this audience as a member of the Class of 1963 it was just as hot as it is today. But as today, no one seemed to mind—especially friends in the audience from Atlanta whose day it was as much as mine, because they had lived every tense moment of my years here as if I were their own. Of how Donald Hollowell, along with Constance Baker Motley and their legal team, made it possible for me to be here—people who were more than legal minds. They were people in whom resided the highest qualities of the human spirit. As was Carl Holman, the gentle poet and tough advocate, my mentor in too many ways to detail here today. As was my mother, a woman of deceptively quiet strength, whose short legs had a hard time keeping up with Vernon Jordan and me as our longer legs propelled us through the campus mobs on that first tumultuous day. But who, along with my father, "the Colonel," had been the one to provide me with all the stuff I needed to stay ahead and to stay here. Class of 1988, permit me to steal a moment of your time today to say thank you to them and to Hamilton Holmes, my friend for life, and his family, from this very special place.

But I have other memories as well—memories that time has not erased, and for that I am grateful, because my impulses as a citizen and as a journalist were the result as much of those times as any other. Those were times of testing and, yes, of triumph. Of pioneering and legend-building. Of armor-building.

Once, when the writer Gail Godwin was asked why she felt the need to modulate suffering with sweet reasonableness and humor, she answered, "Honey, that's what they call character." And so, of character building . . . Of charting new courses.

I know that the University of Georgia at that time made an enormous difference in the lives of so many, even today I still get letters from classmates who tell me of the enduring lessons they took from this place, even though in some cases those lessons were a long time coming, and not just the usual ones taught in an academic setting.

Listen, for example, to this letter I received a few months ago from a Georgia graduate living in North Carolina:

> I entered the university a very ignorant child. Growing up in Virginia, I was not aware of the suffering of Blacks, and I truly had never given it a thought. But your experience

was very visible to me. I watched from the window the night the mob came over the hill from the basketball game, and that shock remains vivid in my mind. For the first time I understood unreasonable cruelty, and I have not been an innocent since that night . . .

I have tried ever since 1961 to treat all people with respect, and now I have a good number of Black friends. I wish I could have known you then. And I wonder how many of the "privileged" white girls in Center Myers have been able to use their potential as you have; when I think of some of the attitudes, there is irony and I have to smile to myself.

You may marvel at her capacity to recall what may seem to you like ancient history, especially since your freshman year might seem like a hundred years ago. But something like the scent of perfume or after-shave lotion or of baking bread, of magnolias or the wood chairs in an empty classroom, dust in the library stacks, or hearing "When Doves Cry" or "What's Love Got to Do with It?" Maybe the first time you yelled, "Go, Dawgs!!!" Any one or all probably call forth a rush of vivid, exciting memories.

It happened to me just the other night, as I listened to the poet Yevgeny Yevtushenko talk with my colleague Robert MacNeil about the reforms of an emerging new era in the Soviet Union—I remembered that Yevtushenko's poetry was one of the passions I pursued here as a part of what thankfully came to be an almost routine existence at Georgia. His passion was still alive as he spoke about the painful period of Russian history in which, he said, Stalin "destroyed memory, our national memory."

Listening to Yevtushenko as I contemplated my return to Georgia, and as Robert Kennedy was being honored in our national memory, I felt, almost palpably, history coming full circle. As Attorney General of the United States, R.F.K., in fact, came to this campus shortly after our admission, and while the wound caused by our admission was still wide open in the hearts and minds of many, he said unflinchingly that the graduation of Hamilton Holmes and Charlayne Hunter would "without question aid and assist in the fight against Communism, political infiltration, and guerrilla warfare." I almost fell over. I mean, I had never thought of it all in quite those terms.

Yevtushenko. Cold war/détente. R.F.K. Desegregation/graduation . . . 1963/1988. Déjà vu, all over again. History coming full circle . . . but not, thankfully, repeating itself. For, as Kennedy and the poetry of this man of conscience filtered through my mind's eye, so did the memory of being one of two Blacks in a graduating class of 1,600. Being more or less lost in the crowd, the presence of Charlayne Hunter and Hamilton Holmes causing nothing like the tumultuous uproar of our admission only two and a half years before. And yet some of the words spoken by the senior senator that day were words wedded to the myths of the past rather than a present and future symbolized by our very presence in that graduating class. The senator spoke of the "majesty of local law," a not-so-veiled reference to the continuing Southern antipathy to the law of the land. At that time, in Clarke County, the "majesty of local law" meant that I could not take a bowling class at the University of Georgia because the bowling alley they used was in Athens and the federal law that desegregated the university did not apply to the town. But it also did not apply to Black citizens from Athens who came to football games in this very stadium. They were still forced to sit in isolation, off in what was then called the "crows' nest."

But despite those words and those facts of life twenty-five years ago, a watchfire was lit, a watchfire celebrating the revelation that amid misunderstanding and confusion—and hate—the simple good fortune of one curious, inquisitive Black girl who once dreamed of being Brenda Starr and found the University of Georgia the place to fulfill that dream, and one gifted young Black man who wanted to be a healer could be attained.

There may be a tendency on the part of some of you to regard the journey here today as a casual undertaking. I hope not. For my journey to this place of graduation was no casual undertaking. And just as I experienced the heady feeling of being a part of the continuum of American history on this day twenty-five years ago, it is no less the case with you today. The University of Georgia, historically unique in its role as a training ground for the state's "tree shakers and jelly makers," to quote another son of the South . . . that institution found itself established as one of the first battlegrounds of a new South—one that cannot be denied, even as it is still aborning. Which means that you, too, as much as Charlayne Hunter and Hamilton Holmes, are pioneers. Now, pioneering has always been an unsettling experience. Residence is taken up in an unfamiliar universe. Old habits of mind must be discarded, often at the risk of pushing ahead without compensating replacements. This would fit a popular definition of courage, but to my mind it is really a question of acknowledging the guiding principles of fundamental human decency and then living by them.

One of the things I would want us all to keep alive in our memory is that as unique and painful as it was, our days here as students would have been a sojourn in unrelieved loneliness had not some others pioneered with Hamp and me. Some I have mentioned. There was Tom Johnson, editor of *The Red and Black*—here today, now publisher of one of the world's leading newspapers.* And there were other pioneers, most of them quiet, undemonstrative people, some members of the faculty and administration, some fellow journalism students, all white. There was Marcia Powell, a loyal friend who has remained so despite the twists and turns that are inevitable in enduring friendships. And Joan Zitselman. And Walter Stovall, a man of bona fide white Southern credentials who boldly sought me out and was rock solid as a companion and friend. I confess I was leery of him when he took a seat next to me during summer school in the Continuing Ed sandwich shop and introduced himself. But when we spotted each other in the fall registration line at Lumpkin Hall, and we hugged each other, I pretty much knew that we had stolen each other's heart. We both took the leap, and he unhesitatingly jumped into my boat with me. He gave up going to the movies because he knew I couldn't get a seat in the segregated theaters. He gave up going to the Varsity because he knew they would not serve me— although he said at the time it was because the chili dogs tasted funny. We married, despite the uproar we knew it would cause, because we loved each other. And while we are now both happily married to other people that we love, I to Ronald and he to Sue [the Susan Floge

* Tom Johnson is now president of Cable News Network (CNN).

who with a friend visited me in the dorm during my first days at Georgia], the reason our marriage didn't work out certainly wasn't because either of us lacked the courage to try in a time of sea changes. I salute Walter for his courage and for continuing to be a good father to our daughter and one of my best friends and collaborators . . . even on this speech. I would wish for you all such courage, conviction, and commitment to ideals and principles.

In the years that have elapsed since the moment I arrived here and ultimately graduated, I have come to understand that in this country of ours only one region has ever been a true melting pot. And that region is the South. Through the events of our toil and our tumultuous history we have become a definable people, *sui generis* in the way we talk, our preference for fried food, and, above all, our manifest humility as we fulfill our hopes and dreams.

When I was offered my first job in television, the news director laid out for me all the qualities I had that he felt would make me a good television journalist . . . and then he added, "Of course, you have a kind of lazy way of talking, but we can fix that." As some of you may have noticed, that really didn't get fixed. I never allowed it. And I am now working for a program where that kind of difference is seen as a positive, a genuine reflection of the diversity of the nation and the world we attempt to report.

But our differences as Southerners are no less true today than they were twenty-five years ago. In those perilous days, we trod, some of us eagerly, others with defiant reluctance, the bitter ground of denial, hatred, and violence.

As we shared our destiny, I believe we came to know each other in new aspects, and I believe we came to acknowledge and respect both each other's abilities and each other's ways of life. In many ways, it was a natural unfolding. In others, it was not.

For centuries, we shared a world of courtesy and difference established on utter tragedy. As Blacks, we gave to the white world, and that world gave to us. But the gifts were ambiguous, weighted as they were with the force of unequal tradition. You were not ours, but we were yours. Then, slowly, painfully, came the furious dawn of recognition. We saw, half hidden in the blazing noonday sun, the true outline of our burden.

It encompassed the mournful glories of Chickamauga and Kennesaw Mountain, the heroic steadfastness of ordinary and extraordinary men in gray and the celluloid myth of Rhett, Scarlett, and Mammy. But the pictures were incomplete, consigning the other figures in our shared history to the obscure background. The slave block at Louisville became a tourist attraction, while the grandchildren of the slaves toiled as ever in the fields. The good servants daring only at their peril to be good patrons, taking refuge in feigned ignorance and the indolent shuffle of moon-faced grins, frustrated but prudently quiet in the face of the iron-clad strictures of Jim Crow, which extended even to a weed-grown cemetery in Covington, where my grandmother sought in tears to discover the location of my grandfather's grave . . . in the "separate but equal" part.

No one here today would pretend that the Old South is dead and buried, that the events of the past twenty-five years, even my presence here today, have transformed our peculiar world into one that is beyond recognition. The Confederate flag still flies in places on this campus, we all love our grits for breakfast, and it would still be unwise for me to spend too much time in certain municipalities a few hours' drive from here. To be sure, there are more than two Black students in this graduating class—there are 300 out of a class of 6,200. Taken together with the number of Black students in the entire student body—1,200 out of 26,000—permit me to say that we have all failed in our responsibility to this institution and to this state for lo these many years. For we cannot say that the university has fulfilled its mission if in addition to what Matthew Arnold called "the best that is known and thought in the world," it has not also prepared you for the real world, one in which, thanks to the events in Moscow this month, holds out the greatest promise in your lifetime of a future devoid of the fear of nuclear holocaust.

But a real world which is a lot smaller, a lot more interdependent.

I do not believe we can function as a secure society if we are not at peace with ourselves. A trip to South Africa that represented a step back in time for me was a jolting reminder. And yet the lessons I learned on this campus that have stayed with me for life have provided me with sharp radar for disharmony and intolerance. And in recent times that radar has been sounding constant alarms. From the college campus, where dissent is now often mean-spirited, to the White House, where former education secretary Terrell Bell recalled that he was "shocked to hear . . . sick humor . . . racist clichés . . ." and other ethnic slurs.

Something—I know not exactly what, probably a combination of things—has changed the consensus we forged in the sixties. And we are opening old wounds and beginning to experience new pain. Again, I remember being in South Africa and reflecting on our experience, feeling on the one hand hopeful that one day, like us, they would find their way to justice and equality, but also thinking about the wearying steps and the inevitable pain of the process. Made even worse there by far more intransigent resistance to equal rights for the Black majority. And while the history of South Africa departs in some significant ways from our own, the history lesson from Dr. Kopp's class rings true as ever, as much as Santayana's.

I came across some words the other day by West African novelist Ayi Kwei Armah, and they, too, struck a chord. "Our way . . . is not a random path," he wrote. "Our way begins from coherent understanding." The reason they struck a chord was because I believe the South's understanding, even when it was wrong, was always more coherent than that of the rest of the country . . . And as we have peeled away the protective coating that has exposed other parts of the country's weaknesses on matters of equity and justice, the South's "coherent understanding" is the one really hopeful sign I see . . .

President Knapp's bold stroke in hiring fifteen new Black faculty members for the upcoming academic year is a part of that equation. When people at the top exercise aggressive leadership and will, even when they don't work miracles, they set a tone and create an atmosphere that make things happen. And that is true in government and industry, in the media and on the college campus—all places where the gap between what should be and what is remains a wide abyss. Where institutional resistance to full equality is agonizingly slow to yield. Where leadership from the top has too often been silent or inconsistent or hypocritical.

For years, as I have visited campus after campus in other parts of the country, I have heard echoes of protestations of administrators,

CEOs, news directors, and others in charge, about their philosophical commitment to diversity and pluralism, but how they "just couldn't find any qualified." Well, Mr. President, did you create these people in Georgia's renowned biotechnology program? Or did you find them where any other executive could have . . . by looking where they were and making them offers they couldn't refuse?

I am convinced that the presence of more Black faculty members here will not only attract more Black students to this campus, but their presence, along with those other Black students, will move this place—our place—to a new phase in its pioneering history. A place that could be a model for a more perfect union. A place in which people of color are on the ascendancy. By the year 2000 one out of three Americans will be a person of color. It really is our turn.

And you, as the dynamic products of this institution that is otherwise growing in so many wonderful ways, you should be an integral part of that. As its supporters and its ambassadors to a waiting and needful world. I say you will, hopefully. Who knows? In twenty-five years, one of you may be standing here as I am, reporting back and taking stock—even of whether Dr. Knapp's promising beginning blossoms into a rainbow of perennials. Because even gardens in the richest of soils need tending. I think, with all our help, your speech could be the one to celebrate the most successful chapter on true integration ever written.

I first came here, in the words of Stephen Vincent Benet, "a brown girl bearing an idle gift." I stand before you now a woman who has drunk from the waters (and the wines) of the world, not at peace but confident of my capacities and yours, praising the shepherds' and the lawgivers' gifts, because we have had our justice after all . . . And if I had it to do all over again, I might hope for less of a struggle, but even so, today, I would welcome the challenge, if for no other reason than to hear the young Black man who approached me at a "Sweet Auburn Avenue" reception in Atlanta the other day and introduced himself to me with the sweetest greeting of them all. He said, "Hello, Charlayne. I'm a fellow dawg."

And so . . . I celebrate this joyous moment with you in a way that few others can, and ask you to join with me today in what Zora Neale Hurston called our continuing "journey to the horizons in search

of people," justice, equity, and love, because, as the poet Gwendolyn
Brooks has written:

> *. . . We are each other's harvest,*
> *We are each other's business,*
> *We are each other's magnitude*
> *And bond.*

Congratulations to you all.